COMPUTERS,

SURVEILLANCE,

AND PRIVACY

COMPUTERS,

SURVEILLANCE,

AND PRIVACY

David Lyon *and*
Elia Zureik, *editors*

University of Minnesota Press

Minneapolis / London

Published by the University of Minnesota Press
111 Third Avenue South, Suite 290, Minneapolis, MN 55401-2520
Printed in the United States of America on acid-free paper

Library of Congress Cataloging-in-Publication Data

Computers, surveillance, and privacy / David Lyon and Elia Zureik, editors.
    p.   cm.
    Includes index.
    ISBN 0-8166-2652-9 (hc)
    ISBN 0-8166-2653-7 (pb)
    1. Electronic surveillance—Social aspects.   2. Computers and civilization.
    3. Information technology—Social aspects.   I. Lyon, David, 1948-   .
    II. Zureik, Elia.
    TK7882.E2C66   1996
    303.48'34—dc20   95-38820

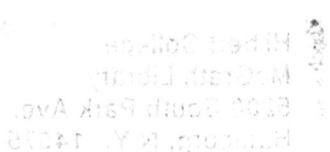

Contents

Introduction

The late twentieth century is witness to widespread, massive, unprecedented change. Economic restructuring, based on new technologies and global operations, political realignments following the end of the Cold War and the reassertion of nationalisms, and social-cultural shifts relating to consumerism, mass media, and ethnic, gender, income, and status conflicts have produced a world quite different from that of the mid-century.

A main feature of this restructuring is the ability of the new technology to handle, through the use of powerful computers, unprecedented amounts of information by both private and public organizations. Surveillance, in the broad sense of the collection and processing of personal data, is a significant aspect of this. On the one hand, governments claim the right to monitor the activities of citizens to ensure fairness and equal access to services and the law, and companies regard personal records as valued commodities to be bought and sold in pursuit of markets. On the other, ordinary people, increasingly aware that their driver's licenses and credit cards are used to keep tabs on them, show some concern that their lives are more transparent, that their privacy is invaded, or that their lives are remotely manipulated.

What is especially new about this is the way that very large-scale systems, often global in scope, interact with the local, the personal, the immediate. Surveillance, again, is one such instance. Huge corporations and governments—sometimes of a supranational kind, think of the European Union—are involved. But daily life claims to unemployment benefits or trips to the shopping mall are affected. Hence the main discourse of resistance to oversurveillance is that of "privacy."

A glance at the table of contents for this book reveals that we have not devoted any specific section to "state surveillance," even though it was the sinister power of government surveillance that spawned the original Orwellian fears of "Big Brother." The globalizing reach of surveillance mentioned above also means that today's surveillance extends far beyond the state, above all to the marketplace.

This book explores these issues from a variety of angles. The contributors all enter the debates about "surveillance" and "privacy," but they do so from different perspectives and come to different conclusions. Several take issue with each other. Most are social scientists—in sociology, political science, communications, public policy, and history—but some come from computer and information science backgrounds. All are concerned not only with analysis but also with the practical, legal, and organizational consequences of their work.

The chapters in this volume originated as papers given at a strategic research workshop at Queen's University at Kingston, Ontario. They have been revised in the light of discussions there, sharpened especially by the presence of several "privacy practitioners" from government offices in Ottawa and Toronto. The workshop was funded largely by the Social Science and Humanities Research Council of Canada, but also by Bell Canada and several departments at Queen's, including the Department of Sociology, the School of Graduate Studies and Research, the School of Policy Studies, and the Centre for Industrial Relations, to whom thanks are due. We hope that the lively, collegial spirit of debate and the quest for appropriate policy that marked the original workshop will be continued and broadened with the publication of the book.

1

Surveillance, Privacy, and the New Technology

David Lyon and Elia Zureik

On 5 July 1993 a package of new telephone facilities was launched in our city, Kingston, Ontario. Similar services have become available in other cities in North America over the past few years. "Call management services" include Call Display, Call Return, Call Screen, and Call Trace. Naturally enough, the marketing pitch assures customers that these features are designed to give them "greater control over calls received." Call Display, for instance, shows on a small screen the number from which an incoming call is being made, so that the customer can choose whether or not to answer. The advantages of such a service for those in vulnerable situations, such as battered wives or recipients of harassing calls, are obvious. Indeed, statistics suggest that rates of abusive calls fall in areas where these services are available. Less positively, those operating hotlines or shelters are concerned that their protection is stripped away by Call Display. According to the Privacy Commissioner's 1992 annual report, telephone "subscribers who wished to preserve the anonymity of their telephone numbers would not have to pay a special charge" (p. 4). It is in this context that the recent ruling by the Canadian Radio, Television and Communications Commission (CRTC) banning the use of automated dialing and announcement devices by telemarketers has been welcomed by privacy advocates (Surtees, 1994). This ruling clearly recognizes that in telecommunications, "privacy is recognized as a consumer's right, and not merely as a commodity for sale" (p. 4).

Although this is mentioned, the telephone company's advertising brochure remains silent about the huge loss of control over personal data that is unwittingly experienced by all telephone customers, including those who do not themselves subscribe to the new features. Nor does the company mention the fact that the really large-scale advantages accrue to the companies using Call Display, not the residential customer. As soon as any call is placed, from any phone, to a store, a

1

car salesroom, or a mail-order firm, the company receiving the call can automatically log the number, use it to activate a reverse directory that gives names and addresses from numbers, and connect those data with any other available personal information the company wishes.

Call Display is becoming an interesting test case of the rapidly growing phenomenon of computer-assisted surveillance. It ushers in a new type of telephone relationship. Most of us think of the phone as a tool for the voluntary communication of limited messages to others whom we have some reason to trust. Now it becomes a means for the involuntary extraction of potentially unlimited personal data by those with whom we have no particular relationship, for commercial purposes that we may or may not approve, triggered only by our making unsuspecting calls.

Call Display thus raises a number of issues far beyond what might be expected with a new telephone facility. For one thing, it depends upon computerized switching of telephones (common channel signaling) and thus demonstrates the tremendous potential of information technology to enable novel configurations of computers with telecommunications. For another, Call Display is another crucial connection marketers require to consolidate their use of personal databases for increasingly precise advertising targets. Used in conjunction with, for instance, sociodemographic data on every one of the 650,000 postal codes in Canada sold by Compusearch Market and Social Research of Toronto, it can allow the creation of remarkably accurate profiles of potential customers (Feschuk, 1992). A third aspect of Call Display as a test case is that in North America no laws exist to limit what personal data can be collected or for what purposes such data may be gathered. Will this be the innovation that pushes governments to act?

Even if they did, would they have any power to halt the trend? Already the terms of a major debate appear, within an apparently innocent telephone service: new technology, surveillance, and social control. They alert us to a set of analytic and political issues of increasing interest and importance. The three concepts relate to each other, but also require unpacking. By *new technology* we mean primarily those information and communication technologies dependent upon microelectronics. We have in mind especially the storage, retrieval, connection, and transmission capacities of such technologies, seen, for instance, in the networking of databases. The development of so-called information superhighways will only accelerate this trend.

One of the most celebrated current examples is the case of the American "Clipper chip" proposed as the new U.S. federal information processing standard for data encryption. What began as a relatively unregulated system for data exchange, the Internet, will, if Vice President Al Gore has his way, become a means of enhancing commercial, educational, and health care networks. This extension raises questions of security and confidentiality that the Clipper chip is supposed to solve. Data packets sent through the Internet will be scrambled by the chip, and only the intended recipients will be able to unscramble them.

The controversial aspect of all this, which has raised the ire of Computer Professionals for Social Responsibility, the American Civil Liberties Union, and others, is that the U.S. government will hold a secret decryption key for each chip, usable by law enforcement and national security agencies. Is this an "innocent" technical device (and will it work), or is it a threat to liberty, democracy, and privacy? As information superhighway projects take shape, these kinds of challenges will multiply.

Surveillance refers to the monitoring and supervision of populations for specific purposes. Of special interest are the ways in which new technologies are augmenting the power of surveillance in the late twentieth century, and thereby influencing the privacy debate. Three things should be noted about this. First, large-scale surveillance by bureaucratic organizations is a product of modernity, not of new technologies. Second, this surveillance has two faces; advantages appear alongside serious disadvantages. Finally, the new technologies facilitate some major magnification of surveillance power; some even argue that they change its character qualitatively. And the purposes?

Social control is the element that most fear with regard to computerized surveillance, and thus it features—alongside privacy—most prominently in discussions of new technology. But if such discussions are not simply to relapse into the paranoid, we must know which technologies are deployed for what purposes and with what results. The zero-sum game of "more technology = less freedom" is simply nonsense.

Surveillance and Society

Surveillance—literally, some people "watching over" others—is as old as social relationships themselves, but this phenomenon has acquired new and distinctive meanings in the modern era. The advent of capitalist production ushered in closer attention to the daily activities of workers in order to achieve higher rates of profit, which was echoed in the arrival of the nation-state, with its growing concern to document the doings of its citizens. By the twentieth century, these trends were epitomized in the clock-in card and assembly line at the factory and the extensive reach of government bureaucracies in all aspects of life, from employment to health and education.

The social sciences have taken note of this increasingly important aspect of social life, from Max Weber's studies of rationalization and bureaucracy to the famous Hawthorne experiments concerning worker productivity. But surveillance also features in other media, from Franz Kafka's *The Trial* via George Orwell's *Nineteen Eighty-Four* to Margaret Atwood's *The Handmaid's Tale,* or from Charlie Chaplin's *Modern Times* to *Sneakers.* Within sociology, surveillance was examined in its own right (rather than as just an aspect of bureaucracy or capitalism) by James Rule in his study of credit card companies and government departments, *Private Lives, Public Surveillance* (1973), but leaped to prominence with Michel Foucault's idiosyncratic but insightful analysis of the history of prisons, *Discipline and Punish* (1977). Theoretically, surveillance is taken up by Anthony Giddens as one of four central institutions of modernity in *The Nation-State and Violence* (1985).

By the 1980s, changing social and technical conditions and developing social theory were converging, stimulating the emergence of a new social science subfield centered on surveillance and its converse, the study of privacy rights. The altered conditions were, on the one hand, the rapid development of information technology and the implementation of computer systems for surveillance purposes, and on the other, the decisive extension of surveillance into the consumer sphere. Each was the outcome of long-term historical trends. Since the Industrial Revolution, the quest for greater control of process and populations lay behind the development of what Beniger (1986) calls "the control revolution," now greatly enhanced through the application of the new microelectronic technologies. And the desire to manage patterns of consumer demand dates back at least to General Motors' Alfred Sloan and may be seen in the huge growth of the twentieth-century advertising industry. Together, these trends meant that surveillance capacities were massively augmented at the same time the scope of surveillance was widened (Lyon, 1988; Webster and Robins, 1986).

In addition, surveillance, now powered and to some degree driven by technological advancements, became an increasingly global and integrated phenomenon. Both commercial and government-related data flow more frequently across national boundaries, and simultaneously the flow is greater between the so-called public and private sectors. Global marketing requires great attention to consumption in different parts of the world, and the use of credit cards and bar-coded passports internationally also means that consumer and personal data move from one territory to another with ease. Such information also passes between organizations once considered discrete and self-contained.

Mention has already been made of the ways that certain companies use government-garnered data, such as Statistics Canada census material, for marketing profiles; equally, data leak from commercial sources—such as those concerned with credit ratings—into government departments—such as those in charge of taxation. The arrival on the surveillance scene of "smart cards" will serve only to advance this process, especially as their current experimental use is for combining medical, pharmaceutical, and insurance data. Information technology thus facilitates a blurring of conventional boundaries.

In the chapters that follow, the contributors analyze the growth of surveillance and discussion about privacy issues in various different areas—the state, the workplace, the consumer marketplace—and chart the cultural and organizational significance of this growth. Needless to say, the essays here represent a limited view, even though most important facets of contemporary surveillance are touched upon in passing. At least two areas deserving of further study are surveillance in the armed services and that conducted by the police. The work of Gary Marx (1988) is central to such endeavors.

Surveillance and Social Theory

As one might imagine, the development of a new social science subfield is fraught with controversy. No settled views on the origins, character, or likely direction of electronically enabled surveillance are available. And although it is possible to characterize the field in terms of recognizable theoretical perspectives, part of the debate also concerns the extent to which these differing modes of explanation are compatible. At the risk of oversimplifying, we believe the three main perspectives may be summed up in terms of their leading motifs: capitalism, rationalization, and power.

In the first, derived primarily from Marxian ideas, the thrust and impetus of surveillance must always be connected with the capitalist drive for greater profit. This may be expressed in different ways, from the constant renewal of technologies to facilitate greater degrees of efficiency and productivity, to the exporting of efforts directed at managing production, to more recent attempts to manage consumption. Thus authors such as Webster and Robins (1986) speak of "cybernetic capitalism" and Rob Kling and Jonathan Allen, in this volume, of "information capitalism." In his contribution to this volume, Oscar Gandy sees the "global capitalist system" now guided by what he calls the "panoptic sort," which uses new technologies to assign differing economic values to different sectors of a given population (see also Gandy, 1993).

Understanding surveillance in this light makes sense. Clear historical patterns may be traced, and the whole process may be seen as having an economic logic. It also makes possible a critical stance in which systematic inequalities are exposed and a critique is made of the major organizations and ideologies that perpetuate the system. However, in its less sophisticated versions, its shortcomings also relate to these factors. It is all too easy to use capitalism as a catchall explanation, without, for instance, noting ways in which bureaucratic and technical logic themselves may play a relatively independent role. And the critical stance may sometimes lack nuance. Surveillance is not an unmitigated evil, but rather a two-faced social phenomenon with which many cheerfully collude for the sake of the advantages that accrue to them. People are willing to sacrifice a little privacy or autonomy for the sake of political participation or consumer convenience. For these reasons, most social and political analysts seeking a framework within which to explain surveillance draw upon a range of perspectives, each of which may contribute some significant insight.

A more Weberian perspective focuses on the processes of rationalization that characterize the development of modern organizations. The capitalist firm and the government bureaucracy evidence similar features, according to this view, features that may not be reduced to the workings of capitalism itself. Surveillance is a means of ensuring the ongoing functioning of the organization, and this may or may not mean that narrowly capitalist goals are pursued thereby (Dandeker,

1990). Moreover, for the Weberian, surveillance is never a process to be explained by one logic. Rather, one must examine each situation in its own right to discover its nature and consequences in that location. The work of James Rule in this volume is testament to such an approach.

The Weberian perspective is sometimes—erroneously—associated with a gratuitous emphasis on technical change. Technological developments, expressing the rationalizing motif, are sometimes taken to be central to an understanding of surveillance. Organizational computer power somehow spells "Big Brother." Although a Weberian approach would indeed accent the unique contribution made by specific new technologies, it is a mistake to equate this with a form of technological determinism. The contributors to this volume repudiate such a position, but it is not uncommon, especially in many popular accounts, to find new technologies branded as the "cause" of new surveillance practices.

Those working from both Marxian and Weberian perspectives have also been drawn into a debate with Michel Foucault that has led to modifications of each viewpoint. Foucault's work centers on the "disciplinary practices" diffused throughout modern social institutions. He sees power as a ubiquitous but not necessarily negative feature of all social relationships. However, the strong impression is given by much of Foucault's work that such power does disadvantage people in the sense that we are all under closer regimes of social control. His history of prisons, for instance, highlights the role of the "panopticon" prison architecture that obliged prisoners to self-control by means of unverifiable observation. Inmates would always be conspicuous within their cells, but never sure when exactly they were under scrutiny. Many have seen this dream of a sort of automated prison realized only with the advent of the invisible gaze of electronic technologies (see Lyon, 1991, 1993).

Foucault's work has been used in various ways in surveillance studies. First, he notes the apparent similarity in surveillance practices within diverse social spheres, such as the factory, school, and prison. This, as we will show in the next section, has raised critical questions about the extent of such commonality, questions on which Weberians would be particularly insistent. Second, Foucault's surveillance theory points up the ways in which surveillance extends into the micropractices of organizations, the "capillary" level, classifying as well as observing subordinates. Third, although Foucault's studies refer primarily to modernity, some take the phenomenon of electronic surveillance (among other forms) to presage a postmodern condition in which virtual "selves" circulate within networked databases, independent of their Cartesian counterparts who use credit cards and are identified by social insurance numbers (see, e.g., Clarke, 1994). Abbe Mowshowitz, in this volume, sees in the widespread use of databases the potential development of "endogenous" forms of social control, where "virtual individuality," group conformity, and other-directedness will now reside in the data themselves. For Mark Poster, whose chapter here best exemplifies the Foucaldian approach, databases have become the new text in Foucault's sense of discourse (see also Poster, 1989, 1990). Lastly, and related to this, Foucault's stress on ubiquitous power raises questions of resistance. What can be done? Without some theory of countervailing powers or resistance, at which Foucault only hints, paranoia remains but a short step away.

As a coda to this cursory glance at surveillance theory, it should be noted that several theorists, including, for example, Oscar Gandy, find help from Anthony Giddens in organizing their explanatory tools. Giddens, as a sympathetic critic of all three theoretical traditions, has attempted to produce an intelligent synthesis of the best of each. His emphasis on surveillance as a modern institution and, from structuration theory, his focus on its enabling as well its constraining features draw the attention back to human beings as "knowledgeable agents" within surveillance situations. His insistence that a "dialectic of control" exists in all such situations, giving subjects the chance to "answer back" to their "surveillers," has prompted further concern with questions of resistance. Although theoretical advance is being made through critical engagement with Giddens's work, the main task confronting those who wish to use that work is to demonstrate its empirical relevance. Does his theory really explain what is happening in the world of contemporary surveillance? This question is likely to remain at the forefront of current concerns.

Surveillance, Work, and the State

The spread of surveillance in society has prompted some writers to argue that workplace surveillance and related concerns about privacy will become the issue of the 1990s (Jenero and Mapes-Riordan,

1992:71). A December 1990 front-page article in the *New York Times* discussed at great length the problems surrounding surveillance and privacy at work, and pointed out that such widespread practices have led American policy makers to urge the introduction of legislation to curb privacy violations at work (Kilborn, 1990). Judith Perrolle's essay in this volume highlights the importance of viewing workplace privacy not as a reified entity subject to the dictates of technology, but as a negotiated activity in which the design of the technology is made subservient to the communicative needs of workers.

Interest in the notions of surveillance and control is intertwined with interest in labor commodification and accumulation, two key ingredients in the analysis of organizations in advanced capitalism. In his seminal essay "Time, Work-Discipline, and Industrial Capitalism" (1982), E. P. Thompson argues that whereas capital acts as a disciplining force vis-à-vis labor, it is the measurement of time that makes such a disciplining process all the more possible. It is no exaggeration to say that the computer has become the defining tool of time measurement par excellence (Bolter, 1984). Thompson echoes the observations of Mumford (1963), who attributes to the invention and subsequent diffusion of the clock a key role in the measurement and commodification of labor in industrial capitalism. Thompson distinguishes between what he calls "task-oriented" time, a feature of preindustrial societies where there is little demarcation between leisure and work activities, and value- or labor-oriented time. In the latter case, time acquires a new meaning dictated by the emergence of the complex division of labor and the need for labor supervision. "In all these ways—by the division of labor; the supervision of labor; bells and clocks; money incentives; preachings and schoolings; the suppression of fairs and sports—new labor habits were formed, and new time-discipline was imposed" (Thompson, 1982:305). In an attempt to ensure its objective in disciplining labor, the bourgeoisie in modern times resorted to the introduction of scientific management techniques and the "propaganda of time-thrift," which, through a mixture of puritanism and industrialism, "converted [people] to new valuations of time; which taught children even in their infancy to improve each shining hour; and which saturated men's [and women's] minds with the equation, time is money" (p. 308).

Giddens develops the notion that by regularizing labor and the structuring of work habits, the clock transformed time from its intangible, subjective dimension to its commodified version, thus refining the labor exchange process under capitalism. The "socially necessary labor time," as Marx has it, became the main ingredient in the conversion of labor to its corresponding exchange value. Giddens goes one step further and points out that the commodification of time is what sets "class-divided" (i.e., feudal and preindustrial) societies apart from industrial (i.e., "class") societies: "The management of 'free' labour-power, concentrated in factory and in office, has no real precedent in class-divided societies" (1981:135). Class-divided societies were dissolved by means of three ingredients. First, there was "the commodification of labor via its transformation into labor-power" (p. 152). Second, there occurred "the transformation of the 'time-space' paths of the day, through its centering upon a defined sphere of 'work' physically separate from the household and separated in objectified time from 'leisure' or 'private time'"(p. 153). Related to this form of transition, there was finally the incorporation of surveillance techniques in various capitalist activities. Although surveillance is perceived to be a "phenomenon of capitalism," Giddens points out, it nevertheless owes its origins equally to the development of the European nation-state, without which industrial capitalism could have not flourished. In essence, surveillance is associated with power, the kingpin of political life, and refers to two elements: "the accumulation of information" and "the supervision of the activities of subordinates by their supervisors" (p. 169). The deployment of surveillance in advanced industrial societies is secured by means of "technical control," the coordination of labor power with technology and the application of systems analysis.

Giddens underscores Foucault's contribution to the analysis of capitalism, which, in the tradition of Max Weber's analysis of bureaucracy and the role of administrative power, highlights surveillance techniques as neglected features of capitalist societies. If capital accumulation is the driving force behind the "economic take-off of the West," the "political take-off," according to Foucault, is made possible through the development of "methods for the administering of men." For Foucault and other writers in the same genre, the importance of the factory lies in its social control function, fashioned after the prison, the hospital, and other "total institutions," which make possible "the replacement of punishment as a violent spectacle with the discipline of anonymous surveillance." Here Giddens rejects Foucault's close equating of the factory with the prison:

But there are two essential differences between the prison and the factory or the capitalistic work-place. "Work" only makes up one sector, albeit nor mainly the most time-consuming one, of the daily life of individuals outside prisons: the capitalistic work-place is not, as prisons are, and clinics and hospitals may be, "total institutions" in Goffman's term. More important, the worker is not forcibly incarcerated in the factory, but enters the gates of the work-place as "free wage-laborer." (1981:172)

The analogy of the factory with the prison, according to Giddens, depicts total institutions as omnipotent and minimizes the important role of the class struggle and the fact that, in the case of the factory, workers and their unions did not succumb passively to the dictates of the industrial panopticon. "Foucault's 'archaeology,'" states Giddens, "in which human beings do not make their own history but are swept along by it, does not adequately acknowledge that those subjects to the power of dominant groups themselves are knowledgeable agents, who resist, blunt or actively alter the conditions of life that others seek to thrust upon them" (1981:172).

Because surveillance is a central component of the modern state and the institutions of industrial capitalism, it is incorrect to think of it as a twentieth-century phenomenon made possible solely by the new information technology and the computerization of the so-called postindustrial society. To view surveillance in this light is to subscribe to technological determinism and to elevate technology above its place; it is to argue that control by means of information is associated with the decline of industrialism and the emergence of postindustrialism. After all, Giddens reminds us, Babbage's 1843 work on the forerunner to the current computer occurred during the zenith of industrialism, long before postindustrialism became fashionable. This is not to say that patterns of control in advanced industrial societies have not been greatly enhanced by the introduction of new and more powerful computer-based surveillance techniques. But surveillance is only one feature of capitalism, and not the most important one. What distinguishes capitalism from previous modes of production is the separation of the "economic" from the "political." This dual feature of the capitalist state leads to a corresponding separation in the agencies and functions of social control: the business enterprise takes on the task of coordinating surveillance based on technical control, whereas the state asserts its control through monopolizing the means of violence. This process leads to an inherent tension in the capitalist state, because the state depends largely upon the accumulation process, yet it does not control (economic) exploitation directly.

Illuminating as Giddens's analysis is, questions may be raised today about the extent to which it touches on some of the niceties of surveillance in its electronic phase. The neat distinctions with which Giddens works may well be breaking down as such new technologies help create new situations. In particular, we draw attention to the Giddensian distinctions between state and economy and between monitoring and supervising. In the first case, the massive interactions between "public" and "private" sector surveillance—direct marketers using census material and government referring to credit ratings, for instance—means that the state/economy divide is not as wide as Giddens sometimes implies. Consumer surveillance now extends economic-sphere collection of personal data far beyond the level of production. In the second case, the use of information technologies for surveillance introduces closely related if not identical techniques for "watching" employees, which suggests that these technologies are facilitating a convergence of previously separable processes (see Lyon, 1992, 1993). Thus Giddens's theoretical work is challenged—as all good theory will be—by altered empirical circumstances, many of which are documented in the chapters that follow.

Surveillance, Privacy, and Public Policy

The "other route" into surveillance studies, apart from social analysis, is from the political analysis of or direct engagement with public policy, above all as it is expressed in the discourse on "privacy." Many people who are concerned with the direct legal and political implications of increasing levels of surveillance seek from political scientists, communications theorists, and sociologists a broader picture of what is occurring. Concerns for what is termed in North America *privacy* and in Europe *data protection* have grown steadily since the 1970s, and are manifest in laws, commissions, and conventions in nearly all the advanced societies. Such legal provisions attempt—unsuccessfully—to keep pace with technological advances in data processing and with the symbiotic growth of surveillance practices in government and commercial settings. Different patterns have emerged in Europe and North America: in the United States, for instance, privacy matters relating to government data come eventually before the courts, whereas in the United Kingdom, data protection covers both public and private spheres and is achieved through the registration of data users with a registrar. Currently, pressure is being exerted by European countries for North Americans to abide by the European Convention on Data Protection, with the likely result that greater legal consistency will result. Thus comparative analysis is crucially important, as the work of Colin Bennett in this volume indicates (see also Bennett, 1992). It is high time, according to Bennett, that we situate the discussion about "dataveillance" and privacy in a new terrain that falls outside the traditional contours of individual rights versus state rights and public versus private use of information. The line separating the latter two is becoming increasingly blurred. For this reason, argues Bennett, regulatory policies currently in place, which are products of the 1960s and 1970s, are not suitable for dealing with information as a social value.

Although much important work has been done on privacy law, the fact remains that privacy itself is a highly contested concept. It is culturally relative, and debate in this field has been plagued by terminological fuzziness. It is also unclear that definitions deriving from, say, John Stuart Mill or even from legal precedents set earlier in this century are equal to the conditions of contemporary surveillance described above. It seems insufficient, for example, to conceive of a sort of trade-off between the interests of citizens and those of the state as far as so-called infringements on privacy are concerned. For one thing, far more is involved than just the "state" (and that itself has been magnified several fold this century), and for another, any "balance" must be thought of in the context of systemically unequal conditions. Simon Davies's bold attempt in this volume to universalize privacy assessment by developing objective statistical indicators for the measurement of privacy is worth considering.

Alan Westin defines privacy as "the claim of individuals, groups, or institutions to determine for themselves when, how, and to what extent information about them is communicated to others" (1967:7). Or, couched negatively, in the words of the Canadian Privacy Commissioner, "A society which casually accepts the existence of dossiers of unknown accuracy in unknown hands on millions of individuals, and with no rights of access and correction, is a society which is recklessly indifferent to preserving that most basic privacy right: the right to some control over what others know about you" (1992:5). The legal definition of privacy right refers to the right to be let alone; the right of a person to be free from unwarranted publicity. Term "right of privacy" is generic term encompassing various rights recognized to be inherent in concept of ordered liberty, and such right prevents governmental interference in intimate personal relationships or activities, freedoms of individuals to make fundamental choices involving himself, his family and his relationship with others. The right of an individual (or corporation) to withhold himself and his property from public scrutiny, if he so chooses. (Black, 1979:1075)

A 1985 task force on privacy and computers delineated three components of privacy: privacy with regard to territory and space, privacy of the person, and privacy as a correlate of human dignity and integrity in the face of massive information collected and stored about individuals (Rankin, 1985:325). It is on the last sense that the privacy rights debate centers. In spite of various attempts to enshrine privacy right in law, the Canadian Privacy Commissioner laments, "the acceptance of privacy as a basic human right has not yet found its way into our statutes" (1992:8). As Priscilla Regan points out in this volume, "biological surveillance," characterized by nonintrusive measures through the use of genetic testing, may yet provide the greatest challenge to our coming up with a workable definition of privacy. According to Regan, to be protected adequately, privacy must be conceptualized as a public good, which may make its consideration as a human rights issue more plausible.

A joint government and private sector survey of three thousand Canadians was conducted in late 1992 to explore the various dimensions of privacy (Ekos Research Associates, 1993). The results revealed that more than 90 percent of those sampled are generally concerned about privacy issues, with about one-half expressing "extreme" concern. Four out of five of the surveyed Canadians believe that computers endanger their sense of privacy; 54 percent express extreme concern over the computer's ability to link personal data stored on several computers; and 60 percent believe that there is now less privacy than there was a decade ago. These concerns are not necessarily based on personal experience, given that only 18 percent of those surveyed said that they had experienced serious privacy invasion. The report speculates that "for most Canadians concern is apparently driven by other factors such as attitudes, ethics, the experience of others, or concern about how these issues might affect them or their families in the future" (p. i).

When asked to give examples of "serious invasions" of privacy, only 3 percent ventured to do so. The category that captured first place was that of crime, followed by disturbance, psychological harassment, information abuse, credit and financial data problems, and finally workplace surveillance. In commenting on these findings, the report notes that inability to name examples of privacy abuse may be due in large measure to the invisible nature of privacy problems.

The study did find, in descending order of importance, that (a) knowledgeable people, as well as those who are least informed, tend to manifest the highest levels of concern; (b) the more transparent the rules are, the less concerned individuals are that their privacy will be violated; (c) having a sense of consent and control over the process of information storage and its release makes people feel comfortable that their privacy will not be violated; (d) those who accept the rationales given for privacy protection, and who see a benefit in it, tend to be less concerned with privacy issues; and (e) perceptions of the legitimacy of institutions that hold information about citizens are correlated with lower levels of concern that these institutions might violate one's privacy.

Among those surveyed, women, minorities, the elderly, and the poor appear to be the most concerned about privacy. Compared with Anglophone Canadians, Francophones, who enjoy privacy protection legislation in Quebec, are more concerned about privacy violation and tend to know more about it. A slightly larger proportion of Francophones, compared with Anglophones, know where to turn in addressing their privacy grievances (22 percent versus 17 percent).

The same survey refers to American data that show that Americans, more than Canadians, believe that consumers have lost all control over information stored on them (61 percent versus 39 percent), yet Canadians report lower incidence of privacy violation than Americans (18 percent versus 25 percent). This has to do with the subjective definition of privacy. In the American case, the most frequently cited example of privacy invasion is police intrusion; for Canadians, it is robbery and burglary.

In descending order of frequency, Canadians define privacy to mean (a) not being watched or listened to (75 percent), (b) being in control of who has access to information (70 percent), (c) controlling what information is collected (63 percent), (d) not being disturbed at home by marketers (42 percent), and (e) not being monitored at work (36 percent).

For Canadians, government legislation is ranked as the main source of privacy protection (72 percent), followed by the application of privacy rules governing both government and business (71 percent). Some 60 percent believe that it is up to business and government to work jointly to come up with necessary guidelines, and 45 percent believe that private citizens are to be entrusted most with protecting themselves against privacy violation. Finally, one-quarter of those sampled said that they would put their trust in the business community to protect them.

A more recent survey by Gallup Canada Inc. regarding government role, privacy, and the information superhighway confirms the above picture. Although 55 percent of those polled said they are familiar with the term *information highway*, 85 percent feared loss of privacy as a result of using the information highway, and nearly half endorse government regulation of access to and operation of the information highway (Rowan, 1994).

Pursuing the meaning of privacy is important in this context, however. Even though it is poorly defined, it serves as a mobilizing concept to express real social anxieties and fears and therefore should be addressed for that reason alone. Dispute over the term is evident in the chapters that follow, although all agree that something significant is at stake. The degree of access to the individual seems to be what the concept refers to at its most basic, but that hardly seems like a primary political virtue. Indeed, in our view it is not. Rather, privacy should be seen as a means to other ends, not as an end in itself. Such ends would include social participation, political autonomy, and the like.

Calvin Gotlieb's controversial proposal, later in this volume, that privacy be abandoned because of lack of political interest, deserves attention. Without doubt, he is correct to note the failure of any leading politicians to make major mileage out of privacy concerns, and because of this, it is indeed unlikely that privacy will feature as a central player on the political stage. Even where it has maintained sufficient interest to be translated into law, it has been argued that, paradoxically, such laws can serve to facilitate the further extension of surveillance rather than to curb its abuses.

Gotlieb's alternative is to treat privacy as a commodity and thus a matter of information management, a responsibility devolving upon all those who process personal data. Although it would indeed be desirable to see privacy concerns rate higher in the priorities of information managers, it could be objected that this will not come about unless privacy and data protection continue to be enshrined in law. If privacy is a means to other vital ends, then reducing its protection to a managerial task alone could jeopardize those ends. As will become evident, more than one contributor to this volume sees the need for continuing debate and struggle on several fronts.

In order for that debate to be meaningful, then, contributions are required from both those engaged in social and political analysis and those struggling directly with surveillance realities in the public policy arena. The social scientists need the jolt of real-world situations and of technological advances to hone their theories such that they connect with what is actually happening, and policy makers and legal experts need the broader, longer-term, comparative picture in order to make sense of the particular and the specific. The strategic research workshop held at Queen's University at Kingston, Ontario, Canada, in May 1993 deliberately drew together participants who could grapple with the issues of surveillance from these contrasting but complementary positions.

References

Beniger, James R. (1986). *The Control Revolution: Technological and Economic Origins of the Information Society.* Cambridge, Mass.: Harvard University Press.

Bennett, Colin. (1992). *Regulating Privacy.* Ithaca, N.Y.: Cornell University Press.

Black, Henry Campbell. (1979). *Black's Law Dictionary* (5th ed.) St. Paul, Minn.: West.

Bolter, David J. (1984). *Turing's Man: Western Culture in the Computer Age.* Chapel Hill: University of North Carolina Press.

Clarke, Roger. (1994). "The Digital Persona and Its Application to Data Surveillance." *Information Society* 10, no. 2.

Dandeker, Christopher. (1990). *Surveillance, Power and Modernity.* Cambridge: Polity.

Ekos Research Associates. (1993). *Privacy Revealed: The Canadian Privacy Survey.* Ottawa: Ekos Research Associates.

Feschuk, Scott. (1992). "They Have Got Your Number." *Globe and Mail*, 1 December, B22.

Foucault, Michel. (1977). *Discipline and Punish: The Birth of the Prison*, trans. Alan Sheridan. New York: Pantheon.

Gandy, Oscar. (1993). *The Panoptic Sort: A Political Economy of Personal Information.* Boulder, Colo.: Westview.

Giddens, Anthony, (1981). *A Contemporary Critique of Historical Materialism*, vol. 1, *Power, Property and the State*. Berkeley: University of California Press.

———. (1985). *A Contemporary Critique of Historical Materialism*, vol. 2, *The Nation-State and Violence*. Berkeley: University of California Press.

Jenero, Kenneth A., and Lynne D. Mapes-Riordan. (1992). "Electronic Monitoring of Employees and the Right to Privacy." *Employee Relations Journal* 18, no. 1.

Kilborn, Peter T. (1990). "Workers Using Computers Find a Supervisor Inside." *New York Times*, 23 December, 1, 16.

Lyon, David. (1988). *The Information Society: Issues and Illusions*. Cambridge: Polity.

———. (1991). "Bentham's Panopticon: From Moral Architecture to Electronic Surveillance." *Queen's Quarterly* 98, no. 3.

———. (1992). "The New Surveillance? New Technologies and the Maximum Security Society." *Crime, Law and Social Change* 18: 159–75.

———. (1993). "An Electronic Panopticon? A Sociological Critique of Surveillance Theory." *Sociological Review* 41: 653–78.

Marx, Gary. (1988). *Uncover: Police Surveillance in America*. Berkeley: University of California Press.

Mumford, Lewis. (1963). *Technics and Civilization*. New York: Harcourt Brace Jovanovich.

Poster, Mark. (1989). *Critical Theory and Poststructuralism*. Ithaca, N.Y.: Cornell University Press.

———. (1990). *The Mode of Information*. Cambridge: Polity.

Privacy Commissioner, Canada. (1992). *Annual Report 1991–92*. Ottawa: Minister of Supply and Services.

Rankin, Murray. (1985). "Privacy and Technology: A Canadian Perspective." In Science Council of Canada, *A Workshop on Information Technologies and Personal Privacy in Canada*. Ottawa: Minister of Supply and Services.

Rowan, Geoffrey. (1994). "Snoopophobia Haunts Information Highway." *Globe and Mail*, 3 May, B–1, B–24.

Rule, James. (1973). *Private Lives, Public Surveillance*. London: Allen Lane.

Surtees, Lawrence. (1994). "CRTC Cuts Off Junk Calls." *Globe and Mail*, 14 June, A1–A2.

Thompson, E. P. (1982). "Time, Work-Discipline, and Industrial Capitalism." In Anthony Giddens and David Held (eds.), *Classes, Power, and Conflict*. Berkeley: University of California Press, 299–309.

Webster, Frank, and Kevin Robins. (1986). *Information Technology: A Luddite Analysis*. Norwood, N.J.: Ablex.

Westin, Alan F. (1967). *Privacy and Freedom*. New York: Atheneum.

Part I

WORKPLACE

Genetic Testing and Workplace Surveillance: Implications for Privacy

Priscilla M. Regan

Employers have always had an interest in hiring workers who are likely to be productive and honest. They have also had an interest in ensuring that workers meet these expectations once hired. To these ends, employers have used a number of techniques in preemployment screening and in workplace monitoring, including video surveillance, call monitoring, keystroke monitoring, drug testing, polygraph testing, integrity testing, and genetic testing. Employer use of these techniques has provoked heated debates involving questions about the necessity of surveillance, the effectiveness of the techniques, and the impacts of surveillance on individual workers. These debates occur in a number of academic disciplines, in personnel offices and boardrooms of corporations, in union halls, and in congressional hearing rooms.

This chapter is concerned with the policy responses that have occurred as a result of a recent trend in workplace surveillance, that of surveillance increasingly focused on the *worker* rather than the *work* itself. As surveillance gets closer to the individual worker, the policy response is to emphasize surveillance as a problem of privacy invasion. But policy outcomes based on concerns about privacy invasions have not curtailed workplace surveillance. Part of the explanation for the weakness of the privacy-based response is that questions about surveillance are raised in the employment context, as illustrated by the policy limitations imposed by the concept of "employment at will."[1] But part of the explanation for the policy response is a result of the difficulties inherent in viewing the privacy claim as an individual claim. This definition serves as a weak basis upon which to formulate policy to protect worker privacy. If the social importance of privacy is recognized and factored into policy debates, this could lead to a broader understanding of the threats of workplace surveillance and to stronger policy to protect privacy.

In general, technology has facilitated the trend toward monitoring the worker rather than the work itself. One new technology—genetic testing—makes possible monitoring of the worker in a way heretofore impossible and in a way that challenges many of our tools for thinking about workplace surveillance. Genetic testing goes further than earlier techniques of workplace surveillance in terms of the information revealed. In his contribution to this volume, James Rule raises the question of whether new forms of surveillance are different from face-to-face patterns of surveillance that have always existed in work relations. Genetic testing does involve a different form of surveillance. Genetic information fundamentally entails individuality. Genetic variations account for many individual variations. Each person's genetic makeup is unique and is thought to offer explanations for behavior and attitudes. Two professors of ethics describe advances in genetic knowledge as creating a situation in which "human beings will be laid genetically bare and thereby rendered vulnerable" (Fletcher and Wertz, 1990:748).

In comparison with other workplace surveillance techniques, genetic testing itself is not necessarily intrusive, and no invasive questions are asked. Genetic testing, then, appears to be a somewhat different case of workplace surveillance. Despite these differences, one likely policy response is to define genetic testing issues as privacy issues. In 1990, Representative John Conyers (D-Michigan) proposed the Human Genome Privacy Act (H.R. 5612), which would give individuals a right to access information about their genetic makeup maintained in federal agency databases and would limit disclosure of such information without the individual's consent.

In order to examine the policy issues posed by genetic testing and the effectiveness of policy responses based on concerns about privacy, this chapter proceeds in four parts. First, I briefly review workplace surveillance techniques in order to place genetic testing within a context for discussion of policy issues. Second, I examine employer interest in genetic testing, as well as some of the policy questions posed by employer use of genetic testing. Because privacy is one of the primary questions raised, the third part of the chapter is devoted to analysis of what is likely to happen in policy debates where the policy goal is protection of individual privacy. Fourth, I suggest a reconceptualization of privacy as a social value and then discuss the policy implications of this view with respect to genetic testing.

Workplace Surveillance Techniques

The 1987 U.S. Office of Technology Assessment (OTA) report *The Electronic Supervisor* (1987: 12–15) develops a categorization for workplace surveillance that highlights the privacy and civil liberties questions that result. The objects of surveillance can be performance, behaviors, or personal characteristics, and a variety of surveillance techniques are available for monitoring performance, behavior, and personal characteristics. As one moves from measuring performance to measuring personal characteristics, there is increased interest in the "worker" rather than the "work" (see Figure 2.1), but the OTA categorization reveals a continuum with no clear boundaries. As surveillance moves along this continuum from work (performance) to the worker (personal characteristics), the type of information collected becomes more "personal." Genetic screening is categorized as a means of monitoring personal characteristics, specifically an individual's predisposition to health risk. However, genetic screening might also reveal information about likely behaviors, including concentration and predisposition to certain kinds of errors, as well as likely performance. In this sense, genetic testing would be a form of surveillance that, if a scoring system similar to that suggested by Simon Davies in his chapter in this volume were to be used, would represent "total surveillance."

Three reasons help to explain why genetic testing is different from earlier forms of workplace surveillance. The first is the nature of the information that is revealed in genetic tests. Genetic testing yields information about the likely course of a person's physical and psychological development. Genetic testing would appear to be a greater invasion of the individual's privacy than other forms of surveillance because of the biological, and inherently personal, nature of the information revealed. A second reason genetic testing is fundamentally different from other surveillance techniques is that the individual has no control over the information revealed; genetic information is not the result of actions that the individual has taken. A person cannot change or modify his or her genetic information; it is integral to the individual. Genetic information is information about inherited characteristics. It is also information that the individual does not necessarily know about him- or herself. Third, genetic information is not "information" in the pure sense, but reveals predispositions and probabili-

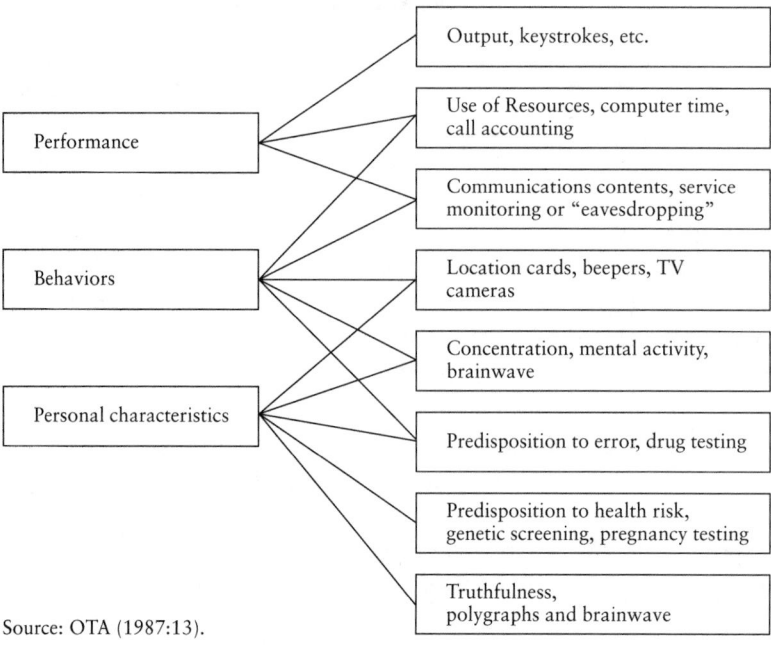

Source: OTA (1987:13).

Figure 2.1. Categories of workplace surveillance.

ties. For the foreseeable future, gene maps will not be able to predict most characteristics.[2] They will not yield information about the presence or absence of most major diseases (cancer or heart conditions) or particular conditions (psychological disorders or alcoholism).[3] Instead, genetic mapping will indicate predispositions. The realization of a condition for which an individual has a genetic predisposition will depend on other genetic predispositions and on a host of environmental factors. Even in those cases where the genetic information yields a clear answer on presence or absence of a disease or condition, medical science may not yet have a cure or treatment.

As one moves along the continuum of surveillance techniques depicted in Figure 2.1, not only is the information collected more personal, but the accuracy or meaning of that information for workplace decisions becomes more problematic. Questions about the relevance and accuracy of information have occurred with many surveillance techniques, especially drug testing and polygraphs. Although polygraphs and genetic testing are different tools for workplace surveillance, they are similar in that they both represent techniques for monitoring the worker rather than the work. Both are categorized as means of surveilling "personal characteristics," and both intrude into what might be termed an individual's "inner processes." Because of these similarities, I will examine briefly below the policy debate about use of the polygraph in employment decisions, to illustrate the kinds of policy questions that are likely to arise concerning genetic testing.

Alan Westin refers to polygraphs as a form of "psychological surveillance," because individuals reveal information that they might not want to reveal or may not even realize they are revealing, and because individuals usually do not understand the effects of their revelations on their privacy. Westin defines the privacy issue as "whether employers or the government should be allowed to require individuals to have their inner processes probed through the machine or test measurements" (1967:134). With polygraphs, the intrusiveness of the machine—the fact that the individual is strapped to a chair with electrodes and wires connecting him or her to a machine that records the body's responses—also raises privacy concerns. The invasiveness and relevance of questions asked in the process are likewise concerns.

Although issues of psychological privacy generally involve potentially sensitive or intimate information and the procedures used affect the person directly, congressional efforts to resolve psychological privacy issues have not been very successful. In the 1960s, congressional debate about personality tests did not result in legislation. When debate about the polygraph was framed as a privacy issue, no legislation was passed. The concept of psychological privacy as an individual right formed a surprisingly weak basis for legislation—surprising because one might assume that as privacy invasions get closer to the sphere of individuality, individual rights claims would be viewed as more credible. But, because the work relationship is not one in which privacy rights are easily accommodated into the concept of "employment at will," and because of difficulties in viewing privacy as an individual claim, policy discussions focused more on questions about scientific accuracy.

In policy discussions about the polygraph, several questions were raised. First, were polygraph tests reliable? Did the polygraph consistently measure the same properties? Second, there were questions about the validity of the test: Were the inferences drawn from the test appropriate, or did the test measure what it was intended to measure? (See American Educational Research Association, American Psychological Association, and National Council on Measurement in Education, 1985; Society for Industrial and Organizational Psychology, 1987.) In a 1983 report, the OTA concluded that "the available research evidence does not establish the scientific validity of the polygraph test for personnel security screening" (1983 b:4). It also concluded that it was not possible to establish an overall measure for or general judgment about the validity of polygraph testing because of the complexity of the polygraph examination itself and because of the different applications in which it was used. Largely in response to these findings, Congress prohibited private sector use of the polygraph test for employment purposes. The result was that many employers turned to paper-and-pencil integrity, or honesty, tests as preemployment screening tests. These raise similar questions about scientific accuracy and appropriateness of use in employment decisions (OTA, 1990a).

Questions about the validity and relevance of information resulting from genetic testing increase by an order of magnitude those raised concerning the polygraph. In an article in *Business & Professional Ethics Journal,* Moseley and colleagues (1991:72–73) suggest that six discrete scenarios can occur as a result of genetic screening: the person screened

1. is *certain* to get X (or "already has it, subclinically");
2. is at some *explicitly specified risk* of getting X;
3. is at *increased, but unspecified, risk* of getting X;
4. will get or is at elevated risk of getting X *if medical/preventive measures are not taken;*
5. will get or is at elevated risk of getting X *if personal lifestyle behavioral changes are not initiated;* or
6. will get or is at elevated risk of getting X *if exposed to some disease vector* (e.g., chemicals in the workplace, radiation, infectious agents).

General questions about validity and relevance of genetic tests are not appropriate to this complexity. Instead, validity and relevance issues regarding genetic tests need to be debated and resolved for each of these scenarios. No test will be perfect, and questions about what level and what kinds of misclassifications (false positives or false negatives) to tolerate will also need to be resolved (Diamond, 1983; Rowinski, 1988).

Genetic Testing in the Workplace

Genetic testing raises several significant and troubling questions, especially concerning its use for employment and insurance decisions (Cavoukian, 1989; OTA, 1990b; American Association for the Advancement of Science, 1991; Privacy Commissioner, 1992) Many of the ethical, legal, and moral concerns about genetic testing are being defined in terms of individual privacy. Currently in the United States, the Human Genome Project, which is jointly directed by the National Institutes of Health and the U.S. Department of Energy, is organizing an effort to determine the locations and chemical sequences of all genes (Bishop and Waldholz, 1990; Cook-Deegan, 1991; Davis, 1990; Kelves and Hood, 1992). The medical and scientific advances that this project makes possible are enormous, but there are also controversies arising about potential adverse or unanticipated consequences. The Human Genome Project is developing the ability to map human genes and provide detailed information about biologically determined features of individuals; the "human genome" contains the basic material from which the human being develops—a complete recipe for a human being. As of June 1995, 3,850 genes had been mapped to their locations on the chromosomes. In 1988, the National Research Council predicted that the mapping project would be completed in fifteen years.[4] Because of the importance of the ethical, legal, and social implications of genetic information—and because resolution of these issues is critical to the ultimate success of the project—Congress and the project coordinators have agreed that at least 3 percent of the budget for the Human Genome Project should be allocated to the study of ethical, legal, and social issues. This amounts to several million dollars a year.

Although biomedical research and technology are primarily involved in genetic screening and testing, once tests have been conducted the results are inherently information about individuals. Information technologies become essential to the collection, use, and exchange of genetic information. Some observers see the logical next step as the development of a database containing information about the genetic makeup of millions of people. This would result in a new form of what Colin Bennett refers to in chapter 11 of this volume as "dataveillance." Some speculate that genetic information will be contained in bar codes, that will facilitate its storage and exchange. The link between information technologies and genetic technologies is direct in two senses. First, the value to an employer from genetic technologies is the genetic *informa-tion* that is revealed. Second, information technologies provide the means of collecting, using, and exchanging genetic information.

In a 1983 report on genetic screening in the workplace, OTA found that few large firms in the United States were using genetic screening in personnel selection. Out of 366 respondents to an OTA survey, only 8 reported that they were currently doing any type of genetic tests; 17 had done so in the past, but 59 had plans to do so in the future (1983a). In 1989, OTA conducted a follow-up survey and found that 13 percent of the health officers from Fortune 500 companies respond-ing reported that their companies had used some type of genetic mon-itoring or screening, either currently or in the past (OTA, 1990b). Twelve health officers—double the number in 1982—reported that genetic monitoring or screening was currently conducted. In 1989, the Northwestern National Life Insurance Company surveyed four hun-dred firms and found that 15 percent planned by the year 2000 to test the genetic status of potential employees and their dependents before making employment decisions (Gostin, 1991:116).

Although the current use of genetic testing is not great, increasing employer health insurance costs and the decreasing costs and increas-ing scientific value of genetic testing are creating more incentives for employers to use genetic tests. Employers are interested in categorizing employees on the basis of a number of risks. Genetic testing as a tech-nology refines and enlarges what Oscar Gandy terms the "panoptic sort" (see chapter 7, this volume). Larry Gostin, executive director of the American Society of Law and Medicine, argues, "If the market-place is the only restraint on this technology's proliferation, decreased prices and demonstrated cost-benefit advantages will make wide-spread adoption inevitable" (1991:117).

In determining the policy questions raised by the use of genetic test-ing, it is helpful to consider the purposes for which genetic testing is likely to be conducted. OTA (1990b) distinguishes between genetic monitoring and genetic screening. Genetic monitoring involves the peri-odic use of genetic tests on current workers to determine genetic changes that may be attributed to the effects of certain products or procedures, primarily exposure to toxic substances. But non-work-related activi-ties (for example, personal habits, age, and environmental exposure) can also cause changes in genetic material. Genetic monitoring, then, casts a wider net than solely work-related activities in its surveillance.

Genetic screening entails the evaluation of the genetic makeup of an employee or potential employee to determine the individual's likely inherited, or genetically based, characteristics. Genetic screening can be used either to determine susceptibility to certain diseases that may be work related or caused by occupational factors or to determine the general health condition of an employee or potential employee. The information revealed by both genetic screening and genetic monitoring falls into James Rule's category of "inferential information" and should be collected only with the consent of the employee.

Arguably, both types of genetic tests provide benefits for workers. Genetic monitoring could be used to enhance the general health and safety of work conditions and could be used to change the working conditions of individual workers who are at special risk. Genetic screening could be used to ensure that workers are placed in appropriate working conditions, so that workers who are susceptible to specific risks in an environment are given jobs that minimize their hazardous exposure. Genetic screening could also be used to promote health awareness programs and to improve employers' health care costs.

At the same time, both types of genetic tests pose policy questions concerning the rights of workers and the interests of employers. Genetic screening for general health conditions—because it encompasses current employees and potential employees, and because it is not necessarily work related—is often viewed as raising more serious policy questions. However, because genetic monitoring can pick up non-work-related chromosomal changes, its use also raises significant policy questions. Primarily, these questions involve possible discrimination on the basis of genetic information, confidentiality questions concerning third-party use of information and ownership of genetic test results, and workers' privacy interests in being able to control employers' access to information about workers.[5] It is the last of these issues that provides the focus for the remainder of this chapter.

Individual Privacy and Public Policy

When questions about genetic testing are defined as questions of privacy, the questions become part of a long debate about the meaning and importance of individual privacy. Most legal and philosophical writing about privacy stresses the policy goal of protecting privacy because of its importance to the individual.[6] Generally, the importance of privacy is rooted in liberal thinking—privacy inheres in the individual as individual, and is important to the individual for self-development or for the establishment of intimate or human relationships (Pennock and Chapman, 1971; Schoeman, 1984). Given that the philosophical justification for privacy rests largely on its importance to the individual as individual, policy discussions about protecting privacy focus on the goal of protecting an individual value or interest. The result has been an emphasis on an atomistic individual and the legal protection of his or her rights.

But defining privacy primarily in terms of its importance to the individual and in terms of an individual right has served as a weak basis for developing public policy to protect employee interests for two primary reasons: First, it emphasizes the negative value of privacy, and second, it establishes a conflict between the individual and society.

Negative Value

American legal and philosophical thinking on privacy as a specific value and right takes as its point of departure an 1890 *Harvard Law Review* article by Warren and Brandeis, in which they define a "right to privacy" as the "the right to be let alone" (p. 75). They anchor the right to privacy in the common-law protection offered intellectual and artistic property, which is based on the principle of "an inviolate personality" (p. 82). The Warren and Brandeis right to privacy is very much an individual right and a right of protection from social intrusion. This right is fundamentally at odds with social interests.

The view of privacy as the "right to be let alone" draws attention to the reasons an individual might want to be let alone. Other than for the establishment of intimate relationships and the development of autonomy, the reason offered most often is to "hide" things the individual does not want known. Two responses seem to follow. First, if one has nothing to hide, then one places no value on privacy. Second, if one has something to hide, the question is, should what one is trying to hide remain private, or do others need to know about it? This second response has placed much attention on what is sometimes referred to as the "pathology of privacy." Arndt, for example, writes:

> The cult of privacy rests on an individualist conception of society, not merely in the innocent and beneficial sense of a society in which the welfare of individuals is conceived as the end of all social organization, but

in the more specific sense of "each for himself and the devil take the hindmost." (1949:70-71)

Many scholars recognize that privacy may be used to protect anti-social behavior (e.g., Fried, 1968; Gerstein, 1970).

Policy difficulties that result from emphasizing the negative value of privacy are seen in Richard Posner's analysis. Starting from Alan Westin's definition of an individual's right to privacy as "the right to control the flow of information about him," Posner turns this into "a right to misrepresent one's character" and notes that "others have a legitimate interest in unmasking this misrepresentation" (1978:20). Posner takes issue with Warren and Brandeis's view that people want to be let alone; rather, he sees them wanting "to manipulate the world around them by selective disclosure of facts about themselves" (p. 22). This gives support to Posner's view that the privacy right in information should not be given to the "possessor of guilty secrets" (p. 22) if "secrecy would reduce the social product by misleading others" (p. 23). The privacy right then turns on the substance or quality of the information one wishes to withhold. But Posner also goes on to say that the "case for protecting business privacy is stronger, in general, than that for protecting individual privacy," because "secrecy is an important method of appropriating social benefits to the entrepreneur who creates them, while in private life it is more likely to conceal legitimately discrediting or deceiving facts" (p. 25). The importance of Posner's distinction is that the benefits to the entrepreneur are regarded as "social," whereas those to the individual are not only individual rather than social, but also assumed to be used largely for negative purposes.

Conflict with "Society"

In his seminal work *Privacy and Freedom*, Alan Westin views privacy and social participation as competing desires and sees each individual as establishing the balance between the two that is best for him or her. Although the norms of society may set some boundaries on that balance, basically it is a "personal adjustment process" (1967:7). Thus, each unique individual may establish a unique balance between privacy and social participation. Charles Fried (1968) likewise analyzes privacy in terms of its importance to the individual. For him, privacy is part of the mutual respect between individuals in a society, but is not an essential ingredient of a society of individuals. In other words, the importance of privacy is in forming the basis of personal relationships between individuals, not in forming a society of individuals or in forming relationships between people and organizations.

The philosophical thinking about privacy that establishes a tension between the individual and society often moves policy debate to a discussion of how privacy conflicts with social interests such as law enforcement, government efficiency, and an honest workforce. Barrington Moore notes: "Privacy cannot be the dominant value in any society. Man has to live in society, and social concerns have to take precedence" (1984:274). Although one could quarrel with the view that social concerns have to take precedence, my quarrel is with whether social concerns and privacy values are necessarily antithetical. Many have framed them as such. The assumption is that privacy and society are antithetical, but does this have to be the case? As John Dewey points out, framing debate in terms of an individual interest in competition with a social interest does not make for fruitful discussion of social issues:

> One of the obstructions in the path is the seemingly engrained notion that the first and last problem which must be solved is the relation of the individual and the social:—or that the outstanding question is to determine the relative merits of individualism and collective or of some compromise between them. In fact, both words, individual and social, are hopelessly ambiguous, and the ambiguity will never cease as long as we think in terms of an antithesis. (1927:186)

Framing privacy as a conflict between individual and society is not just philosophically difficult, as Dewey suggests, it is overly simplistic. People are both public and private; we operate in both contexts and see both as important. The two spheres are not necessarily contradictory or in conflict; instead, there is a dynamic relationship between the two. A simple dichotomy between individual and society, or between private and public, also fails to take into account the reality that in the modern world people operate in a range of contexts that can be more or less public or private.

One response to the problem of resolving conflicts between individual and society has been to argue for community interests over individual interests. Amitai Etzioni, as well as others, advocates a communitarian movement, because "the pendulum has swung too far toward the radical individualistic pole" and there is a need to have a "judicious mix of self-interest, self-expression, and commitment to the commons—of rights *and* responsibilities" (1993:26). But if privacy continues to be valued primarily for its importance to the individual or its self-interest, then the community or communitarian values might be viewed as restraints on privacy, as reasons to restrict the area of privacy rather than as a basis for a shared interest in privacy. Privacy is more likely to be regarded as one of those individual rights or demands that must be curbed rather than as part of the commons. A proposal, then, to introduce community as a space between public and private does not appear to resolve questions about privacy's conflict with society; instead, it raises new questions about the definition of the commons.

The Social Importance of Privacy

Is privacy only important to the individual for his or her self-development or is privacy also of social importance? Calvin Gotlieb argues in chapter 8 of this volume that most people do not care enough about privacy to value it—that they make individual calculations about the value of privacy in particular settings or circumstances and trade it off for other values, often convenience. But one explanation for this is that privacy is viewed in an individualistic way. Broadening our understanding of privacy to include its social importance would remove it from a purely individualistic calculation. Colin Bennett also suggests that new forms of dataveillance are straining the traditional theory of information privacy.

I argue that privacy's importance does not stop with the individual and that a recognition of the social importance of privacy will clear a path for more serious policy discourse about privacy and for more effective public policy protecting privacy. Privacy has value beyond that to the individual for his or her dignity or for the development of personal relationships. Most privacy scholars emphasize that the individual is better off if privacy exists. I am arguing that society is better off as well when privacy exists, because privacy serves common, public, and collective purposes. If you could subtract the importance of privacy to one individual in one particular context, privacy would still be important because it serves other important functions beyond those to the particular individual.[7] These three concepts provide bases for discussing a more explicitly social importance for privacy—privacy as a common value, privacy as a public value, and privacy as a collective value.

Common Value

Some values, although arguably protecting individual interests, are regarded as so fundamental that all individuals in common have a similar interest in them. For example, although different people exercise the right to free conscience differently, believe in different things, and belong to different religions, all individuals have a common interest in this right. The same is arguably true for privacy. Even though people may define privacy differently, may draw different lines to divide public and private, and may have different sensitivities with respect to what is known about them, they all have a common interest in there being a right to privacy. In much the same way that people of different religious beliefs have a common interest in a right of free conscience, people of different privacy beliefs have a common interest in a right of privacy.

Both a philosophical argument and an empirical argument can be made to support the claim that privacy is a common value. John Dewey's discussion of the distinction between the private and public spheres helps to establish the theoretical argument. Dewey argues that the source of a "public" is "the perception of consequences which are projected in important ways beyond the persons and associations directly concerned in them" (1927:39). Michael Walzer's argument about liberalism and the art of separation is also instructive in looking at privacy within a common social context rather than from the perspective of an atomistic individual. He writes:

> The goal that liberalism sets for the art of separation—every person within his or her own circle—is literally unattainable. The individual who stands wholly outside institutions and relationships and enters into them only when he or she chooses and as he or she chooses: this individual does not exist and cannot exist in any conceivable social world. (1984:324)

He goes on to argue that the relevant art of separation in the modern world is not to separate individuals but "institutions, practices, relationships of different sorts"; the goal is not the "freedom of the solitary individual" but "institutional integrity" (p. 325).

The concepts of common perceptions and institutional relationships are relevant to the issues of workplace surveillance. Survey data support the claim that there are common perceptions about privacy. From the 1970s to 1990, general concern about threats to personal privacy from technology increased (Harris and Westin, 1979, 1990; Harris, 1983).[8] The privacy Americans voice concern about in these surveys is not privacy for intimacy, friendship, and trust, but privacy within the context of their relationships with institutions. This is reflected in the 1978 and 1990 responses to several survey items. For example, in 1990, 93 percent agreed with the statement "I have someone I can share my personal problems with when I need to"; in 1978, the figure for this item was 94 percent. In 1990, 90 percent agreed "I am generally able to be by myself when I need to be"; the figure for this item in 1978 was 88 percent. People seem to believe that the privacy of their personal or human relationships is not endangered.

Public Value

Privacy has value not just to individuals as individuals or to all individuals in common, but arguably to a democratic system as well. Privacy can be considered one of Madison's "permanent and aggregate interests of the community" (1961:78). In thinking of privacy in this way, parallels can be drawn to John Stuart Mill's discussion of the public value of individuality (1859/1939:998). For Mill, the private sphere of the individual is important not only to individual development but also to the type of public sphere or society that Mill wanted. A similar utilitarian argument for the importance of privacy is made by Ruth Gavison, who sees privacy as important in "the promotion of liberty, autonomy, selfhood and human relations, and furthering the existence of a free society" (1980:423). She recognizes the importance of privacy both to the individual and to society:

> We desire a society in which individuals can grow, maintain their mental health and autonomy, create and maintain human relations, and lead meaningful lives. . . . some privacy is necessary to enable the individual to do these things, and privacy may therefore both indicate the existence of and contribute to a more pluralistic, tolerant society. (p. 455)

Thus, privacy is important, as liberty is from Mill's perspective, because it enables the development of the type of individual that forms the basis of a certain type of society.

Hannah Arendt's discussion of the public and private realms also offers some insights into the public value of privacy. She notes that privacy originally meant a deprivation of something, "the privative trait of privacy," for example, being deprived of entering the public realm, and later took on importance as an individual protection, "to shelter the intimate" (1958:38). In order for the common to develop in the public realm, however, there must be the "simultaneous presence of innumerable perspectives and aspects in which the common world presents itself and for which no common measurement or denominator can ever be devised" (p. 57). In order for the common to develop, the private realm is essential. If the private realm is destroyed, the public is destroyed as well, because the human is destroyed. Arendt then points to the older, nonintimate, traits of privacy that are important to the development of the common public world; without initiative and a hiding place where we can be neither seen nor heard, the public would become shallow.

The importance of privacy to the common public world becomes apparent when one considers the computerized databases available and the exchanges of information taking place in the late twentieth century. The more people know about the details of one's personal life and transactions, the more individual or unique one becomes and the more difficult it is to construct a "public" or, in Arendt's term, a "community of one's peers." In this way, privacy may be essential to justice and equality, because in order to have justice or equality, some commonality among individuals is necessary. The more fragmented or differentiated people become, the harder it is to put them together in a society or body politic. In this way, privacy can be viewed as essential to Rawls's circumstances of justice in which "mutually disinterested persons put forward conflicting claims to the division of social advantages under conditions of moderate scarcity" (1971:128). The more that is known about the uniqueness or distinctive characteristics of others, the harder it will be to have "mutually disinterested persons."

Collective Value

The concept of collective value used here is derived from the economists' concept of collective or public goods, which are those goods or values that are indivisible or nonexcludable—that no one member of society can enjoy the benefit of without others also benefiting (Head, 1962; Olson, 1965; Ostrom and Ostrom, 1971). Clean air and national defense are examples of public or collective goods. If a good is a collective good, then it is inefficient to provide the good through the market; a market solution will result in a suboptimal supply of a collective good. Two aspects are important in defining a collective good: one is whether the good can be easily divided so that those who want the good, or want to pay for the good, can do so and those who do not want it can opt out; and second is whether there are spillover effects or externalities that make it difficult to isolate the enjoyment or damage of a particular activity. The question then is whether privacy can be considered a public good on either of these dimensions.

Currently, a number of policies and policy proposals treat privacy as a "private good" and allow people to buy back or establish the levels of privacy that they wish. For example, when you subscribe to a magazine, you can indicate that you do not want your name and information about you incorporated in a mailing list and sold for direct mail purposes. Similarly, with Caller ID telephone service, one policy proposal is that individuals may be able to "block" the display of their numbers. From this it appears possible that we can indeed "divide" privacy into components and allow people to establish their own privacy levels. But three factors limit the effectiveness of this individual or market-based solution for privacy: the interests of third-party record holders, the nonvoluntary nature of many record-keeping relationships, and computer and telecommunication technologies.

Vast quantities of personal information about individuals now are held by third-party organizations, including credit reporting agencies, insurance companies, schools, employers, mail-order companies, hospitals, and video rental stores. In each case, the personal information becomes part of a record that is largely the property of the organization, not of the individual.[9] The organization uses this information for its own administrative and marketing purposes, and often sells that information to yet another organization. Information about the transactions that people have with one organization or one type of organization is valuable to other organizations. What results is a lucrative market in the sale, packaging, and resale of people's characteristics and transactions. Although people are often given opportunities to remove themselves from this market, few avail themselves of those opportunities, largely because they do not have adequate information on how this market in personal information operates or what its implications for privacy might be (Culnan, 1993). At the same time, it is not in the interests of the third-party record keepers to give people complete information about the market and its privacy implications, because it would lower the value of their product if people denied organizations the ability to use personal information as a commodity.

Another element that gives privacy a collective, or indivisible, quality is that the nature of the relationships that generate records and information is changing. It is hard to define these relationships as truly voluntary. In some cases—as with tax records and social security records, one is required by law to be a part of the system—one cannot set the level of privacy that one desires; instead, some minimum level of privacy, or means to exercise privacy, is established as part of the relationship. In other systems, such as those involving credit records or bank records, the relationship might be regarded as somewhat voluntary, in that one can choose not to have a credit card or a bank account, but necessary enough that the government has intervened to legislate some level of privacy protection. As more record-generating relationships are regarded as necessary parts of modern life, the list of laws also grows, establishing minimum levels of privacy expectations for those relationships. The nonvoluntary nature of some relationships is complicated further because the individual is not technically a party, or the responsible party, in some relationships. For example, medical records that result from a transaction between a patient and a doctor are sent to a health insurance company for payment. But because the health insurance company has its relationship with the patient's employer, not directly with the patient, employers can argue that they have legitimate interests in the content of those records.

These institutional-individual relationships are not necessary only for the individual to function in modern life, but also for the functioning of a modern economy and society. For example, if large majorities were to opt out of the credit system, the consumer economy would slow down and be less efficient. If some ill people were to opt out of the health system because they do not believe their medical records receive adequate protection, there would be spillover effects on everyone's health. If citizens refused to participate in the census, or misrepresented themselves in the census, the funding of major public programs and the apportionment of congressional districts would be affected.

The complexity and interrelatedness of the computer and communication infrastructure that underlies these record exchanges also make it more difficult to divide privacy. This may appear counterintuitive, in that computer software makes it easier to program specific instructions into systems. At the same time, however, the design of the overall communication or information system becomes more important in defining what is possible. Privacy levels or possibilities are integral to the overall system design. The level of privacy possible is dependent in part on the hardware and software of the communication system. Somewhat similarly, it is also difficult to isolate one record from a system of records and give that record a particular level of privacy. Error rates in credit reporting systems and criminal justice systems are evidence of the problems of buying "effective" individual privacy without also monitoring or auditing the entire system for a level of record quality. Privacy is becoming less an attribute of individuals or records and more an attribute of social relationships and of information systems or communication systems.

The Social Importance of Genetic Privacy

It is interesting to consider whether genetic privacy can be viewed as being of broader social importance along the dimensions discussed above. Genetic information fundamentally entails individuality. It would thus seem that on this issue it would be difficult to develop common perceptions. But science does have its limitations, and these limitations make possible, if not necessary, common perceptions. Because genetic testing will indicate predispositions, which will depend upon other genetic characteristics and environmental factors, people will have limited knowledge, but not accompanied by the power or wisdom to act. It is unlikely, certainly in the near term, that people will know their particular, self-interested privacy concerns about their genetic information. The issue of genetic privacy therefore makes possible Rawls's "mutually disinterested persons."[10] Before scientific and technological advances make possible a complete genetic map, no individual will know his or her particular interest. John Fletcher and Dorothy Wertz note that "genetics is a great equalizer, and eventually, everyone will understand that they suffer from diseases and burdens having a strong to moderate genetic determinant" (1990:757). Similarly, a neuroscience professor argues that our traditional concepts of individual diversity and commonality will need to be rethought, "recognizing that our approximately 100,000 genes are mostly uniform, so that our genetic heritage binds us together more tightly than it divides us" (Grisolia, 1991:46). The privacy issues raised by genetic mapping and testing can be defined therefore as important to all individuals in the same way. Hence there is an opportunity in these debates to begin the discussion with a recognition of the social importance of privacy, because there initially will be common or reciprocal interests in genetic privacy.

Recent survey data support the existence of common perceptions. In a 1985 *Business Week*-Lou Harris survey, 89 percent of respondents answered that employers should not have the right to use genetic tests for hiring decisions; 82 percent responded that an employer's knowledge of a job applicant's potential to have a serious disease in the future is not an acceptable reason for that applicant to be denied work; 65 percent said they believed that employers should not be able to exclude employees or potential employees from certain jobs based upon the results of genetic tests that would indicate an employee's vulnerability to heart attack or stroke because of stress; and 79 percent said that insurance companies would not be justified in using genetic tests to refuse life or health insurance coverage. In general, this poll found that if the genetic testing were not to be related to employment or insurance decisions, then about 50 percent of the respondents were willing to be tested for incurable or fatal diseases that they might develop at some point in their lives (OTA, 1990b:171-72). A 1992 Louis Harris poll conducted for the March of Dimes found respondents very approving of the use of gene therapy to treat or cure genetic diseases, but also found that 63 percent believed an employer should not know that someone is a carrier of a defective gene or has a genetic disease.

In terms of genetic privacy's importance as a public value, consider the formation of Arendt's "community of one's peers." With knowledge of genetic information, even if that information does not give a complete and dependable picture of an individual, the notion of "peers" may be made obsolete. Differences among individuals, rather than shared or common characteristics or circumstances, are likely to be emphasized. Within a democratic society, some level of equality among individuals is assumed. Genetic information, especially regarding intelligence, could lead to elitism, a hierarchy based upon genetic characteristics. Any possibility of eugenics challenges traditional democratic assumptions. As an article in *U.S. News & World Report* concludes, "The most obvious danger is that genetic screening, like race, will provide one more excuse to divide the world up into superior and inferior, us and them" (Leo, 1989:59). There is then a public value to genetic privacy that might necessitate total restrictions on certain genetic tests or certain uses of genetic information.

Consideration of genetic privacy as a collective or public good also raises interesting questions. One scholar who has written extensively about the ethical issues posed by genetic testing notes that there are three levels of issues raised by the human genome initiative: individual/family, society, and species. The species level raises fundamental questions: "the fact that powerful new technologies do not simply change what human beings can do, but also change the way humans think, especially about themselves" (Annas, 1990:647). Can some members of society have genetic privacy and others not? If policies were to allow people to buy various levels of genetic privacy protection, then it is likely that those wanting a high level of genetic privacy would be perceived as trying to hide something. The suspicion would be that genetic privacy is a "guilty man's privilege" (Gerstein, 1970) that would be used to hide genetic weaknesses. If this were to occur, then the level and degree of genetic privacy would likely be set at a lower level than people would optimally prefer.

Consideration of the future of health insurance in an age of genetic mapping illustrates the public good component of the genetic privacy. In an article published in the *New Republic* in 1990, Robert Wright argues that laws establishing that DNA is private and that no one can look at genetic information without the individual's permission will not be enough. He recognizes that if insurance companies offer discounts to people with "good" genes, those people will voluntarily divulge their genetic information and the cost of insurance for everybody else will go up. Even if the government were to prohibit people from revealing genetic information to insurance companies, if people know their genetic information they would not want to buy insurance against diseases they are not likely to get (Wright, 1990:26). With this scenario in mind, genetic privacy may not be in the interest of any particular individual but may be in the collective interest. In discussing the possibility of using genetic information as the basis for insurance groupings, the president of the Association of Academic Health Centers regards this as "a specter so unpalatable and unjust that our society could not tolerate it" (Bulger, 1991:C4).

Somewhat ironically, the issue of genetic screening, which initially was seen as having the potential to destroy our common notions of privacy and individuality, may instead be an issue through which it will be easier to begin to discuss the social importance of privacy. Arguments can be made that genetic privacy is a common value, a public value, and a collective value. Given these values, the kinds of public policies that would be appropriate would involve government restrictions on the collection and use of certain kinds of genetic information in certain circumstances. This would result in a higher level of protection for individual privacy than would be likely if the goal were only to protect individual interests.

Notes

1. According to this concept, the employment relationship is traditionally viewed as a contract between two equal parties, with the employer buying the labor that the employee wants to sell. Each party to the contract enters it freely and can break it at a later time—the employer can fire or the employee can quit. This contract concept does not recognize the differences in bargaining power that exist between an individual employee and an employer, especially a large corporate employer. For discussion of the policy implications, see U.S. Congress, Office of Technology Assessment (1987: chap. 1).

2. There are some important exceptions to this. In 1989, researchers located the gene involved in most cases of cystic fibrosis; with current screening methods the tests yield probabilities, not certainties, about the presence or absence of the gene. The genetic basis for Down's syndrome and sickle-cell anemia have been known for some time, and tests are available for screening for these genes in a fetus. Some caution against a "gene of the week" psychology that may accompany genetic advances. For discussion of scientific developments and ethical concerns in this area, see Joyce (1990).

3. For example, research seems to indicate a connection between certain genetic patterns (not necessarily the presence or absence of a particular gene) and a susceptibility to developing certain kinds of cancers. More detailed knowledge of the genetic basis of cancer will increase our ability to recognize cancer development and cancer risk factors, and will influence approaches to prevention and therapy (Bankowski, 1988).

4. The project is interested first in "mapping" and then in "sequencing" the human genome. *Mapping* refers to knowledge about the location of a gene on a chromosome. Information comes from family linkage studies and bio-

chemical measurements. Sequencing is a more involved and detailed process entailing the breakdown of the biochemical parts of DNA into its component parts, nucleotides. Sequencing makes possible the ability or opportunity to develop drugs or treatments on the molecular level (Fletcher and Wertz, 1990:754–55)

5. In an interesting and thorough analysis of the discrimination questions posed by the use of genetic information, Larry Gostin (1990) concludes that although it is likely that the Americans with Disabilities Act of 1990 would cover discrimination based upon future disability, as would be revealed by genetic testing, an amendment to the ADA may be necessary to cover any uncertainty. There was little congressional attention to genetic discrimination during hearings and floor debates, and at this juncture it would be left to the courts to decide if discrimination based upon a predicted disability revealed by genetic tests comes under the scope of the ADA. For other discussions regarding the applicability of the ADA to genetic conditions, see Orentlicher (1990); for an earlier discussion of discrimination questions, see Peirce (1985).

6. The following sections are derived from a lengthier and more developed argument about the social importance of privacy that is contained in Regan (1995, see especially chap. 8).

7. Conversations I had with Helen Nissenbaum at Princeton University's Center for Human Values were important in the development of this distinction.

8. In 1990, the survey conducted by Louis Harris & Associates did not include the preamble, "Now let me ask you about technology and privacy." See Harris and Westin (1990:2).

9. In *United States v. Miller*, 425 U.S. 435 (1976), the Supreme Court rejected Miller's claim that he had a Fourth Amendment reasonable expectation of privacy in the records kept by banks "because they are merely copies of personal records that were made available to the banks for a limited purpose," and ruled instead that "checks are not confidential communications but negotiable instruments to be used in commercial transactions." In response to this decision, Congress passed the Right to Financial Privacy Act of 1978, providing bank customers with some privacy regarding records held by banks and other financial institutions. The records of customers' rental transactions in video stores were similarly regarded as the property of the video store with no protection for the individual, until Congress passed the Video Privacy Act of 1990.

10. Rawls discusses the question of eugenics and social justice as follows: "In the original position, then, the parties want to insure for their descendants the best genetic endowment (assuming their own to be fixed). The pursuit of reasonable policies in this regard is something that earlier generations owe to later ones, this being a question that arises between generations. Thus over time a society is to take steps to preserve the general level of natural abilities and to prevent the diffusion of serious defects. . . . I mention this speculative and difficult matter to indicate once again the manner in which the difference principle is likely to transform problems of social justice" (1971:108).

References

American Association for the Advancement of Science. (1991). *The Genome, Ethics and the Law: Issues in Genetic Testing* (proceedings of the Conference on the Ethical and Legal Implications of Genetic Testing, June 14–16). Washington, D.C.: American Association for the Advancement of Science.

American Educational Research Association, American Psychological Association, and National Council on Measurement in Education. (1985). *Standards for Educational and Psychological Testing.* Washington, D.C.: American Psychological Association.

Annas, George A. (1990). "Mapping the Human Genome and the Meaning of Monster Mythology." *Emory Law Journal* 39: 629–64.

Arendt, Hannah. (1958). *The Human Condition.* Chicago: University of Chicago Press.

Arndt, H. W. (1949). "The Cult of Privacy." *Australian Quarterly* 21 (September).

Bankowski, Zbigniew. (1988). "Genetics, Medicine and Ethics." *World Health* (December), 3–5.

Bishop, Jerry E., and Michael Waldholz. (1990). *Genome: The Story of the Most Astonishing Scientific Adventure of Our Time.* New York: Simon & Schuster.

Bulger, Roger J. (1991). "How the Genome Project Could Destroy Health Insurance." *Washington Post,* August 4, C4.

Cavoukian, Ann. (1989). "Genetic Engineering: The Ultimate Threat to Privacy." Remarks made on behalf of the Information and Privacy Commissioner/Ontario at Access '89, meeting of the American Society of Access Professionals, April 14.

Cook-Deegan, Robert Mullan. (1991). "The Human Genome Project: The Formation of Federal Policies in the United States, 1986–1990." In Kathi E. Hanna (ed.), *Biomedical Politics.* Washington, D.C.: National Academy Press.

Culnan, Mary J. (1993). "Consumer Attitudes toward Direct Mail, Privacy, and Name Removal: Implications for Direct Marketing." Paper prepared for the Symposium on Consumer Privacy, Chicago/Midwest Direct Marketing Days, Chicago, January 20.

Davis, Joel. (1990). *Mapping the Code.* New York: John Wiley.

Dewey, John. (1927). *The Public and Its Problems.* Chicago: Swallow.

Diamond, Ann Lucas. (1983). "Genetic Testing in Employment Situations." *Journal of Legal Medicine* 4, no. 2: 231–56.

Etzioni, Amitai. (1993). *The Spirit of Community.* New York: Crown.

Fletcher, John C., and Dorothy C. Wertz. (1990). "Ethics, Law, and Medical Genetics: After the Human Genome Is Mapped." *Emory Law Journal* 39: 747–809.

Fried, Charles. (1968). "Privacy." *Yale Law Journal* 77: 475–93.

Gavison, Ruth. (1980). "Privacy and the Limits of the Law." *Yale Law Journal* 89: 421–71.

Gerstein, Robert S. (1970). "Privacy and Self-Incrimination." *Ethics* 80: 87–101.

Gostin, Larry. (1991). "Genetic Discrimination: The Use of Genetically Based Diagnostic and Prognostic Tests by Employers and Insurers." *American Journal of Law & Medicine* 17, nos. 1–2: 109–44.

Grisolia, James Santiago. (1991). "The Human Genome Project and Our Sense of Self." *Impact of Science on Society* 41, no. 161: 45–48.

Louis Harris & Associates. (1983). "The Road after 1984: A Nationwide Survey of the Public and Its Leaders on the New Technology and Its Consequences for American Life." Survey conducted for Southern New England Telephone, for presentation at the Eighth International Smithsonian Symposium, December.

Louis Harris & Associates and Alan F. Westin. (1983). "The Dimensions of Privacy: A National Opinion Research Survey of Attitudes toward Privacy." Survey conducted for Sentry Insurance, December.

———. (1990). *The Equifax Report on Consumers in the Information Age.* Atlanta, Ga.: Equifax.

Head, J. G. (1962). "Public Goods and Public Policy." *Public Finance* 17 no. 3: 197–219.

Joyce, Christopher. (1990). "Your Genome in Their Hands." *New Scientist,* August 11, 52–55.

Kelves, Daniel J., and Leroy Hood (eds.). (1992). *The Code of Codes.* Cambridge, Mass.: Harvard University Press.

Leo, John. (1989). "Genetic Advances, Ethical Risks." *U.S. News & World Report,* September 25, 59.

Madison, James. (1961). "Federalist Paper #10." In *The Federalist Papers.* New York: Mentor.

Mill, John Stuart. (1939). "On Liberty" (1859). In Edwin A. Burtt (ed.), *The English Philosophers from Bacon to Mill.* New York: Modern Library.

Moore, Barrington, Jr. (1984). *Privacy: Studies in Social and Cultural History.* Armonk, N.Y.: M. E. Sharpe.

Moseley, Ray, Lee Crandall, Marvin Dewar, David Nye, and Harry Ostrer. (1991). "Ethical Implications of a Complete Human Gene Map for Insurance." *Business & Professional Ethics Journal* 10, no. 4: 69–82.

Olson, Mancur. (1965). *The Logic of Collective Action.* Cambridge, Mass.: Harvard University Press.

Orentlicher, David. (1990). "Genetic Screening by Employers." *Journal of the American Medical Association* 263, no. 7: 1005, 1008.

Ostrer. (1991). "Ethical Implications of a Complete Human Gene Map for Insurance." *Business & Professional Ethics Journal* 10, no. 4: 69-82.

Ostrom, Vincent, and Elinor Ostrom. (1971). "Public Choice: A Different Approach to the Study of Public Administration." *Public Administration Review* 31 (March/April): 203–16.

Peirce, Ellen R. (1985). "The Regulation of Genetic Testing in the Workplace: A Legislative Proposal." *Ohio State Law Journal* 46, no. 4: 771–843.

Pennock, J. Roland, and John W. Chapman. (1971). *Privacy* (Nomos XIII,

Yearbook of the American Society for Political and Legal Philosophy). New York: Atherton.

Posner, Richard A. (1978). "An Economic Theory of Privacy." *Regulation* (May/June): 19–26.

Privacy Commissioner of Canada. (1992). *Genetic Testing and Privacy.* Ottawa: Minister of Supply and Services Canada.

Rawls, John. (1971). *A Theory of Justice.* Cambridge, Mass.: Belknap Press of Harvard University Press.

Regan, Priscilla M. (1995). *Legislating Privacy: Technology, Social Values, and Public Policy.* Chapel Hill: University of North Carolina Press.

Rowinski, Laura. (1988). "Genetic Testing in the Workplace." *Journal of Contemporary Health Law and Policy* 4: 375–413.

Schoeman, Ferdinand David (ed.). (1984). *Philosophical Dimensions of Privacy: An Anthology.* Cambridge: Cambridge University Press.

Society for Industrial and Organizational Psychology. (1987). *Principles for the Validation and Use of Personnel Selection Procedures* (3rd ed.). College Park, Md.: Society for Industrial and Organizational Psychology.

U.S. Congress, Office of Technology Assessment (OTA). (1983a). *The Role of Genetic Testing in the Prevention of Occupational Disease* (OTA-BA-194, April). Washington, D.C.: U.S. Government Printing Office.

———. (1983b). *Scientific Validity of Polygraph Testing: A Research Review and Evaluation* (OTA-TM-H-15, November). Washington, D.C.: U.S. Government Printing Office.

———. (1987). *The Electronic Supervisor: New Technology, New Tensions* (OTA-CIT-333, September). Washington, D.C.: U.S. Government Printing Office.

———. (1990a). *The Use of Integrity Tests for Pre-Employment Screening* (OTA-SET-442, September). Washington, D.C.: U.S. Government Printing Office.

———. (1990b). *Genetic Monitoring and Screening in the Workplace* (OTA-BA-455, October). Washington, D.C.: U.S. Government Printing Office.

Walzer, Michael. (1984). "Liberalism and the Art of Separation." *Political Theory* 12 (August): 315–30.

Warren, Samuel D., and Louis D. Brandeis. (1890). "The Right to Privacy." *Harvard Law Review* 4 (December 15).

Westin, Alan F. (1967). *Privacy and Freedom.* New York: Atheneum.

Wright, Robert. (1990). "Achilles' Helix." *New Republic,* July 9–16, 21–31.

Privacy and Surveillance in
Computer-Supported Cooperative Work

Judith A. Perrolle

In considering the effects of computerized surveillance in the workplace, analysts have tended to make two assumptions that obscure complex relationships among surveillance, privacy, and group processes. When privacy is implicitly defined as the absence of organizational surveillance of individuals, the importance of mutual surveillance for the functioning of small groups is ignored. When group work is approached as if it were a matter of coordinating the tasks of individual group members, the social processes by which small groups form solidarity and exert informal social control over members' behavior are ignored. Designers of computer-supported cooperative work (CSCW) systems are beginning to create software to facilitate groups of people working together on the same task, rather than simply to coordinate groups of individuals working on separate tasks.[1] In doing so, they have inadvertently created new possibilities for organizational surveillance of employees.[2] In addressing workplace privacy concerns, it is important for CSCW designers to appreciate the ways these issues affect groups, not just individuals.

Privacy

Privacy as the freedom to be left alone by other individuals and by social groups has been distinguished from privacy as freedom from the intrusions of formal institutions and authorities into personal life. Analysts of computerized surveillance in the workplace have tended to focus on the latter, neglecting the social characteristics of privacy as a small group phenomenon. Privacy involves more than the ability to keep information about oneself away from authorities who might use it to control one's behavior; it also involves the ability for individuals, small groups, and organizations to negotiate mutual demands on time, space, and actions.

47

According to Barrington Moore Jr. (1984), privacy involves both the right of individuals to be left alone by others (family, neighbors, coworkers, and so on) and freedom from the intrusions of formal bureaucratic institutions and authorities. The former is guaranteed in all societies through social rules that specify the situations in which people's behavior is to be ignored—in other words, when they are to be free of informal social control. Often this does not mean isolation from others, just being left alone. The latter sense of privacy is formally established in law in modern democratic societies and defines limits on surveillance and institutionalized social controls (such as the police). There is also a third sense of privacy in which social groups are left alone by formal authorities and are free to pursue their own goals, including exerting social control over their members. This is similar to what Ferdinand Schoeman (1992) refers to as the "context" in which privacy is an issue. Families and religious groups have traditionally had this sense of privacy in the United States, although this is now being eroded in some areas, such as child abuse. This third sense of privacy seems particularly relevant to the topic of computer-supported cooperative work, because working groups need some autonomy from their organizations in order to engage in the processes by which small groups form and influence their members' behavior.

Privacy as Freedom to Be Left Alone

The desire for "protection or escape from other human beings, emerges when an individual becomes subject to social obligations that that individual cannot or does not want to meet" (Moore, 1984:268). Preindustrial societies evolved a variety of mechanisms through which individuals could avoid temporarily and in more or less socially accepted ways the demands of their communities. By our own standards, the opportunities for privacy were often limited—all bodily functions, for example, might be performed in front of other people. "Being sick" is a modern example of privacy in this sense. If we are ill, we can stay home and avoid social interaction. However, the urgings of our friends to "get well," the invasion of our bodies by medical personnel, and organizations' insistence on "notes from our doctors" are social control mechanisms that limit our freedom to be sick privately in the interests of getting us back to our normal social roles (Parsons, 1951: chaps. 7, 10).

When our right to be sick is interfered with by the health care system and by our employers, we experience invasion of privacy in Moore's second sense. This form of privacy involves the concept of the individual's rights against external authorities. In modern societies, people seek privacy from organizations and institutions as well as from one another. The privacy debate over computer use for government and corporate record keeping is about this second sense of privacy—the right of individuals to be left alone by their government and by the economic organizations of their society. This right of privacy is often in direct conflict with the norms governing our obligations to work and to obey society's laws and regulations.

The legal concept of privacy in the United States is based on the idea that the individual, rather than the group, is the basic unit of society.[3] In 1890, attorneys Samuel Warren and Louis Brandeis published a landmark legal opinion extending the common-law right to life to "the right to be let alone" to enjoy life. The right to property was extended to the right to own intellectual property—including information about one's personal life. Contemporary analysts have located privacy in the Bill of Rights of the U.S. Constitution. The right to exchange information is based on First Amendment freedom of speech. Private telephone conversations are protected by the Fourth Amendment's ban on unreasonable searches and seizures. The 1973 *Roe v. Wade* decision extended Fourteenth Amendment protection to the right to give and receive information. U.S. Congressman Sam Ervin has noted that "privacy is a catchword for the control that the individual exercises over information about himself" (1983:160).

Privacy as Control over Information about Oneself

Ownership and control are attached to information as to anything else—through possession legitimated by law and custom. We are now going through a period of social and technological change in our fundamental conception of intellectual property that may transform the social definition of information as radically as the emergence of private ownership transformed land use in the centuries before the industrial revolution (Perrolle, 1987). Our concern about surveillance and privacy in CSCW is only a small part of our response to great change in the conditions of work and life in contemporary societies. By asserting our right to "own" information about ourselves, we have already agreed that information is a form of property. And most of us recognize the rights of employers and governments to exert control over employees and citizens. The source of our anxiety is not the principle of formal institutional surveillance and control over us—that is implicit in our acceptance of life in a modern capitalist nation. Rather, we are upset by the technological possibilities for a vastly expanded exercise of corporate and government ability to keep track of us.

Culture, defined as the entire way of life shared by a people, includes implied social contracts as well as formal rules and laws. Much of culture's content is public domain information—ideas, beliefs, languages, history, scientific knowledge, and so forth. Smaller groups have subcultures with their own shared bodies of knowledge and rules of behavior. By tradition, some personal information about individuals is public property of their societies or subcultures. For example, few people would consider private their physical location while crossing a street. Most of us agree that this information should be freely available to drivers and other pedestrians without our permission. This sort of surveillance supplies the information we must have about one another in order to live as social beings. Different cultures and subcultures have developed quite different implied social contracts regarding the personal and the public. Within some families, for instance, members give one another considerable personal privacy; in others, individual members' actions and communications are subject to constant scrutiny.

Organizations have subcultures that define implied social contracts for employee and management behavior.[4] Yet, because these corporate cultures differ among themselves, it is impossible to anticipate precisely what sorts of intrusiveness and what areas of personal privacy will be desired by CSCW users. This can be seen in the very different results of experiments with active badges. Information about where an individual worker is at all times during working hours is defined as public information in some organizations and as private in others. It seems clear that the introduction of active badges into the latter type of organization will be enormously disruptive, with employees objecting to change in their tacit social contract. In the former type of organization, active badges will provide technological support for information that already "belongs" to the organization and its subgroups. This shows the futility of trying to analyze privacy issues related to new technologies based on inherent properties of the technologies. It is the cultural context that defines privacy, both through formal negotiations that result in laws, regulations, and employment contracts and through the informal social interactions that produce implied social contracts.

Privacy as Negotiated Access Restrictions

Privacy is a complex, multilayered set of arrangements, both formal and informal, that regulates the exchange of information about individuals and groups. If the purpose of CSCW is to support the actual activities of cooperative groups, some attention must be paid to the ways groups negotiate privacy. This involves investigation of at least two levels of privacy: the individual's privacy from the demands of the group and the organization, and the group's privacy from the organization. The former includes, for example, questions about how accessible individuals must be. The latter includes issues such as how company time and resources may be used by work groups.

The totally private individual does not exist in the workplace, or in any other formal or informal social organization. Groups of all sorts depend on information about their members' behavior in order to define group membership, create solidarity and commitment, develop and enforce standards of conduct, and perform group tasks.[5] But in exerting social control over their members, informal social groups develop unwritten agreements about how much and what kinds of freedom members will have. Individuals agree on how to avoid intrusions on one another's time, space, and behavior without interpreting "being left alone" as isolation or rejection of social relationships. This often involves contradictions in behavioral norms. Because isolating oneself from the group is a form of deviance, members agree in principle not to do so. But in actual practice, members tacitly negotiate the circumstances under which failing to interact with others or neglecting to inform others of one's whereabouts or actions is allowed or even encouraged.

Individually Negotiated Privacy

Individuals frequently negotiate privacy in the workplace by claiming to be busy at some task of higher priority than interacting with managers or coworkers. They can also claim to be engaged in a culturally agreed-upon private activity, such as going to the bathroom or being on their lunch hour. In the case of the lunch hour, most organizational cultures define such times as freedom from official intrusions but vulnerable to social demands of coworkers. Negotiations over "Shall we go to lunch?" or "Can I call you about it on Sunday morning?" are a nontrivial part of how newly formed work groups begin to establish limitations on members' access to one another. Nonverbal cues (see Druckman, Rozelle, and Baxter, 1982) such as a closed office door or looking at one's watch or one's work after returning a greeting are subtle indicators of a desire to be left alone. People tacitly learn and unconsciously interpret these signals as they negotiate mutual intrusions.

In electronic communications subtle cues are lost (Kiesler, Siegel, and McGuire, 1991), but technology can sometimes be used as a substitute. For example, answering machines can be used as call-screening devices, so that you can know that someone has sent you a message without letting them know that you have just received it. You can then decide whether to be "at home" or not. But, by putting the power to decide if a conversation will take place in the hands of the receiver, answering machines remove some of the social controls on communication. If you don't answer your phone when someone calls, the penalty is that you don't always get the message. With an answering machine, you acquire the power to receive information without the obligation of speaking to others. Telephone tag is a new version of the game of who is more important than whom. It is an example of how the quest for individual privacy involves issues of status, power, and autonomy as well as freedom from intrusion.

Group-Negotiated Privacy

Social interaction theorists sometimes refer to group privacy as a "backstage" area in which the group's behavior is not on public view (Goffman, 1961). Social interaction in their shared private spaces provides groups with social control over group resources and activities away from the surveillance of organizational authorities. Limiting access by outsiders helps a group define its membership and boundaries. Having its own resources to allocate to or withhold from members helps a group maintain internal social control. Backstage activities, such as making mistakes and wasting company time in socializing, are necessary and inevitable, and they do not exist in the group's front-stage presentation of itself and its completed work. Eating together, planning recreational activities, and holding personal conversations are important ways in which small groups develop solidarity and enhance member commitment. They are often formally defined as a waste of company time and resources, and so must occur within a sphere of group privacy.

It is important to realize that the implied social contracts negotiated by groups often contradict the formal rules of their organizations. For example, whispered asides do not exist in *Robert's Rules of Order*. What makes an aside private is not that other people cannot hear it, but that it is ignored as "not part of" whatever discussion is going on. One thing that asides usually do, however, is indicate a lack of respect for whoever is speaking at the moment. They are part of the informal way audiences communicate with a speaker. In most electronic communications systems we have not really worked out the conversational problem of turn taking, and we seem to have lost the nonverbal indicators of boredom and disinterest. Thus, we are unable to negotiate an informal end to someone's speech using customary body language and noises. If we formalized group meetings completely, individual participants would lose some of their power to reject demands on their time and attention.

The Case of Electronic Mail

Electronic mail is a particularly interesting case of negotiated privacy. At the societal level, we have not yet formalized a uniform set of access restrictions for it. If it is defined as being equivalent to paper mail, the privacy of its contents is guaranteed by law. As with e-mail, actual protection of mail privacy depends on people's respect for it. Given that mailboxes are relatively easy to pry open and that many workplaces deliver mail to open mailboxes in public rooms, one's colleagues may be physically able to browse through one's mail. But, because mail is socially defined as private property, they would hate to be caught doing it. Alternatively, if we agree that e-mail messages are equivalent to things posted on bulletin boards, then it is acceptable for others within one's organization to look through one's e-mail—though it would be unacceptable for a stranger to wander through the organization reading the walls.

The ways individuals are expected to respond to e-mail messages are also negotiable. Paper mail takes time to arrive and can be answered after a socially acceptable delay. Express mail and faxes have shortened expected response time. We have lost one means of negotiating extra time, the polite fiction: "The mail hasn't arrived yet." Telephones, which used to demand immediate attention, have been modified by voice mail and answering machines to lengthen expected response time. The time demands of e-mail are currently being negotiated. I have been experimenting with reading my e-mail once a week; under pressure from my colleagues, I am beginning to attend to it more often. Through subtle exercise of normative power, my colleagues are gradually wearing me down, and I seem likely to join the ranks of the information overloaded. In many organizations, electronic mail runs constantly on employees' desks, and new messages beep for attention; I hope that my organization will not be one of them. The decision about what form electronic mail will take at my university will be made by the administration in consultation with computer vendors and a faculty committee. Unfortunately, the choice seems to have been defined by all involved as a technical rather than a social issue.

We have also not decided on a single definition of to whom the contents of e-mail messages belong. Most companies claim ownership of communications on their systems and reserve the right to examine them. Most individuals and small groups are used to being able to have private conversations in the workplace, and resent employer eavesdropping. Attempts to solve the privacy problem in electronic mail design must be sensitive to the social characteristics of privacy and realize that actual groups negotiate a variety of different solutions. They should also realize that trying to make all communications formal and public can inhibit what individuals say to one another, can make it more difficult for groups to function, and can increase the intrusiveness of organizational authorities into individual working life.

A Theoretical Basis for Negotiated Privacy

The negotiation of privacy in computer-supported cooperative work is essentially a small group political process involving critical issues of how organizational power and autonomy are distributed. An absence of public negotiation of goals and behavior is characteristic of authoritarian, intrusive workplaces. CSCW systems that restrict discussions to technical questions of how to accomplish predefined group tasks distort privacy negotiations by embedding relationships of power and authority into the software itself.

Reification

Reification, the embodiment of social relationships in objects, distorts negotiation by making the power of those who design, implement, own, and manage computer systems appear as a natural feature of the working environment. Instead of seeing who is exerting what sort of control over the activities of whom through CSCW, we seem to be in a world of relationships between persons and objects. Our privacy is intruded on by technology rather than by people with whom we can negotiate access restrictions.

Individuals and groups can adapt and learn to function as new technologies do. After all, a species that learned to repress its biological characteristics in order to work on assembly lines and awake to alarm clocks should be able to get used to even the worst of CSCW designs. Our experiences in the workplace can even be transferred to our nonworking lives, just as our patterns of leisure and social life have taken on many of the scheduled, goal-oriented characteristics of modern workplace activity. For example, I once observed the application of a token ring protocol to the activity of a group that had just met at a conference and had gone to a Chinese restaurant. A piece of paper was passed around the table, and each individual added a choice to the list. The usual small group process did not develop very fully. Instead of beginning to learn one another's preferences and interaction styles while observing the spontaneous emergence of possible group leaders, we obtained food efficiently and talked like strangers. Today I cannot remember those present or what we spoke about, yet I vividly recollect other conference dinners from many years ago where enthusiasm and emotional warmth began a process that resulted in professional collaborations and friendships.

As the process of reification occurs, rational procedures and technologies begin to replace social interactions. The result is a diminished capacity for individuals to commit themselves to groups and for groups to engage their members in collective endeavors. Although individuals may appear to obtain more privacy, it occurs at the cost of their being isolated from groups. At the same time, individuals and groups lose much of their ability to negotiate privacy as a part of their working lives. If CSCW designers mistake isolation for privacy, the social basis for cooperation will be reified instead of supported.

Nondistorted Communication

Jürgen Habermas's (1979, 1984) theory of communicative action views communication as a fundamental basis for society. In what Habermas calls the ideal speech situation, all participants have equal opportunities to participate in nondistorted, rational discourse. In situations where some participants use their social status or their power and authority to inhibit the conversation of others, distorted communication occurs. Because computer interfaces remove individuals from the physical presence of others, social context cues to status and power are obscured, reducing some of the means by which distorted communication occurs. Yet computer interfaces can reify unequal social relationships in their design, making power and authority appear as features of a world of objects. When this occurs, opportunities for computer-mediated nondistorted communication are limited (Perrolle, 1991).

In order to approach Habermas's ideal speech situation, individuals in a negotiation make four sets of claims regarding their competence to participate. The first type of claim involves a speaker's linguistic competence—everyone must be making sense in a language all can understand. In computer-mediated communications, difficulties with typing or otherwise using the system may be interpreted by others as indicators of incompetence. Because typing is slower than speaking, CSCW interfaces using video or voice to replace the keyboard enable individuals and groups to converse more competently. Defining part of the CSCW system (such as databases, interface characteristics, or even the basic design) as outside the area of a group's expertise reduces that group's ability to negotiate competently. Designer attitudes that users are incompetent to talk sensibly about technical issues is a rejection by designers of users as competent negotiators of their own privacy.

The second type of claim made in nondistorted communication involves the nature of external reality. In ideal speech situations, speakers interrogate one another to establish claims about what is true. In bureaucratic organizations, truth is located in formal rules and official knowledge. In computerized organizations, databases and technology often reify and limit the objective world of working groups and individuals. To the degree that CSCW systems limit the universe of discourse subject to negotiation, groups lose autonomy. Besides reducing opportunities for privacy, this can have a negative effect on groups' decision making and can restrict an organization's ability to solve problems outside of predefined possibilities.

A third claim that participants in nondistorted communication must trust is that each intends to have a rational conversation, rather than to intimidate or mislead others to his or her own advantage. In situations where great differences in status or power distort face-to-face communication, the tendency of computer-mediated communication users to focus on statements of fact and not intentions can facilitate social interaction. In the absence of visual cues, the contributions of low-status individuals are not automatically ignored. Yet when conversations take place under the control of organizational authorities, some intentions are reified. Research on the perception of intention indicates that people easily attribute intention to objects (Dasser, Ulbaek, and Premack, 1989). Perceptions of CSCW systems as neutral technology with user-friendly intentions obscures managerial intent, such as getting the most work out of employees for the least expenditure in wages and benefits. In other words, any managerial intentions to exert maximum control over employees by surveillance of any lapses in performance will tend to be reified in CSCW systems.

Finally, nondistorted communication must be conducted in socially appropriate ways. Research indicates that computer-mediated communication alters the social norms governing conversation by removing elements of emotion and social control (Kiesler et al., 1991). It also provides the possibility of more equal participation by obscuring the visual and verbal status distinctions that give higher-ranking or more aggressive people an advantage in face-to-face speech. For example, in face-to-face conversation, women are expected to allow themselves to be interrupted by men (Zimmerman and West, 1975). Similar conversational norms allow high-status people to interrupt low-status ones (Molotch and Boden, 1985). In circumstances where opportunities for participation are enhanced and opportunities for one speaker to control another are reduced, computer-mediated communication facilitates privacy negotiations. Emotionally based arguments, which often sway opinions in face-to-face situations, are less likely to influence the outcomes of computer-based discussions. With ordinary mechanisms of social control missing, participants in computer-based discussions have more freedom to develop new and unconventional implied social contracts. The price that small groups pay is a reduction in their ability to develop strong feelings of solidarity.

Surveillance as Reification and Distortion of Negotiated Privacy

Computer surveillance threatens to undermine the social character of privacy in the workplace by providing a technological means to reify large areas of social interaction and distort the small group processes by which individual and group workplace privacy is negotiated. The reification process begins when informal social interactions and implied social contracts are made more formal, more explicit, and more subject to surveillance.

Whenever individuals are being informally watched or listened to, they are somewhat inhibited by what they imagine others' reactions to be. This is how informal social control works in groups. We tend to try not to upset the people around us, especially if they have the means to retaliate in some way. Gossip and other private communications are an ordinary part of both group and organizational office politics. In informal conversation it is one person's word against another's as to what was said and by whom. A private comment can be publicly denied. However, once a conversation gets recorded (for example, in a paper memo or in an e-mail message), it assumes a more formal existence. As people begin to suspect they will be held accountable for their spontaneous utterances, their freedom to express themselves is inhibited. Although this may be an improvement in the case of malicious gossip, it also destroys the backstage area where so much of group work is actually done.

When groups become more formal, as has been a characteristic of workplaces since the Industrial Revolution, bureaucratic structures of surveillance by persons in formal positions of authority tend to replace the informal negotiations of small group members in defining an individual's sphere of privacy. But even under formal rules of work, organizations develop informal agreements about actual behavior that differ substantially from job descriptions and company regulations. Professional and technical employees in particular are able to avoid the close formal surveillance applied to factory or clerical workers. Many systems now being developed to provide computer support for cooperative work make it technically possible for companies to monitor information about all activities occurring in the workplace or using the company network, including where each person is at all times and what he or she is doing. In the worst case of formalized communications, we would get a CSCW version of "work to the rule" in which everyone does exactly what is set out in his or her job description and no more, and organizations would stop functioning due to lack of informal structure and activity.

In general, technological and bureaucratic forms of surveillance are common in settings where there is low trust. Organizations that use these forms of surveillance also create low-trust workplaces. Conventional computerized workplace surveillance depersonalizes relationships of power and authority, reifying them in managerial technologies. It also relocates trust from the employee's personal reports of his or her own behavior to objective measurements of performance. If employees are not trusted in the first place, the machine may be preferred to the human evaluator. In the most extreme cases—such as lie-detection technology—employees' accounts of even their intentions are no longer trusted by employers. In its most benign form, computerized surveillance in such workplaces replaces the social indignities of being given orders by another person with the impersonal neutrality of the machine. In its worst form, computerized surveillance establishes relationships of intrusive oppression as part of the external reality of the workplace. It would be technically possible, I imagine, to combine visual surveillance of workplace bathrooms with automated drug testing technology. But for such an Orwellian scenario to be implemented, we would have to be living in a world where social trust had broken down so far that we would find children carrying guns to school to protect themselves. In such a world, the prospects for any sort of cooperative work, computerized or otherwise, seem dim. The challenge for CSCW is to provide computer surveillance systems that support instead of reify social interaction.

Designing CSCW for Negotiated Privacy

The ideal of computer support for nondistorted communication among equals in cooperative workplaces has had a powerful appeal to the community of CSCW designers. From the theoretical perspective that privacy consists of negotiated access restrictions, one of the most important human factors in CSCW design is the impact that the system has on users' abilities to negotiate through unreified, nondistorted communications. Negotiating privacy in CSCW is essentially a small group political process involving critical issues of how organizational power and autonomy are distributed. This cannot be determined by software designers, although they can certainly be concerned with supporting the process and with avoiding the potential for abuses.

Supporting Interactional Cues

Designs to support individual privacy negotiations must implement some version of the interactional cues with which individuals make inquiries about one another's accessibility. Bellcore's Cruiser system creates a virtual hallway through which people can stroll and observe who is in their offices. "Privacy blinds" appear as bars across office images, allowing people to observe one another's presence while indicating a desire not to be disturbed. There may be other, less expensive ways to implement negotiated intrusions, perhaps by developing simple status indicators of prioritized requests for attention and for being left alone. Other CSCW features, like active badges, can facilitate negotiated privacy if they have "off" switches.

Privacy for Groups

Group-negotiated privacy can be supported by such features as group work spaces accessible only to group members. Flexibility in the design of these backstage areas will give user groups the opportunity to experiment in negotiating their own structure and expectations. Automated meeting schedulers could be made less than automatic, allowing users and user groups to indicate several different states of "being available" depending on the nature of the meeting being scheduled.

Avoiding Reified Authority

Reification of authority relationships in electronic surveillance could be avoided if users were to be notified whenever their e-mail files were read or backed up. Although this would not prevent surveillance, it would remind all parties involved that the surveillance is being done by people, not by technologies. If e-mail privacy is part of an organization's implied social contract, notification of intrusions could at least serve as a basis for discussion of organizational behavior.

Supporting Nondistorted Communication

If we take Habermas's requirements for nondistorted communication seriously as a basis for negotiated privacy, CSCW systems should be extremely user-friendly, approaching the ease of face-to-face discussion, to facilitate user competence. CSCW designers should remain aware that the world represented by computer software and databases is a socially negotiated one. Insofar as possible, CSCW should not preempt definitions of the subject matter and conduct of work by restricting group activity to preexisting databases and work procedures. Intentions to control cooperative work groups should be implemented explicitly, preferably through discussions with both employees and managers of organizations that will be using the systems. Finally, attention should be paid to the variety of implied social contracts for appropriate behavior in the workplace, so that CSCW communication systems allow group norms to emerge out of group process. This is quite a different problem from trying to develop formal protocols for small group interactions. Even if we could create a standardized group process by capturing and formalizing group behavior, in doing so we would destroy its capacity to generate new social forms out of participant negotiations. There is no technological fix for negotiated privacy.

Conclusion

Designers and implementers of CSCW systems should keep in mind that privacy is not merely absence of information or isolation from interacting with others. Privacy in small groups is the result of a dynamic process in which people negotiate mutual intrusions and avoidance while remaining connected to one another in a context of power and status relationships. If privacy issues are viewed only as relationships between individuals and formal authorities, the effectiveness and quality of life of working groups will be undermined.

Notes

1. For more on the design of CSCW software, see Baecker (1993), Bowers and Benford (1991), Conference on Computer-Supported Cooperative Work (1988, 1990, 1992), Easterbrook (1992), European Conference on Computer-Supported Cooperative Work (1991), Greenbaum and Kyng (1991), Greenberg (1991), Greif (1988), Kensing and Winograd (1991), Marca and Bock (1992), Power (1993), and Sharples (1993).

2. For in-depth discussion of organizational surveillance, see Computer Professionals for Social Responsibility (1991), Deutsch (1986), Hoffman (1980), Law Reform Commission of Canada (1986), Marx and Sherizen (1986), Mendes (1985), Shepard and Duston (1987), and U.S. Congress, Office of Technology Assessment (1987). For discussion of pending legislation, see U.S. Senate, Committee on Labor and Human Resources (1993). A 1994 U.S. Senate bill (S-984) that would have restricted workplace surveillance to performance evaluation only died in committee.

3. For reviews of the legal status of privacy, see Seipp (1978) and Westin (1967). Also, for a history of the legal status of electronic surveillance (mostly in criminal cases), see National Commission for the Review of Federal and State Laws Relating to Wiretapping and Electronic Surveillance (1976).

4. For an introduction to corporate culture, see Deale and Kennedy (1982), Ouchi (1981), Schein (1985), and Smircich (1983).

5. There is a large sociological literature available on small groups, including Homans's (1950) and Olmstead and Hare's (1978) theoretical approaches. Good reviews of the classical literature are presented in Cartwright and Zander (1968), Crosbie (1975), and Hare (1962). Studies of programs to train employees for cooperative work groups can be found in the education literature; see, for example, Dahlstrom (1994) and Slavin (1983).

References

Baecker, Ronald M. (ed.). (1993). *Readings in Groupware and Computer-Supported Cooperative Work: Assisting Human-Human Collaboration.* San Mateo, Calif.: Morgan Kaufmann.

Bowers, John M., and Steven D. Benford, (eds.). (1991). *Studies in Computer Supported Cooperative Work: Theory, Practice, and Design.* New York: Elsevier.

Cartwright, Dorwin, and Alvin Zander (eds.). (1968). *Group Dynamics: Research and Theory.* New York: Harper & Row.

Computer Professionals for Social Responsibility. (1991). *First Conference on Computers, Freedom, and Privacy* (March 25–28).

Conference on Computer-Supported Cooperative Work. (1988). *CSCW '88: Proceedings of the Conference on Computer-Supported Cooperative Work* (September 26–29, Portland, Ore.). New York: Association for Computing Machinery.

———. (1990). *CSCW '90: Proceedings of the Conference on Computer-Supported Cooperative Work* (October 7–10, Los Angeles). New York: Association for Computing Machinery.

———. (1992). *CSCW '92: Sharing Perspectives. Proceedings of the Conference on Computer-Supported Cooperative Work* (October 31 to November 4, Toronto, Ont.). New York: Association for Computing Machinery.

Crosbie, Paul. (1975). *Interaction in Small Groups.* New York: Macmillan.

Dahlstrom, Carl A. (1994). "A Study of Participants' Experiences in an Organizational Entry Program with a Major Cooperative Team Component." Unpublished manuscript, University of Maryland, College Park, Department of Curriculum and Instruction.

Dasser, Verena, Ib Ulbaek, and David Premack. (1989). "The Perception of Intention." *Science* 243 (20 January): 365–67.

Deale, T. E., and A. A. Kennedy. (1982). *Corporate Culture.* Reading, Mass.: Addison-Wesley.

Deutsch, Steven. (1986). *The Context for Exploring Workplace Monitoring,* (report prepared for the U.S. Congress, Office of Technology Assessment). Washington, D.C.: U.S. Government Printing Office.

Druckman, Daniel, Richard M. Rozelle, and James C. Baxter. (1982). *Nonverbal Communication: Survey, Theory, and Research.* Beverly Hills, Calif.: Sage.

Easterbrook, Steve (ed.). (1992). *CSCW: Cooperation or Conflict?* New York: Springer-Verlag.

Ervin, Sam, Jr. (1983). "Justice, the Constitution, and Privacy." In Dennie Van Tassel and Cynthia L. Van Tassel (eds.), *The Compleat Computer.* Chicago: Science Research Associates.

European Conference on Computer-Supported Cooperative Work. (1991). *ECSCW '91: Proceedings of the Second European Conference on Computer-Supported Cooperative Work.* Boston: Kluwer Academic.

Goffman, Erving. (1961). *The Presentation of Self in Everyday Life.* Garden City, N.Y.: Doubleday.

Greenbaum, Joan, and Morten Kyng (eds.). (1991). *Design at Work: Cooperative Design of Computer Systems.* Hillsdale, N.J.: Lawrence Erlbaum.

Greenberg, Saul (ed.). (1991). *Computer-Supported Cooperative Work and Groupware.* London: Academic Press.

Greif, Irene (ed.). (1988). *Computer-Supported Cooperative Work.* San Mateo, Calif.: Morgan Kaufmann.

Habermas, Jürgen. (1979). *Communication and the Evolution of Society.* Boston: Beacon.

———. (1984). *The Theory of Communicative Action* vol. 1, *Reason and the Rationalization of Society,* trans. Thomas McCarthy. Boston: Beacon.

Hare, A. Paul. (1962). *A Handbook of Small Group Research.* New York: Free Press.

Hoffman, Lance J. (ed.). (1980). *Computers and Privacy in the Next Decade* (proceedings of the Workshop on Computers in the Next Decade, February 25–38, 1979). New York: Academic Press.

Homans, George C. (1950). *The Human Group*. New York: Harcourt Brace.

Kensing, Finn, and Terry Winograd. (1991). *The Language/Action Approach to the Design of Computer Support for Cooperative Work* (Report CSLI–91–152). Stanford, Calif.: Stanford University Center for the Study of Language and Information.

Kiesler, Sara, Jane Siegel, and Timothy W. McGuire. (1991). "Social Psychological Aspects of Computer-Mediated Communication." In Charles Dunlop and Rob Kling (eds.), *Computerization and Controversy: Value Conflicts and Social Choices*. Boston: Academic Press, 330–49.

Law Reform Commission of Canada. (1986). *Electronic Surveillance*. Ottawa: Law Reform Commission of Canada.

Marca, David, and Geoffrey Bock. (1992). *Groupware: Software for Computer-Supported Cooperative Work*. Los Alamitos, Calif.: IEEE Computer Society Press.

Marx, Gary T., and Sanford Sherizen. (1986). *Social Aspects of Changes in Worker Monitoring and Computer/Communications Privacy and Security Practices* (report prepared for the U.S. Congress, Office of Technology Assessment). Washington, D.C.: U.S. Government Printing Office.

Mendes, Meredith W. (1985). *Privacy and Computer-Based Information Systems*. Cambridge, Mass.: Center for Information Policy Research.

Molotch, Harvey L., and Deirdre Boden. (1985). "Talking Social Structure: Discourse, Domination, and the Watergate Hearings." *American Sociological Review* 50 (June): 273–88.

Moore, Barrington, Jr. (1984). *Privacy: Studies in Social and Cultural History*. Armonk, N.Y.: M. E. Sharpe.

National Commission for the Review of Federal and State Laws Relating to Wiretapping and Electronic Surveillance. (1976). *Commission Studies*. Washington, D.C.: U.S. Government Printing Office.

Olmstead, Michael, and A. Paul Hare. (1978). *The Small Group*. New York: Random House.

Ouchi, W. G. (1981). *Theory Z*. Reading, Mass.: Addison-Wesley.

Parsons, Talcott. (1951). *The Social System*. New York: Free Press.

Perrolle, Judith A. (1987). *Computers and Social Change: Information, Property, and Power*. Belmont, Calif.: Wadsworth.

———. (1991). "Conversations and Trust in Computer Interfaces." In Charles Dunlop and Rob Kling (eds.), *Computerization and Controversy: Value Conflicts and Social Choices*. Boston: Academic Press, 350–63.

Power, R. J. D. (ed.). (1993). *Cooperation among Organizations: The Potential of Computer Supported Cooperative Work*. New York: Springer-Verlag.

Schein, Edgar H. (1985). *Organizational Culture and Leadership*. San Francisco: Jossey-Bass.

Schoeman, Ferdinand David. (1992). *Privacy and Social Freedom*. Cambridge: Cambridge University Press.

Seipp, David J. (1978). *The Right to Privacy in American History*. Cambridge, Mass.: Center for Information Policy Research.

Sharples, Mike (ed.). (1993). *Computer Supported Collaborative Writing.* New York: Springer-Verlag.

Shepard, Ira M., and Robert L. Duston. (1987). *Workplace Privacy: Employee Testing, Surveillance, Wrongful Discharge and Other Areas of Vulnerability.* Washington, D.C.: Bureau of National Affairs.

Slavin, R. E. (1983). *Cooperative Learning.* New York: Longman.

Smircich, L. (1983). "Concepts of Culture and Organizational Analysis." *Administrative Science Quarterly* 28: 339–58.

U.S. Congress, Office of Technology Assessment. (1987). *The Electronic Supervisor: New Technology, New Tensions* (OTA-CIT-333, September). Washington, D.C.: U.S. Government Printing Office.

U.S. Senate, Committee on Labor and Human Resources. (1993). The Privacy for Consumers and Workers Act: Hearing before the Subcommittee on Employment and Productivity, U.S. Senate, One Hundred Third Congress, first session on S. 984, June 22.

Westin, Alan F. (1967). *Privacy and Freedom.* New York: Atheneum.

Zimmerman, Don, and Candace West. (1975). "Sex Roles, Interruptions, and Silences in Conversation." In Barrie Thorne and Nancy Henley (eds.), *Language and Sex: Difference and Domination.* Rowley, Mass.: Newbury House.

High-Tech Workplace Surveillance: What's Really New?

James B. Rule

Writing about high-tech workplace surveillance is a hazardous business. The hazard stems from two things: first, the strong feelings that most people have on the subject, and second, their conviction that the essential direction of social change is apparent to them. Nearly everyone, it would seem, has some emotional associations to workplace supervision—perhaps because nearly everyone has experienced it, in one form or another. Moreover, most people seem convinced that computing and other technologies are changing the character of workplace monitoring, in ways that they clearly discern. Against these strong currents, those who seek to base their conclusions on empirical research may find it hard to swim.

We can begin with certainty about one thing: the tension between managers' desire to know about employees' work and employees' interest in maintaining control over (and hence a measure of privacy regarding) that work has an extremely long history. As early as the beginning of the nineteenth century, Robert Owen and Jeremy Bentham developed elaborate rationales for the improvement of work, and ultimately of workers, through intensive surveillance of the workplace. In the Enlightenment thinking of their time, these schemes were seen as progressive—as steps in the overall amelioration of the human condition. Today, intellectuals are apt to view innovations in workplace surveillance more nervously—as potential threats to the experience of work and the dignity of the worker.

Thus in the past ten years we have had a spate of writings conveying alarming views of workplace surveillance, most of them with special attention to the role of computing. Books on the subject include Barbara Garson's *The Electronic Sweatshop* (1988), Robert Howard's *Brave New Workplace* (1985), and, most influential of all, Shoshana Zuboff's *In the Age of the Smart Machine* (1988). All these works inveigh against what are seen as the distinctively erosive qualities of computerized surveillance in relation to the experience of work.

These accounts often find a ready resonance in the experience of today's workers. Few if any employees in modern organizations can avoid noticing that provision of information about themselves seems to be a taken-for-granted condition of the employment relationship. In many cases, these data intakes appear to have plausible and even unexceptionable explanations—for example, the need of employers to adjust tax withholding or insurance coverage to correspond to the realities of staff members' lives outside the workplace. But in other cases, employees find themselves the subjects of data collection the purposes of which are unclear or even threatening. Why does the employer need to know all the information required in attitude tests used to select employees, or to assess their potential for advancement? Why are employees' telephone calls, or their use of electronic mail, or their movements about the workplace subject to monitoring? What are the intended purposes of such measures—and can these purposes be justified?

Such apprehensions grow more acute when employees consider the sophisticated ways in which individual data elements can be woven into *inferences* about their future within the organization. Often abetted by the insights of social science, sophisticated management techniques make it possible to predict future developments in an employee's performance that are no part of his or her intentions at an earlier moment—who will become pregnant, who will be at risk for certain potentially disabling diseases, who is apt to favor a union organizing drive. To the employee, the notion of being judged on the basis of anticipated behavior or events yet to unfold will seem unjust and manipulative. To the employer, the efforts to make such judgments may seem like nothing other than prudent concern for the long-term well-being of the organization.

For students of workplace monitoring at the end of the twentieth century, the tension between these perspectives poses a special analytic problem: How are the forms of surveillance implemented by computing and other novel technologies *different* from face-to-face patterns of surveillance long familiar in work relations? Are they inherently more intrusive? Are they distinctively more degrading? Does the availability of the new technologies bring about an *absolute* rise in the level of workplace monitoring? Do inferences about employees' future states or performances undertaken by modern, high-technology methods raise any ethical or policy issues that are distinct from those raised by earlier, less sophisticated judgments made by employers? Or do they simply involve replacement of more familiar, traditional forms of supervision by others?

These questions are unavoidable in any attempt to explore the policy or action implications of workplace surveillance. If analysts cannot show what is distinctive about the new forms of workplace surveillance, they can hardly hope for any particular form of action or policy in response. And, as I hope to show in the pages that follow, such distinctions are by no means easy to defend.

Foucault and Discipline

We get little help in this respect from the work that is no doubt most widely associated with the subject—that of Michel Foucault. Among all of Foucault's many ideas, perhaps the best known are those on the historical encroachment of "discipline"—the notion that the growth of modern social forms has entailed, and continues to entail, relentless and incremental growth in monitoring and control by central authorities. Bentham's panopticon, for Foucault, was nothing other than the embodiment of a pervasive dynamic whose grip on human life was to be felt in all settings. From prisons and asylums to schools and workplaces, central authority was increasingly and oppressively extending itself, apparently stifling individual autonomy and freedom of action. Thus for Foucault, Bentham's panopticon was simply the model of a whole world *in statu nascendi*.

Foucault's vision is afflicted with serious flaws, not the least of which are its historical inaccuracies. As Richard Hamilton notes:

Nowhere in Foucault's work does one learn a simple and rather important fact about the panopticon. A leading criminology text, one Foucault could have used, describes Bentham's effort as follows: "The plans were drawn up, but fortunately for penology this monstrosity was never built." This fact is clearly indicated in Foucault's original source, that is, Bentham's *Works*.

Hollywood, in its many prison movies, has provided a more accurate portrait than that of Foucault's fiction. Most prison movies, it will be remembered, show cell blocks, not panopticons. . . .

Few hospitals, factories, schools, or barracks, moreover, are based on the Bentham plan. The only panopticon-style prison building existing in the United States today is found in Stateville, Illinois where four such structures were built between 1916 and 1925. Foucault's book contains a picture of one of these Stateville buildings but gives no indication that it is the unique example of the style in the United States. (1991:6–7)

But Hamilton's carefully researched dissection of Foucault's arguments labors under a serious disadvantage. What Foucault offers is simply what people in the American West used to call "a great yarn." Beginning with the hair-raising account of the execution of the would-be assassin of Louis XV, and proceeding through a long array of intriguing examples of the rise of subtler forms of control, Foucault conjures up an all but irresistible image of encroaching, but nonintrusive, domination. The trouble is, these images, however captivating, cannot help us answer a question akin to the one entertained above: Are workers—or anyone else—really subject to *more* control, or to *more severe* forms of control, than their predecessors?

Downplayed in Foucault's analyses is the fact that social control is an all but universal social process. It is hard to conceive, even in principle, of any enduring social arrangements without some characteristic forms of social control. Like many other social institutions and processes, the scale on which social control is organized grows with the growth of other modern social forms. So we have nationwide institutions of policing, instead of strictly local ones, or giant corporate personnel systems, rather than direct, face-to-face confrontation between bosses and workers. Moreover, we know that the two broad forms of control may play off against one another; as large-scale controls rise, smaller-scale local ones lose their grip—for all sorts of familiar sociological reasons.

But we have no a priori grounds to conclude that the control of modern, highly centralized institutions is more relentless, more severe, or more total *in its effects on the individual* than large-scale, modern forms of control. True, the modern forms raise distinctive value issues because the collective consequences of their abuse are likely to be more sweeping. An entire nation-state dominated by a dictatorial regime is a greater loss, in value terms, than a feudal principality dominated by an oppressive lord. But which form of control is inherently more destructive from the standpoint of individual experience is far from clear.

The New York Study

If judgments on these matters are not to be rendered a priori, our only recourse is empirical inquiry. To this end, some colleagues and I have been looking at surveillance patterns revealed in a current study of computerized firms in Greater New York. This study, the first part of which was carried out with Paul Attewell between 1985 and 1989, involves interviews in some 161 establishments. These were randomly selected so as to include the greatest possible variety of private sector organizations—having in common only that all relied to at least some degree on computing.

Thus our sample includes both the familiar computerized banks, manufacturing firms, and insurance companies *and* such less predictably computerized sites as medical practices, restaurants, and one horse-breeding farm. At every site, we collected data on each of what we identified as discrete computerized *applications* in use at the site. An application, as we defined it, was a set of activities that ran on its own software and had its own database.

As Peter Brantley and I have noted, our data show first of all that computing is, indeed, employed as a means of employee monitoring (Rule and Brantley, 1992). Out of a total of 181 firms in the sample, we identified some form of computerized surveillance in 73. These 73 firms yielded a total of 101 *applications* involving surveillance. Of these 101 applications, the majority (62.5 percent) were readily classified as part of one of three basic organizational processes: analyses of sales, logging and tracking of work orders, and monitoring of inventory.

Unlike the images of all-pervasive systems of surveillance conveyed in works such as Zuboff's, the vast majority of these instances of computerized surveillance consisted of simple markers of single acts of job performance. One of these cases, for example, was a monitoring system maintained by a Manhattan security company to keep track of the computerized alarm systems installed on its clients' premises. One feature of the system was a "pulse" emitted by the equipment that indicated whether the maintenance staff had serviced the equipment at the client's establishment, as they were supposed to do. To us, this represented an authentic instance of the use of computing to monitor job performance. Yet it hardly conveyed a very complex or rich form of information—basically just a binary signal as to whether the required service had been performed.

What are we to make of cases like these? Certainly they are authentic instances of the use of computing to monitor job performance—and such straightforward applications were very common in our sample. But what moral or sociological difference can we ascribe to such practices in relation to their parallels in old-fashioned, face-to-face supervision? It would be hard to argue, it seems to me, that checking procedures like these are inherently more intrusive, demeaning, or work degrading than conventional ones.

Certainly one would not expect to find cases like this one recounted in the works of Foucault, or even those of Zuboff. They are too banal, too unremarkable in relation to their noncomputerized precedents. Yet they are far more common in our sample of Greater New York firms than anything like the surveillance systems described by these two authors. Indeed, among the establishments in our sample, we found few if any of the highly complex, comprehensive, pervasive systems of computerized work monitoring hinted at by Zuboff.

If we are searching for cases to sustain an argument that there is something distinctive about computerized surveillance, something giving special cause for concern, then we must look further. The most effective cases, it would seem, would be ones involving forms of supervision that could not be accomplished in any way but by computer. And certainly our study affords some cases that seem very distinctive in this way. Consider the report from our interviewer of one of the two computerized restaurants in our study:

> After a waiter or waitress takes an order at a table by hand, he or she goes to one of the five work terminals and [submits] that order by number (all of the . . . items on the menu have inventory numbers). This entry is the sole record of the contents of the order and it is okayed or changed only by a manager working the role of expeditor in the kitchen. . . .
> Nothing can be made or leave the kitchen without a computer slip saying that such and such an order has been logged into the computer (the computer will later print out the customer's bill).

One reason for instituting this system, the manager informed us, was to prevent a specialized form of theft in which items were produced from the kitchen that never appeared on diners' bills. Waiters and waitresses would apparently receive significant tips for arranging such special favors.

A bit later in the interview report, the interviewer comments:

> Waiters can serve their customers faster. Their duties have changed to making sure they can key in orders quickly and accurately, though they have fewer duties in tallying up their tabs. . . . They are supervised differently now from before, since what they order is scrutinized by the expeditor and any special arrangements for orders must be okayed by that manager.

A case like this has greater impact, I think, than the previous one. Why is this? Perhaps because it represents a response to a surveillance problem (from the perspective of management) that seems insoluble with conventional means of watching. It appears to establish tight but unobtrusive controls over workers who might otherwise exercise more discretion over their work—and it makes one wonder whether it might represent a model for all sorts of other surveillance practice in a variety of other work settings.

Does this perception withstand critical scrutiny? I am not so sure. Could we say that no such innovation could—or would—have occurred, without the new technologies? What if management had simply appointed one employee as a human intermediary, to accept orders from the dining room and convey them to the kitchen? Such a possibility is far-fetched, some would say. Even if a human version of the same system were possible in principle, it is not a realistic possibility. Surveillance of this degree of supervision would not have occurred, some would argue, had not computing made it so drastically less expensive than the human alternative.

Perhaps this is so. But if the argument here is that computerization always makes surveillance on balance more intense, I remain skeptical. How do we know that the forms of surveillance that are *losing* ground in the course of these changes are inherently more acceptable than those coming into use? Again, there is no a priori reason to conclude that computerized monitoring is either more severe or more destructive to human values than conventional forms. Some staff interviewed in the New York study, for example, actually welcomed certain forms of computerized checking on their work as a way of "covering their asses"—that is, a way of putting it on record that they had done what was expected of them. This was the case, incidentally, with some of the staff in the restaurant described above. The computerized transmission of orders to the kitchen did at least obviate disputes endemic in restaurants between kitchen and servers, disputes as to what, exactly, had been ordered, and when.

Computerization as a Goad to Rationalization

So, in my view, conclusions that computerized work surveillance must necessarily represent a *net* loss for key human values are problematic. But does this mean that there are *no* generalizations to be made about the role of computerization in the supervision of work?

There is no need to turn away from the subject with such an intellectual shrug. Judging from the information turned up in the New York study, I do believe that computerization creates certain new *occasions* for the monitoring of work. These occasions arise, it seems to me, when computerization provides either the opportunity or the goad necessary for managers to rationalize areas of work life that previously were left to chance and happenstance. In other words, I am suggesting that something about computing enables and encourages those in charge to take more analytic views of their organizations as wholes.

Computerization in effect reclaims and draws attention to information of all kinds that would, in a noncomputerized world, be "wasted." By assembling and analyzing such disparate data, managers in effect extend the reach of their interventions beyond where they would extend in a conventional environment. And sometimes such interventions involve surveillance over staff performance. Consider the account of a small printing firm interviewed in our original sample in the mid-1980s. In the interviewer's words:

> Since [the company does] a lot of rush work, customers call concerning the status of their order. They have instituted a system to track an order through five stages: originating in the office, art department (where off-sets are made), pressroom, collating and binding. A person in each of these areas keeps a log of all jobs that have been completed in that area. They give that to a clerk at the end of each day and it is entered into the computer each morning. In this way, when a customer calls up, one of the customer service reps can call up the order and know which of these five stages has been completed and can then estimate how much longer the order will take.

This is a classic instance of what we have called a "job tracking system," one of the three main kinds of computerized activities that account for the majority of cases of surveillance turned up in our sample. And the effects seem to have been similar to those of many other job tracking systems: by making more accessible and accountable to management the movement of *things,* and the activities associated with those things, computing opens the *people* implicated in these processes to closer scrutiny. Thus, in the words of our interviewer, this system has enabled the owner of this printing company to collect data on how long each job takes. He is beginning to use this to look more closely at jobs that take a long time. He first goes to the foreman in production and tries to find out where the holdup was; sometimes it is machinery, sometimes human error.

As far as we could tell, the creation of the order monitoring application described here was not the result of any interest in staff supervision. The fact that it seems to have led to closer staff monitoring was an unintended consequence, though not necessarily a trivial one.

This theme—the role of computing in bringing together information that would otherwise exist, but not be available to management in a usable way—comes up over and over again in our interviews. The results are often a surprise, even to those who initiate the computerization process in question. And again, these surprises often involve new forms of scrutiny over work performance.

A Basis for Action

Here some distinctive value issues arise, for I see no "natural limit" to these processes, no level of organizational scrutiny inherently too great for the abstracting and summarizing processes of computerized analysis to attain. And concomitantly, I see no human quality, no area of human behavior inherently too "private" to become subject to such attentions. I do not mean by this that work as it is today is necessarily more closely monitored than in other periods; rather, I mean that we need to consider in advance what criteria to apply to the acceptability of workplace monitoring—in both computerized and conventional forms.

Any such formula must be appealing enough to win broad public support, yet clear enough to be workable in practice. In the absence of such a formula, we run the risk that the steady stream of innovation in technology and management practice will continue to endanger the privacy of workers of all kinds.

The search for such a principle is not easy. Certainly, we can expect no help from Foucault. If his words are taken at face value, the relentless extension of "discipline" is beyond the ability of anyone to parry. It is a pervasive and all-conquering cultural dynamic, not something that can be moderated or directed through any kind of enlightened action.

Yet a variety of ad hoc, practical measures are available that can at least diminish the possibility of management peremptoriness in these matters. One might, for example, require that the use of computers or other sophisticated devices for surveillance be approved through collective bargaining. Such a measure is already lawfully binding in Germany.

But such institutional adjustment, desirable though it is, still leaves us without a principle to apply. How much is too much? What *kinds* of workplace surveillance, computerized or other, ought to be admissible? Almost no one, I suspect, would wish to prohibit any role whatsoever for computerized surveillance. After all, it would be a bizarre world in which managers could not take stock of whether or not staff are performing at all. And if informal, face-to-face surveillance is reasonable, then it would seem impossible to object *categorically* to surveillance carried out by computer. As I have sought to show, computerized surveillance is so widely directed to the same sorts of practices and behaviors as conventional surveillance that it is difficult to specify where, precisely, it becomes objectionable.

It will not do, for example, to suggest that only those forms of workplace surveillance—computerized or conventional—are admissible that can be shown to be *relevant* to job performance. True, such a principle would free workers from the dangers of managers' capricious or purely arbitrary demands. But the trouble is that innovations in our ability to know about work and workers constantly render new areas of activity and personality "relevant"—even those most apparently "personal." Thus, for example, if research shows that workers of certain personality types are more likely to question authority, we can well imagine that managers will contrive to use tests that will allow them to choose the other kinds of workers for employment or promotion. Or, similarly, if research were to establish a connection between some aspect of workers' sex lives and productivity, then management would be justified in insisting on reliable information on the subject.

In short, it is easy to devise scenarios for "rational" uses of personal information, either abetted by computing or not, that most people would find highly unacceptable. Yet, again, few if any would wish to defend the position that management has no business monitoring productivity. We still need a principle to distinguish between personal data that management might reasonably be allowed to collect and what should be considered excessive.

Here is my proposal. Management ought to be permitted to collect any data that directly describe performance of employee duties. But collection of information of an inferential kind—for example, information aimed at predicting employees' future productivity—could be collected only with the consent of the employee. Thus counting of widgets, or keystrokes, or loans made by loan officers, or the profitability of those loans after the fact, would be admissible, whether the counting is done by computer or some other method. What would not be admissible would be unilateral attempts to screen out those with hostile attitudes toward management, or those whose work patterns are somehow *associated* with theft, or those who are likely to become pregnant. All of these characteristics could arguably be related to employee "productivity"—at some point, in the near or distant future. But such strictly inferential uses of personal data, it seems to me, are a natural point at which to draw the line as to how far computerized workplace surveillance ought to extend.

Note

I wrote this essay while I was a Mellon Fellow in the School of Social Science, Institute for Advanced Study, Princeton, 1992–93.

References

Garson, Barbara. (1988). *The Electronic Sweatshop*. New York: Simon & Schuster.

Hamilton, Richard. (1991). "The Disciplined Society: Notes on Foucault." Unpublished manuscript, Ohio State University, Sociology Department.

Howard, Robert. (1985). *Brave New Workplace*. New York: Viking.

Rule, James B., and Peter Brantley. (1992). "Computerized Surveillance in the Workplace: Forms and Distributions." *Sociological Forum* 7, no. 3.

Zuboff, Shoshana. (1988). *In the Age of the Smart Machine: The Future of Work and Power*. New York: Basic Books.

Part II

MARKETPLACE

5

Social Control and the Network Marketplace

Abbe Mowshowitz

Computer communications technology offers new ways of forming, maintaining, and modifying social relations. In particular, computer networks facilitate and support social networks. Interconnected local, national, and international computer networks provide the technological means through which people can share experiences and engage in joint activities, *regardless of where they reside.* Networking thus tends to promote a shift in the nexus of social action from traditional, local groups to dispersed groups based on a variety of affinity relations.

Normally, affinity relations involve relatively weak social bonds. People who come together but once a month to trade stamps or discuss books are clearly not as tightly bound to each other as family members or close friends who have many aims in common and a deep pool of shared experience. Nevertheless, affinity groups—collections of individuals with limited common objectives—do shape the attitudes and behavior of their members, especially when the members belong to several such groups with closely related objectives. This shaping of behavior is the essence of *social control,* social structures and mechanisms for ensuring compliance with behavioral norms.

The ability of traditional affinity groups to shape behavior is limited for two reasons. The first is the restricted nature of the groups' shared goals and experiences. The second reason may be described as a proximity constraint—frequency of interaction usually varies inversely with distance, for reasons having to do with travel costs, effort, and local alternatives. Networking eliminates the proximity constraint and increases the size of the population from which affinity groups can be formed. A larger population means that more such groups can be formed, and the greater the number of affinity groups to which an individual belongs, the greater the likelihood that certain objectives and activities will fall within the purview of several groups. This overlap in objectives and activities between groups tends to reinforce affinity relations, and thus to strengthen the social control exercised collectively by the groups.

The technology of computer communications can be used—for better or worse—to extend and intensify the role of affinity groups in the exercise of social control. Nowhere is this control more likely to be elaborated and refined than in the rapidly expanding market for network-based products and services, the *network marketplace.*

Advertisers and political strategists exploit existing affinity relations in the targeting of direct mail. Computer networks facilitate far more powerful and effective targeting than was available previously in the service of advertising, marketing, and campaigning. The growth of such networks will call forth a diverse array of affinity groups and, at the same time, will stimulate the elaboration and perfection of methods for shaping the behavior of individuals within such groups. These evolving methods in the network marketplace signal new directions in social control.

My main objective in this essay is to analyze the possibilities for social control afforded by the network marketplace. Throughout human history, communication technologies have played an important role in shaping social and political institutions (Innis, 1951). These technologies have been used to liberate and to enslave the human spirit, and it is little wonder that much controversy and emotionally charged debate surrounds the latest entrant in the field. Computer-mediated communication could very well support coercive forms of control—indeed, it does already. In describing and analyzing the possibilities for social control in the network marketplace, I aim to provide a sound analytic framework for assessing their social, economic, and political significance.

Because the network marketplace defines the context in which these new forms of social control are developing, the discussion will now turn to a characterization of this marketplace and a sketch of the forces propelling and shaping it. The focus will then shift to an examination of the use of consumer data in targeted advertising, especially direct advertising by means of electronic communication—the network variant of direct mail. This examination will lead directly to a discussion of mechanisms of social control. In particular, I will address the creation of a new form of endogenous control based on affinity groups, formed and maintained by targeted advertising. I conclude the chapter with a look at changes in the process of individuation that may be called into play in the network marketplace.

The Emerging Network Marketplace

A great deal of the basic infrastructure for an information marketplace already exists.[1] The telephone system serves as the basic carrier of information, and various specialized or value-added commercial networks (e.g., SprintNet, Tymnet, Prodigy, CompuServe, and America Online) make use of the telephone system to provide information products and services to businesses and consumers. Cable operators are likely to play an increasingly important role in the future, especially as video entertainment is incorporated into the product mix. However, the current infrastructure is not sufficient to support a truly universal network marketplace. To remedy this deficiency, the Clinton administration has launched the National Information Infrastructure (NII) initiative.

Although the initiative does not spell out the details of the infrastructure, the intention, according to one seasoned observer, is to create an "all-pervasive network that will enable the generation, accession, storage, processing, transmission, and receipt of voice/audio, video, still images, graphics, text, data, and multimedia" (Smoot, 1994:26). This network is what is popularly called the "information superhighway."

Responsibility for the NII initiative is twofold (Roberts, 1994). Major research and development initiatives will be the responsibility of the newly established National Science and Technology Council; NII activities will be coordinated primarily by the Commerce Department. The principal actor within the Commerce Department will be the National Telecommunications and Information Administration. This body will be responsible for three major activities concerned with, respectively, telecommunications policy, applications and technology, and information policy.

The administration's approach to stimulating the development of NII is characterized by five major principles set out by Vice President Gore at the end of 1993 (Roberts, 1994:29). These principles are (1) to encourage private investment, (2) to provide and protect competition, (3) to provide open access to the network, (4) to avoid creating information "haves" and "have-nots," and (5) to encourage flexible and responsive government action. Specific initiatives of the administration include support for the main provisions of the House and Senate telecommunications deregulation bills.

The mechanisms for ensuring open access have yet to elaborated. Accessibility means both the ability to connect to the network and the ability to obtain resources on the network. Ensuring nondiscriminatory access to the physical facilities of the network is comparable to guaranteeing everyone the right to telephone service. The question of access to resources is more complicated, because the network will be host to radically different types of resources, ranging from specialized business services to mass-market products for individual consumers. A method is needed for determining which network resources are to be made universally accessible. One might also ask what products and services will be developed within the administration's framework of private investment and competition. If profitability is the only criterion, the variety and quality of the resources on the network might come to resemble the programming on commercial television.

The magnitude of the NII initiative is evidenced by the Clinton administration's announced goal of connecting to the network all of the classrooms, libraries, hospitals, and clinics in the United States by the year 2000 (Gillespie, 1994). Whatever the actual timetable, the administration's efforts will certainly hasten the construction of the information superhighway.

As indicated above, a limited network marketplace already exists. Many information commodities are already being delivered to customers on various "secondary information highways." For example, electronic mail (e-mail), the electronic exchange of free-form text between users, is a rapidly growing service available on a number of computer networks, including the Internet, with its estimated thirty million users; electronic data interchange (EDI), exchange of structured business forms between computers, is now widely used in commercial transactions; on-line databases offering legal, financial, and statistical information, bibliographies, news reports, and more, are now part of a multibillion-dollar industry; and specialized consumer services such as teleshopping and home banking are growing in importance.

These examples testify to the existence of network infrastructure and to its potential exploitation for the delivery of products and services to organizations and individual consumers.[2] The precise form the infrastructure will take in the future and the mix of information commodities that will obtain are difficult to foresee.[3] As noted above, for example, there are two different network systems offered by the telephone and cable industries, respectively. Each of these industries has the capacity to offer a variety of network-based information commodities, and each is likely to place its own peculiar stamp on the offerings. However, it is just a matter of time—years rather than decades—before the vast majority of homes, as well as businesses, in the industrialized world will be plugged into an extensive marketplace for information commodities, supported by an array of interconnected networks.

My aim in this section is to sketch the consumer segment of the emerging network marketplace. This calls for an examination of the factors likely to affect the growth of consumer markets for computer-based information commodities. I will address these factors with a view to projecting the growth of these markets, taking account implicitly of the principal suppliers and their relative economic and political power positions.

Computer networks, the principal delivery systems for such commodities, have much in common with earlier network-based systems.[4] The networks and services associated with the telephone, the automobile, and radio and television are especially revealing. In particular, it is instructive to compare the diffusion of personal computers with the spread of telephones, automobiles, and radios and television sets. Although quite different in their respective functions, each of these devices acts as a kind of gateway to an array of services that are critically dependent on a network for delivery or support. The delivery and support roles of networks in the diffusion of products offer clues to the future of the network marketplace.

Plugging into the network marketplace is getting easier, but it is still a fairly complex process for the average consumer. There are four major stages in this process:

1. obtaining the equipment—hardware and software—needed to connect to a network;
2. learning how to use the equipment to access network offerings;
3. becoming familiar with the products and services available and then selecting the ones desired; and
4. mastering the use of the chosen products and services.

Economists analyze the growth of markets in terms of supply and demand. In the case of the market for information commodities, *sup-*

ply refers to the network-based products and services offered by vendors, whereas *demand* signifies consumers' needs and desires for products and services. Considerations of supply and demand can also be used to account for a consumer's decision to enter the process described above. Growth in supply encourages consumers to buy, and, conversely, increasing demand prompts suppliers to improve or enlarge their offerings. The influence of these mutually stimulating factors—supply push and demand pull—is examined below.

Supply Push

The extent and diversity of product and service offerings, as well as their cost and ease of use, strongly affect consumers' willingness to connect to networks. Thus, an inventory of existing offerings can give some indication of the likely shape and rate of growth of the emerging marketplace.

I mentioned a few examples of currently available network-based information commodities above. Of these, banking and message exchange are especially important, because they have the potential to reach a mass market. A number of banks currently offer services that enable their customers to obtain account information and initiate transactions (such as transferring money or paying bills) from terminals or personal computers in their homes. As noted earlier, several commercial networks offer electronic mail and conferencing facilities. Another service with potential mass-market appeal is teleshopping, or ordering from an "electronic catalog." This alternative to conventional shopping may be especially attractive to families in which both partners are employed and thus have relatively little time to shop.

Providing on-line access to information is a critical function of computer networks. Thousands of databases are now available on commercial networks such as SprintNet (formerly Telenet) and Tymnet. According to Williams (1994), from 1975 to 1993 the number of databases grew twenty-five-fold (from 301 to 7,538), and the number of records in these databases increased a hundredfold (from 52 million to 5.572 billion). Usage figures exhibit the same kind of rapid growth: the number of on-line searches of databases provided by major U.S. vendors was 51.78 million in 1992, sixty-nine times the 1974 figure of .75 million (Williams, 1994).

On-line databases contain information on travel (e.g., airline schedules), investments (e.g., stock market quotations), current events, and many other specialized subjects. Bibliographic systems such as Knight-Ridder's Dialog and InfoPro's ORBIT are widely used by professionals and managers in large corporations, government agencies, and universities. As the volume of on-line sales increases, it will be possible for on-line vendors to offer more consumer-oriented databases at affordable prices.

Some specialized services may figure prominently in the emergence of a mass market. Tax preparation, financial planning, and a variety of file management services are currently available. Educational and training services, in the form of distance learning programs, are becoming important network applications.

Entertainment is just beginning to be exploited, but it may develop rapidly and open the door to a mass market for network-based services. Chess and other games have been played over computer networks for some time, but few commercial forms of entertainment have been produced. One commercially promising venture is the network distribution of video movies. This is a landmark development the coming of which has been anticipated for some time. In 1987, for example, I observed that "network-based video libraries . . . could establish a marketing link with the mass media" (Mowshowitz, 1987).

A July 1992 ruling of the U.S. Federal Communications Commission (FCC) cleared the way for the transmission of video material over the telephone network (Weber and Coy, 1992). Moreover, Bellcore (the research arm of the regional telephone companies) has developed a technique that makes it technologically feasible to distribute video to the home over ordinary twisted-pair copper cables. This technique achieves a transmission rate of 1.5 megabits per second. Thus, it is possible for the telephone companies to provide video services now—there is no need to wait for the installation of higher-capacity fiber-optic cables. Shortly after the FCC ruling, Bell Atlantic Corp. initiated an experiment to test video service to the home. The service is expected to work like a "video jukebox"—movies will be stored in digital form and transmitted within seconds of a viewer's request.

Moves by the telephone companies to enter the video arena seem to have already galvanized the cable industry into action. For example, cable company Tele-Communications (TCI) has joined forces with media firm Time Warner and software producer Microsoft to form Cablesoft. This new joint venture has been established for the purpose of delivering interactive television programming to the home via the cable network. The cable-television business in the United States generates annual revenues of $25 billion. Video rentals amount to $8 billion per year. Intense competition between the telephone and cable industries to provide video jukebox service to the home will hasten the development of the network marketplace. As entertainment assumes greater significance among network offerings, the development of the network marketplace may come to resemble that of TV broadcasting during the explosive phase of its growth.

Demand Pull

The cost of entering the network-based information marketplace is now within reach of the average consumer. A configuration consisting of a CPU, monitor, printer, modem, and communications software can be purchased for about the same price as some common household appliances. Other fixed costs, in addition to the one-time equipment purchase, are the monthly charges for a telephone line. If one uses one's regular home telephone for communicating with the networks, there may be no additional fixed cost. Variable costs include telecommunications charges (for connect time) and fees for vendor services obtained on the networks. Of course, these costs depend on nature of the services used (some on-line databases are more expensive than others) and the extent to which they are used. It would appear that equipment costs are no longer a major impediment to the growth of a mass market for network-based information services. Moreover, as the telephone is a standard item in all but the poorest homes, line charges are not a problem either.

Fees for using databases, payment systems, and other network offerings are probably still too high to attract the average consumer. The growing popularity of databases distributed on CD-ROM is partly attributable to the relatively high price of on-line services. Be that as it may, the current mix of services may be unattractive at any price—vendors are faced with the classic chicken-and-egg problem of price versus volume. Assuming that consumers perceive the usefulness of particular commodities, growing volumes of use should bring prices below the threshold for a mass market. Joint marketing ventures may also help to cut the price-versus-volume knot.

A consumer must have a certain level of sophistication (knowledge or skill) in order to enter the network marketplace. The requisite sophistication consists of knowing what equipment to get, how to use it, and what services to obtain with it. This knowledge, or the lack thereof, plays an important role in consumer decisions to shop in the network marketplace. Obtaining the appropriate equipment often entails perplexing choices between alternative systems and/or components. Selecting communications software may also be daunting, because many different packages are available. When these hurdles have been overcome, there is still the problem of deciding what services to get. Selection of equipment would be much simpler if integrated systems were available—systems that bundle together all the components and software needed to communicate with the networks. Greater standardization of products and services would make it easier for the consumer to choose appropriate offerings.

Another requirement of the would-be consumer is the ability to use the equipment and software needed to access the network marketplace. This typically means knowledge of the rudiments of an operating system and the basic functions of the communications software and the skill needed to navigate among the network services (e.g., knowing how to use the query language of a bibliographic database). These knowledge requirements may very well be a greater obstacle to general use than the cost of products and services. An obvious—albeit partial—remedy would be the availability of easy-to-follow, step-by-step instructions for operating hardware and software, and for accessing network offerings.

In addition to knowing what to get and how to use it, a prospective customer for network-based information commodities will have to have a reasonable idea of what to do with these offerings. Their utility to the user must be evident and convincing. A few people will buy anything, but sheer novelty will not sustain a mass market. When the novelty wears off, consumers will want to know how information commodities, like other types of commodities, can help advance their careers, further their educations or the educations of their children, make their lives easier and better, and entertain them. The potential rewards in the network marketplace are now sufficiently clear to the stakeholders to ensure that reasonably priced, easy-to-use access platforms will be made available in the very near future. Moreover, the inclusion of entertainment services such as video jukeboxes and interactive television will go a long way toward persuading consumers to make the network connection permanent.

The growth rate of the information marketplace is likely to be influenced by the ways in which network offerings affect social and political relations. For example, networks make it possible for some people to substitute telecommunication for job-related transportation. Telecommuting could provide a major stimulus to the network marketplace. Instead of commuting to work, one could access a computer system in the office from a terminal or personal computer in the home. This is attractive to some employers and employees, but certainly not to all. Experience suggests that telecommuting can induce significant changes in an individual's relations with superiors, coworkers, and subordinates, as well as in an individual's rights and bargaining position with respect to an organization. Thus, the growth of telecommuting may be affected by efforts to regulate potentially predatory business practices, such as the formation of "electronic sweatshops" and the use of contract employment designed to avoid the overhead costs of health care and other employee benefit programs. In addition, attitudes toward changes in modes of social interaction are likely to affect the spread of telecommuting.

Demand for network services such as electronic mail and computer conferencing also depends in part upon the ways in which social relations are affected. The success of various grassroots networking initiatives and the French Teletel network testifies to the powerful influence of social interaction on the demand for computer-mediated communication (Rheingold, 1993).

Consumer Response

Electronic shopping from home is still relatively rare, but the success of home-shopping TV networks suggests that consumers may be primed to accept this type of service. The home-shopping television viewer has no control over the order in which products are advertised. If he or she decides to order something, the usual procedure is to call a toll-free number, indicate the product desired, and arrange for payment (typically by credit card).

Regarding consumer acceptance, electronic shopping differs from the television variety in two important respects. First, establishing contact with a computer network is somewhat more complicated than turning on a TV set. Second, placing an order involves communicating by means of a keyboard. These difficulties will likely dampen consumer enthusiasm for electronic shopping, despite the freedom to browse that it offers.

Home banking services have been marketed aggressively for some years—just how aggressively is revealed by a typical introductory offer: one bank gave new users a subsidy for purchase of a modem, an allowance for use of Dow Jones News/Retrieval, and no service charge for two months. These items, together with the software and glossy instruction manual provided free of charge to the customer, represent a substantial cost to the offering bank. Despite many disappointments (Sigel, 1986), home banking is steadily growing. The banks are pushing the service as a means of reducing their internal processing costs and as a vehicle for marketing a variety of financial services.

The story of videotex (the transmission of data for display on television monitors or personal computers) in North America and most of Western Europe is one of promises unfulfilled. A number of marketing trials have been mounted, but none has been an enduring success. Typical trials in the United States have been launched as joint ventures involving a telecommunications company such as AT&T or Nynex, a media enterprise such as CBS or the Knight-Ridder newspaper chain, and an equipment manufacturer such as DEC or IBM. The respective roles of the participants correspond to their main business lines: the telecommunications company provides the network services, the media enterprise is responsible for the product and service offerings, and the equipment manufacturer provides the terminal and other devices needed to access the videotex computers.

Videotex is just one incarnation of the idea of home delivery of information commodities. It appears to be moribund now, but will almost certainly be revived in other forms. Rheingold (1993) attributes the failure of videotex to its essentially broadcast character, databases furnished by a small number of information providers to a more or less passive public. The success of Minitel in France demonstrates the feasibility of an alternative approach to the delivery of information and services to a mass market. Minitel became popular because of the communication facilities it offered.

As noted earlier, consumer acceptance is dependent on the development of a sufficiently rich universe of offerings, and it appears that facilities for lateral communication between subscribers constitute an important offering. The other marketing requirements of affordability and consumer sophistication can be met fairly easily through economies of scale and integration of hardware and software, respectively.

Network-Dependent Products and Services

The growth of the network marketplace is dependent on the elaboration of network infrastructure and support services. Although this marketplace is linked to a brand new technology—namely, computer communications—it has much in common with older network-based marketplaces. It is instructive to compare the market for information commodities with the markets for other network-based products and services, in particular, the markets based on automobiles, telephones, and radio and television. The following vignettes focus on the use of these instruments by individual consumers to gain access to network-based products and services.

The automobile is an instrument of personal transportation. However, its utility to the consumer is dependent on a network of roads and service facilities. Automobiles are relatively expensive. For most individuals, the purchase price is topped only by that for a home. The use of the automobile, made possible by the creation of an extensive road network, has contributed to the spatial separation between residence and place of work.

The telephone is an instrument of personal communication. Like the automobile, its use depends on a network, in this case one made up of transmission and service facilities. The purchase price of a telephone is relatively low—most of the expenses incurred in the use of the telephone derive from variable service costs. Telephone communication serves many functions in contemporary society. In particular, it plays a major role in sustaining family and other social relations over great distances, an indispensable function in a highly mobile society.

The radio or television set is an instrument of personal information and entertainment. Its utility to the consumer is dependent upon a network of broadcasting stations and distribution facilities (e.g., cable systems). The prices of television and radio sets fall somewhere between those of automobiles and telephones. These instruments, as gateways to the programming of the broadcasting and cable networks, have become permanent fixtures in most homes, and their use as sources of news and entertainment have altered patterns of communication and interaction within the family.

Personal Computer as "Great Integrator"

The personal computer or terminal device, as gateway to the network marketplace, has the potential to integrate the features of the automobile, the telephone, and the radio or television set. Personal computers, by making it possible to substitute communication for transportation, can assume some of the automobile's functions as an instrument of personal transportation. In particular, these devices can serve to extend or refine the automobile's role in distancing the home from the workplace. By means of transportation-communication trade-offs, personal computers can thus increase the flexibility of living and working arrangements.

The personal computer can also absorb the telephone's functions as an instrument of personal communication. Electronic mail and computer conferencing exemplify the new, network-based services that can be accessed by means of a personal computer. Devices that merge computing and communications, allowing the user to process text and send facsimile and electronic mail messages, for example, are already available, and more powerful "personal communicators" that combine these and other features (e.g., video transmission) with the voice communications of ordinary telephone service are on the way.

Finally, the personal computer can assume the function of radio or television by serving as an instrument of personal information and entertainment. Personal computers can provide access to entertainment offerings at least as rich as those currently accessible through television receivers. The distribution of video over the telephone lines and the interactive television services over cable mentioned earlier are indicative of the marriage of television and the personal computer.

The purchase price of a personal computer—the cost of admission to the network-based information marketplace—can be as little as the price of a television set and as high as the price of an automobile. Other costs incurred in using the personal computer as a gateway device are analogous to those associated with using an automobile (e.g., highway tolls, restaurant and motel charges) or a telephone (e.g., subscription fees and long-distance charges). The characteristics of the automobile, the telephone, and the radio or television set, in relation

Table 5.1. Network-dependent instruments

Instrument	Network dependence	Entry cost	Function
Automobile	Roads and service facilities	High	Personal transportation
Telephone	Transmission and service facilities	Low	Personal communication
Radio/TV	Broadcasting and service facilities	Medium	Personal information and entertainment
Personal computer	Transmission, device interface, service facilities	Medium to high	All of above

to the integrative potential of the personal computer, are summarized in Table 5.1.

Because the personal computer integrates the principal network-dependent features of the automobile, the telephone, and the radio or television set, it is reasonable to suppose that it will evolve along the lines of a network access device. So far, the spread of the personal computer appears to have followed the course of the telephone in the early stages of its history. With the availability of video entertainment through computer networks, the diffusion of the personal computer is likely to accelerate, assuming a trajectory reminiscent of the very rapid diffusion of the television set. As the volume and diversity of the information commodities available on computer networks increase, the network marketplace will become a true mass market.

Consumer Data and Targeting

Computer networks provide new opportunities for the use of techniques developed in political campaigning and commercial advertising. To see how the network marketplace may yield new mechanisms (and perhaps even new forms) of social control, we must first examine these techniques. Campaign managers and advertising executives have a common goal: to persuade their respective constituencies to buy something. In one case, it is a candidate for office; in the other, it is a product or service. Necessary, if not sufficient, conditions for accomplishing such a goal include (1) having a good understanding of a constituency's desires and capacities, and (2) having adequate means for communicating with the members. In this discussion a constituency is taken to be a relatively large group of individuals, of a size that makes it impractical to rely on face-to-face campaigning or advertising.

Understanding the Constituency

In practice, the confluence of campaigning and advertising lies in differentiating a population into subgroups according to certain characteristics. Potential voters are differentiated according to voting preferences; prospective buyers are segmented according to buying preferences. The reason for doing this is the same in both cases, namely, to increase the likelihood of message acceptance through the dissemination of highly tailored material designed to appeal to the respective concerns and interests of a set of homogeneous subpopulations. Thus, for example, New York City's Democratic Party, in a mayoral contest, might target Jewish registered voters with one type of campaign literature and black registered voters with very different literature. In the former case, control of street crime and solidarity with the state of Israel might be stressed, whereas in the latter the literature is more likely to focus on the elimination of discriminatory police practices and the creation of job opportunities for inner-city residents.

The same kind of targeting is done in the advertising of products and services. Income, age, gender, ethnicity, and profession are examples of factors that are known to be predictors of buying behavior. By targeting advertising material to subgroups of potential buyers identified according to factors of this kind, the vendor of a product or service can substantially increase the probability of making sales. There is little point, for example, in sending brochures advertising expensive sports cars or luxury cruises to individuals earning the minimum wage, or in touting the virtues of a feminine hygiene product to an all-male audience.

Communicating with the Constituency

Targeting as a means of directing tailored messages to narrowly defined subpopulations is an outgrowth of research on voting behavior. Journalists and broadcasters have made use of profiling techniques based on this research to predict election results. Moreover, these techniques have proved effective in disseminating advertising in political campaigns. Before the advent of computer networks, most campaign literature or advertising material was distributed mechanically, through the regular mail service or specialized carriers—thus the term *direct-mail advertising.*

This form of advertising produces what is often pejoratively called junk mail, unsolicited and unwanted letters that many recipients consign to the trash after the merest glance at the envelopes. Nevertheless, direct-mail advertising has proved an extremely cost-effective way of generating sales. Evidently, what is junk for one person has value for another.

Computer networks make it possible to simplify, extend, and refine direct-mail advertising. Networking facilitates the capture and distribution of information, and can serve as a powerful marketing instrument. Electronically placed orders allow for virtually effortless capture of client data. The standardized protocols of electronic data interchange (EDI) are designed for such capture, but some client data can also be extracted from (free-format) electronic mail messages, especially from headers. Distribution of information is similarly effortless. With electronic addresses and a message on file, a simple command sequence suffices to direct copies of the message to any subset of addresses.

Networking thus turns the order-to-delivery chain into a veritable gold mine. Client data are the ore that can now be profitably extracted and refined into the gold of direct marketing services. Networks combine data storage and retrieval with distribution. This gives rise to a medium that integrates the features of computerized libraries, broadcasting, and telecommunications. In this environment it is possible to capture, store, process, and retrieve data; to match and merge files resident on computers anywhere in the network; and to disseminate information to devices attached to the network. Moreover, it is possible for network users to communicate with each other. In short, computer networks combine the features of broadcasting and interactive communications with the processing power of computer systems.

The enhanced opportunities afforded by computer networks for selling marketing data and related services will lead to ever more sophisticated products. An interesting example of a prenetworking product was a marketing database crafted by Lotus Development Corporation in cooperation with Equifax Inc. This product, called MarketPlace, was announced in 1990 and later withdrawn because of adverse public reaction. According to the announcement, the Market-

Place database contained information on eighty million American households. Information on a household included name, address, shopping habits, and income level. All this was to be furnished on CD-ROM. Lotus planned to charge $695 for software and an initial set of five thousand names. Each additional set of five thousand names was priced at $400.

MarketPlace was an attempt to provide small and medium-sized businesses with an inexpensive version of the marketing data products currently offered to large firms by companies such as Dun & Bradstreet. It is especially interesting here because it illustrates an intermediate step in the evolution of networking services. Most consumer database services rent tailored mailing lists to their clients (e.g., retailers) for one-time use. By contrast, the customers of Lotus's MarketPlace were to be allowed unlimited use of the information provided on CD-ROM. This would allow the customer to use the CD-ROM databases to create highly targeted mailing lists at will. These databases, together with the MarketPlace software, represent the acquisition and processing components needed for targeting messages. In a computer communications network, the databases and processing software would form part of a powerful direct advertising system.

The announcement of MarketPlace provoked a strong public outcry. Although similar information on American households had long been available to large firms, MarketPlace was evidently perceived as a more serious threat to privacy by virtue of its low cost, ease of use, lack of control over dissemination to third parties, and ability to provide relatively fine-grained identification of subpopulations. Perhaps the most threatening of all these features was the lack of control over dissemination afforded by the purchaser's right to unlimited use of MarketPlace's CD-ROM databases. But the threat posed by such a feature would be quite limited compared with the possibilities of using similar data in a networking environment. Marketing, in the context of computer networks, may very well become a powerful form of social control.

New Forms of Social Control

The specter of Big Brother has haunted computerization from the beginning. Computerized personal record-keeping systems, in the hands of police and intelligence agencies, clearly extend the surveillance capabilities of the state. Less obvious is the extension of control signaled by administrative record-keeping systems. These systems support the gatekeeping functions of corporations and government agencies. In this capacity, they contribute to what Rule et al. (1980) have called "bureaucratic surveillance." This type of surveillance induces people to conform to behavioral norms by means of a system of rewards and punishments. One is rewarded by qualifying for a car loan or a life insurance policy or social security benefits; one is punished by being denied credit or by having one's application for unemployment benefits rejected.

Both varieties of surveillance support a kind of exogenous social control. The activities of police and administrative agencies do not form part of the normal social relations of individuals in the community. These agencies may play a very important role in people's lives from time to time, but it is largely a formal role. Whether acting as enforcers, referees, or gatekeepers, these agencies are outsiders—they are interveners, not regular players.

In the era of the stand-alone computer, surveillance was the only effective way to enlist information technology in the cause of social control. Computer networks offer additional possibilities. One is an electronic version of Bentham's panopticon, or perfect prison, in which citizens may be monitored at a distance by agencies of the state or other powerful interests (Rheingold, 1993; see also the chapter in this volume by Gandy). The panopticon is a form—albeit extreme—of exogenous control. Because it is imposed on a group by outsiders, the members of the group can in principle mobilize to oppose it. Such mobilization becomes much more difficult when control is integrated within the structure of the group itself.

Powerful new mechanisms of endogenous social control become possible with computer networks.[5] These mechanisms arise from the limitless opportunities within networks for the formation and transformation of groups and the ease with which individuals can enter and leave such groups. The operative principle in these mechanisms is group membership, a basic feature of social control in any human community.

Human beings typically belong to a variety of social groups, both formal and informal. By virtue of such membership, one is constrained to behave more or less in accordance with group norms. Family, neighborhood, church, working relations, friends, clubs, voluntary associations, political parties, and government units are familiar examples of the groups to which individuals may belong. Each of these, in its own peculiar way, requires observance of certain norms of conduct. Modes of enforcement vary with the type of group. Adherence to norms of conduct within the family is maintained largely by bonds of affection and loyalty; voluntary associations can use persuasion, group pressure, or sanctions ranging from censure to banishment.

Computer networks open up new possibilities for group formation by providing the means for maintaining the continuity of association at a distance. The means consist of facilities for exchanging information (message transfer) and for sharing experience (common files). Both are essential to maintaining the social relations and the common effort of a group whose members are geographically dispersed. Information exchange is essential for coordination of activities and reinforcement of group loyalties; the means for sharing experience through a collective memory is indispensable to all but the simplest of collective activities.

As indicated earlier, the network facilities required for association at a distance are already available. Network applications such as e-mail offer efficient and inexpensive means of exchanging messages with correspondents all over the world. Ordinary postal service—called "snail mail" by devotees of electronic messaging—has in its time served as an instrument of group cohesion and cooperative activity. Electronic mail is a far more powerful instrument. Coupled with collective memory and management facilities—offered, for example, by computer conferencing software—the power of electronic mail is many orders of magnitude greater than conventional postal service.

Affinity groups based on consumption constitute the most likely arena for elaboration of the new forms of social control made possible by computer networks. Direct marketing, with its buying profiles and dissemination of targeted advertising, promises to integrate exogenous and endogenous control mechanisms. Commercial advertising or political propaganda, distributed on a one-to-many basis, exercises some measure of exogenous control by reinforcing the beliefs and prejudices of the recipients. The effectiveness of such procedures can be enhanced enormously through the use of carefully constructed behavioral profiles based on prior knowledge of the target population.

When the targeting is precise enough to define an affinity group (such as users of a specialized product, supporters of a peculiar cause, persons with an unusual characteristic), endogenous mechanisms may come into play. If the members of the target group are connected to the network and know how to use facilities such as e-mail or computer conferencing, they can establish communication links with each other. Advertisers can then try to stimulate and reinforce interaction and cooperation among the members of such groups by distributing newsletters, holding electronic conferences, and so on. Once such an affinity group is defined, it will very likely develop its own norms and standards, reflecting in part the aims of the advertiser. At this point endogenous control mechanisms work hand in hand with exogenous ones.

The evolving forms of social control have much in common with medieval ones. Medieval social control, like that ascribed to the networking environment, was based on the status conferred by group membership. Localized groups such as family, neighborhood, and guild served as keepers of tradition and enforcers of behavioral norms. Interaction was largely face-to-face. The localized, face-to-face relations defining medieval life are different from those obtaining through the medium of computer networks, but from a control perspective, the differences may be less important than the similarities. Networks offer virtual localization—the shared characteristics and objectives of an affinity group that is not confined to any particular place and whose members need not interact at the same time—and this type of localization may be more significant to group solidarity than the form of communication (e.g., face-to-face, telephone, e-mail) or the physical proximity of the members.[6]

Virtual localization in the social environment of a computer network dramatically increases an individual's opportunities for membership in groups. In medieval times, a person's social relations were confined to the population of a restricted area. Now the population a person can draw upon has global reach and encompasses millions. This global population is also available to advertisers and marketers through computer networks. The possibility of multiplying virtually localized groups at will strengthens the advertiser's hand and reinforces the social control aspect of affinity groups.

Rheingold (1993) has described a number of virtual communities that have come into being on computer networks. These communities—from the computer conferences of the WELL (Whole Earth 'Lectronic Link), to the devotees of Multi-User Dungeons, to the scholarly or activist groups on the Internet—are mostly the result of grassroots initiatives. Thus far a frontier mentality has dominated the world of computer-mediated communication, and there is little evidence of virtual communities resulting from network extensions of direct advertising. But as the market for information commodities grows, it is likely that the number of independent suppliers will shrink, and the dominant survivors will be very large private companies. The network marketplace is a high-stakes game, and penny-ante players will be shunted aside to make room for the high rollers. At best, the freewheeling pioneers will wind up on cyberspace reservations.

This radical transformation will go unnoticed by most people, because they will be defined by the virtual communities created by advertising profiles. The marketplace will give them just what they think they want.

Virtual Individualism

More than twenty years ago, in a piece written for a special advertising supplement of the *New York Times*, Isaac Asimov argued that the advent of computer-based, direct-mail advertising heralded a new form of individualism:

> So increasingly narrow and accurate will be the target that each recipient will begin to feel himself all the more an individual through the direct mail advertising he gets. What he receives will be so likely to be of interest to him and to be slanted to his particular needs that, even if he does not buy, he will feel that someone has gone to the trouble of knowing what he might want.
>
> [The world of the future will be one] in which every person can be identified, and dealt with as an individual, . . . handled by the only device fast and versatile enough to deal with hundreds of millions on a one-by-one basis—an advanced computer. (1973)

In 1973, when Asimov wrote these words, computer networking was still in its infancy.[7] The idea of packet switching, a key technology in the efficient use of a network's communication infrastructure, was introduced by the RAND Corporation in 1964. This idea was put into operation in 1969 in the ARPANet, a packet distribution network established by the Advanced Research Projects Agency of the U.S. Department of Defense. Commercial networks such as General Telephone and Electronics's Telenet (now SprintNet) started operations in the mid-1970s. This perhaps explains why Asimov pictured the computer as a stand-alone information processor, rather than as an element in a computer communications network. In any case, his vision of a new individualism could only have been reinforced by taking account of the coupling of computers and communications.

For Asimov, the process of individuation will unfold in relation to the targeted advertising one receives. The more an advertising message reflects a person's particular needs and desires, the more it will help that person to become an individual. But even in the limiting case described by Asimov as "being made part of a non-duplicated coding system," the advertising received would be for a product intended to be used by a number of consumers, thus implicitly defining an affinity group. Although products could be designed for specific persons, affinity groups would still be defined—in this case for users of products in a family of related ones (e.g., all Ford cars with a given engine size, body style, and other features).

Consumers in the network marketplace will be members of many different affinity groups that will persist for varying periods of time. Moreover, the consumer may very well switch from one group to another—autonomously or under the guidance of some invisible hand. To the extent that personal identity is bound up with ever-changing memberships in affinity groups, individuality becomes transformed into virtual individuality. At any given moment, a person's identity can be inferred from the intersection of the affinity groups to which he or she then belongs.

This vision of individuality is an extension and refinement of the notion of other-directedness defined by Riesman (1956). Unlike the inner-directed personality who interprets experience on the basis of internalized norms and values, the other-directed personality looks to others, especially peers, to determine the appropriateness of behavior. "What can be internalized . . . is not a code of behavior but the elaborate equipment needed to attend to . . . messages [from a wide social circle] and occasionally to participate in their circulation" (Riesman, 1956:42). Dependence on others for self-definition is implicit in the notion of individuation through affinity group membership. Asimov's new individual is, like the other-directed person, "at home everywhere and nowhere, capable of a rapid if sometimes superficial intimacy with and response to everyone" (Riesman, 1956:41).

The new element in virtual individuality is the possibility of switching between affinity groups in an essentially unbounded universe. This possibility, afforded by the network marketplace, could have far-reaching consequences for social control, because the switching may be self-directed or may be guided by external agents such as commercial advertisers or political campaigners. External agents can switch individuals between virtual groups by altering profiles or by modifying groups directly (e.g., splitting the membership of a group or merging two groups together). Moreover, such external agents can count on group solidarity to reinforce marketing imperatives.

Clearly, group membership as a control mechanism functions both exogenously and endogenously. Virtual individualism, unlike police and bureaucratic surveillance, does not directly confer power on political or managerial elites. Nevertheless, it may become Big Brother's most powerful ally, as Big Brother is transformed into a virtual presence in an information market oligopoly.

Notes

1. The discussion in this section is based on Mowshowitz (1987).

2. In earlier work, I have treated information products and services as examples of "information commodities" (Mowshowitz, 1992a). According to this view, the market value of such commodities derives from their potential contribution to production processes. See also Gotlieb (1985) for a discussion of economic aspects of information, especially the role of information in decision making.

3. The U.S. Department of Commerce (1991) presents a comprehensive treatment of telecommunications infrastructure, networks, and the services to be supported by the new technology.

4. For a general discussion of computer communications technology, see Stallings (1985).

5. Exogenous forms of social control may be enhanced too. Networks amplify the power of matching and profiling—search techniques used to identify individuals or groups who engage in certain practices or behaviors. See Marx and Reichman (1984) for a discussion of matching and profiling in connection with the "discovery of secrets."

6. Virtual localization is a natural concomitant of virtual organization (see Mowshowitz, 1986, 1992b, 1994, for definition and discussion of virtual organization). Over the past decade, several observers, myself included, have called attention to new forms of organization made possible by information technology. Hiltz (1986) has coined the term "virtual classroom" to characterize an organized learning environment that is not bound to the physical limits of the conventional classroom; Giuliano (1982) uses the term "virtual office" to describe the organization of an information-age office in which

activities are similarly unconstrained by the conventional strictures of time and space. "Virtual community," defined by Rheingold (1993) as a computer-mediated social group, has the same meaning as my own term "virtually localized group." A virtual community or virtually localized group is what results from a process of virtual localization.

7. For further details on the development of computer networks, see Stallings (1985), Stamper (1989), and Wittie (1991).

References

Asimov, I. (1973). "The Individualism to Come." *New York Times,* January 7, special advertising supplement.

Gillespie, R. G. (1994). "Legislation and the NII." *Educom Review* 29: 22–25.

Giuliano, V. E. (1982). "The Mechanization of Office Work." *Scientific American,* September, 149–64.

Gotlieb, C. C. (1985). *The Economics of Computers.* Englewood Cliffs, N.J.: Prentice Hall.

Hiltz, S. R. (1986). "The Virtual Classroom: Using Computer-Mediated Communication for University Teaching." *Journal of Communication* 36: 95–104.

Innis, H. A. (1951). *The Bias of Communication.* Toronto: University of Toronto Press.

Marx, G. T., and N. Reichman. (1984). "Routinizing the Discovery of Secrets: Computers as Informants." *American Behavioral Scientist* 27: 423–52.

Mowshowitz, A. (1986). "Social Dimensions of Office Automation." In M. Yovits (ed.), *Advances in Computers,* vol. 25. New York: Academic Press, 335–404.

———. (1987). "On the Growth of Consumer Markets for Teleservices." In J. M. Noothoven van Goor and G. Lefcoe (eds.), *Teleports in the Information Age.* Amsterdam: North-Holland, 87–93.

———. (1992a). "On the Market Value of Information Commodities: I. The Nature of Information and Information Commodities." *Journal of the American Society for Information Science* 43: 225–32.

———. (1992b). "Virtual Feudalism: A Vision of Political Organization in the Information Age." *Informatization and the Public Sector* 2: 213–31.

———. (1994). "Virtual Organization: A Vision of Management in the Information Age." *Information Society* 10: 267–88.

Rheingold, H. (1993). *The Virtual Community.* Reading, Mass.: Addison-Wesley.

Riesman, D. (1956). *The Lonely Crowd.* Garden City, N.Y.: Doubleday.

Roberts, M. M. (1994). "Building the NII: Challenges for Higher Education." *Educom Review* 29: 28–31.

Rule, J. B., D. McAdam, L. Stearns, and D. Uglow. (1980). "Preserving Individual Autonomy in an Information Oriented Society." In L. J. Hoffman (ed.), *Computers and Privacy in the Next Decade.* New York: Academic Press, 65–87.

Sigel, E. (1986). "Is Home Banking for Real?" *Datamation* 32: 128ff.

Smoot, O. (1994). "The NII and the New World Trade Agreement." *Educom Review* 29: 26–27.

Stallings, W. (1985). *Data and Computer Communications.* New York: Macmillan.

Stamper, D. A. (1989). *Business Data Communications.* Redwood City, Calif.: Benjamin/Cummings.

U.S. Department of Commerce. (1991). *The NTIA Infrastructure Report: Telecommunications in the Age of Information.* Washington, D.C.: U.S. Government Printing Office.

Weber, J., and P. Coy. (1992). "Look, Ma—No Cable: It's Video-by-Phone." *Business Week,* August 31, 94.

Williams, M. E., (1994). "The State of Databases Today: 1994." In *Gale Directory of Databases,* vol. 1, *Online Databases.* Detroit, Mich.: Gale Research, xix-xxix.

Wittie, L. D. (1991). "Computer Networks and Distributed Systems." *Computer* 24: 67–76.

6

How the Marriage of Management and Computing Intensifies the Struggle for Personal Privacy

Rob Kling and Jonathan P. Allen

In the early 1990s, Lotus Development Corporation announced plans to market a CD-based database of household marketing data called MarketPlace:Household. Lotus MarketPlace:Household would have given anyone with a relatively inexpensive Apple Macintosh access to personal data on more than 120 million Americans.

Lotus withdrew MarketPlace:Household from the market in 1991 after receiving more than thirty thousand complaints from consumers about the privacy implications of the product. This interesting story of a victorious consumer revolt has been told many times, but how are we to understand why this kind of technology with substantial surveillance potential was developed in the first place? Was this product a strange, one-time attempt to introduce a piece of technology that could change corporate surveillance and social control practices in our society, or was it merely a highly visible example of a larger societal trend? And how do we explain why some modern organizations might find it attractive to develop and use this kind of technology? Why is the continuing development of information technologies that impinge on personal privacy a continuing struggle in contemporary advanced industrial societies?

Most studies of computers and privacy focus on the problems surrounding particular laws, kinds of systems (e.g., credit reporting), or kinds of practices (e.g., computer matching).[1] Even broad-ranging studies such as those presented in *The Politics of Privacy* (Rule et al., 1980), *Protecting Privacy in Surveillance Societies* (Flaherty, 1989), and *The Rise of the Computer State* (Burnham, 1983) have focused on describing the rise of elaborate social surveillance systems and their legal and administrative frameworks. When authors explain the link between new technologies and changes in surveillance at the broader

104

societal level, they tend to focus on the needs of bureaucracies, public and private, to improve the fairness of their services and to control their clientele and environments more efficiently. Classic works such as Rule's (1974) *Private Lives and Public Surveillance* stress the mandates of various organizations to enforce norms of behavior—to make their clients' behavior more predictable and more acceptable.

We argue that the explanation for the development and adoption of commercial surveillance technologies such as the ill-fated Lotus Market-Place: Household database involves more than a generic "need" to enforce norms of client behavior or to improve bureaucratic efficiency. It would be enticing to have one overarching logic to explain the development of new surveillance systems of all kinds. For example, in his chapter in this volume Oscar Gandy develops the concept of a panoptic sort as the overarching logic for precision marketing systems (see also Gandy, 1993). He examines the characteristics of panoptic sorts, but skirts the question of how they develop over time. In contrast, we examine how the expansion of existing information systems and the development of newer surveillance systems are driven by a particular set of social dynamics.

Laudon (1986a) makes a valuable distinction between "environmental" and "institutional" explanations of the adoption of computer technologies by organizations. Environmental explanations portray organizations as responding rationally to objective uncertainties created by their environments, such as having a large number of clients or facing severe financial losses from doing business with specific people who are not well known to their staffs. Institutional explanations, however, suggest that technology adoption strategies may operate independent of environmental pressures to be efficient. Institutional explanations focus on the ways that organizations computerize seeking to maintain legitimacy and external support, or the ways that computerization reflects the values and interests of specific organizational actors. In his study of the adoption of a nationwide criminal records database, Laudon found that although the initial adoption of the technology was well explained by environmental models, institutional explanations led to a better understanding of how that surveillance technology was ultimately implemented, routinized, and used. Explaining the expanding use of surveillance technologies in commercial organizations more generally, we argue, will require institutional explanations as well.

We view the expansion and use of new computer technologies for large-scale record keeping as the by-products of a set of social practices that we refer to as *information entrepreneurialism,* which flourishes when *information capitalism* characterizes a major part of the system of economic exchange. Information entrepreneurialism may be described as the active attempts of coalitions within organizations to organize corporate production to take advantage of changes in key social relationships and information technology. Information entrepreneurial practices are made efficacious by some of the major social transformations in industrialized society over the past century: the increasing mobility of populations, the growth of nationwide organizations, and the increasing importance of indirect social relationships. Information entrepreneurial practices are also encouraged by the development of more cost-effective technologies for managing large-scale databases. But environmental factors such as social mobility and computer improvements cannot completely explain the diversity of surveillance technology uses across industries, or even between organizations. The internal structures of organizations have been affected tremendously by the rise of professional management, trained and rewarded to pursue managerial strategies that depend upon data-intensive analysis techniques. Organizations selectively adopt technologies that serve the interests of coalitions that can afford them and are considered legitimate. The internal configuration of symbolic analysts inside of organizations, dynamically and opportunistically pursuing information capitalist practices, is an important institutional explanation of modern society's push to increase the surveillance of indirect social relationships.

Information entrepreneurialism stresses the taken-for-granted, institutionalized beliefs of managers and the rewards they reap for pursuing data-intensive strategies of production. It highlights the active pursuit of gain through legitimate patterns of action—the "offensive" side of new surveillance technologies. Information entrepreneurial practices are made possible, legitimate, and rewarding by the rise of a larger institutional system we refer to as *information capitalism.*

In the rest of this chapter, we examine information entrepreneurial practices in the context of information capitalism, computerization, and the surveillance of indirect social relationships. In the first section, we address information entrepreneurialism as an institutional explanation of computer and privacy practice in the commercial world. In the second section, we discuss some of the major social transformations that enable information entrepreneurial practices to be rewarding for participants, combined with the important role of quantitatively oriented professional management in disseminating information capitalist strategies. In the final section, we tie information entrepreneurialism to key policy debates about computerization and privacy, using precision marketing and the rise of "data brokers" as examples of the link between surveillance technology and information entrepreneurialism.

The Engine of Information Entrepreneurialism

In the next twenty years, we expect computer technologies designed to support large-scale personal databases to be absorbed into and then to accelerate an interesting social trend—the expansion of information entrepreneurialism, or organizational practices involving the use of data-intensive techniques (including computerization) as key strategic resources for corporate production (Luke and White, 1985; Kling, Olin, and Poster, 1991; Kling, Scherson, and Allen, 1992; Kling, Ackerman, and Allen, forthcoming). The owners and managers of agricultural, manufacturing, and service firms increasingly rely upon imaginative strategies to "informationalize" production. Sometimes they sell information as a good or service, in the way that magazines can sell or rent their mailing lists as a sideline or that a few major airlines sell the use of their reservation systems. Or they may use refined information systems to focus their production and marketing. Because of the potential value of these diverse approaches, computerized information systems have joined factory smokestacks as major symbols of economic power.

As an organization shifts its managerial style to be more information entrepreneurial, analysts organize, implement, and utilize information systems to improve marketing, production, and operations. Information systems multiply, as cost accounting, production monitoring, and marketing research become key resources in advancing the organization's competitive edge.

Just as entrepreneurial behavior must be embedded in a larger system of capitalist institutions and rewards, information entrepreneurialism is embedded and encouraged within a larger institutional system of information capitalism. Capitalism is a dynamic system, and the information capitalism metaphor includes both information and the traditional dynamism of capitalist enterprise. The information capitalist metaphor is expansive because information entrepreneurialism is also used by nonprofit organizations such as public agencies, special interest groups, and political campaigns.

Information capitalism is a useful metaphor because it marries information with capitalism's dynamic and aggressive edge. Capitalism, as an institutional system, depends upon structures that facilitate reinvesting profit into developing organizations. Capitalism is nourished by the hunger of entrepreneurs, their agents, and their customers. Capitalism is stimulated when consumers lust after lifestyles of the rich and famous rather than when they rest content with emulating the lifestyles of the happy and innocent poor. Capitalism can reward the kind of entrepreneurial angst that stimulates some players to develop new products or more effective ways to market or sell older ones. Although there are numerous complacent managers and professionals in capitalist economies, there are also prospects of sizable rewards for their competitors who can develop new angles on making a business work. This underlying edge to capitalism comes from the possibility of rewards for innovation and the risk of destruction or displacement when the complacent are blindsided by their competitors. A by-product of the way that capitalism civilizes and rewards greed is a system in which some participants opportunistically innovate in the "search for more."

Information entrepreneurs innovate in numerous ways, including through the development of more refined financial management, market analyses, customer service, and sales of information-based products. Only a small fraction of these diverse innovations enhances the surveillance capacity of organizations, but this is an important fraction.

The concrete forms of capitalist enterprises have changed dramatically in industrialized countries in the past two hundred years. Until the late 1840s, capitalist enterprises were usually managed by their owners. Whereas some firms, such as plantations, hired salaried supervisors, managerial hierarchies in businesses were small and numbered in the dozens at their largest. In contrast, some of the largest U.S. firms today can have more than a dozen levels separating the salaried chief executive officer from the lowest-level employee, and they can be managed by tens of thousands of specialized managers. Alfred D. Chandler (1984), the business historian, characterizes this newer form of capitalism as "managerial capitalism," in contrast with the older and simpler "personal capitalism." Managerial capitalist enterprises became large enough producers to give countries such as the United States, Germany, and Japan strong presence on world markets. A more recent shift in the organization of U.S. industrial firms has many manufacturing most or all of their products outside the United States, often in Asia and Mexico. Robert Reich (1992) refers to this emerging shift in capitalist organization as "global capitalism."

Information capitalism refers to a different, but contemporary, shift in the ways that managers exploit information systematically. We view information capitalism as the overarching economic system that enables organizations to profit from the use or sale of information. Information capitalism's legal basis is anchored in the body of law that assigns property rights to information—such as laws concerning copyright, patents, and trade secrets. But it is also anchored in the laws that regulate ownership over information about people. Information capitalism is not a fundamentally new economic system, it is a different view of capitalism that focuses on business practices and social relations change when various kinds of information are treated as important goods and services. Information capitalism is not a static system. Shifting laws regulating the nature of property rights in specific kinds of information can change the detailed character of information capitalist practices.[2]

Firms that are organized by the various forms of capitalism coexist in the same economy. There are numerous small businesses in the United States that are managed only by their owners at the same time that the U.S. industrial economy is increasingly characterized by global capitalism. Similarly, the shift to information capitalism is most pronounced in those organizations where information entrepreneurs dominate. The organizations that employ an information entrepreneurial managerial approach are most likely to exploit effectively the use of sophisticated computer-based surveillance technologies, such as database systems.

Computerization promises to provide more in the particular ways that information can help inventive entrepreneurs, managers, and professionals reach out in new ways, to offer new products and services, to improve their marketing, and to tighten their control over relations with their customers (McFarland, 1984; Ives and Learmouth, 1984). But the key link between information entrepreneurialism and technologies for large-scale databases consists of the possibilities for enhanced information processing that computerization provides to analysts whose managerial strategies profit from significant advances in computational speed and/or the ability to manage huge databases.

Point-of-sale terminals, automated teller machines, credit cards, and the widespread appearance of desktop computing are some of the visible by-products of information entrepreneurialism. Platoons of specialized information workers—from clerks to professionals—are hidden behind these information technologies, which have become critical elements of many businesses and public agencies. Chain fast-food restaurants provide one good example of information entrepreneurialism in action. Viewed as a service, fast-food restaurants sell rapidly prepared food for relatively low prices and stimulate high rates of customer turnover. They are simply furnished, provide no table service, and are staffed by low-paid workers (often teenagers) to keep costs low. They offer a traditional service managed in traditional ways to act as a low-cost service provider. Fast-food chain restaurants differ from other low-cost restaurants in that they buy in immense volume, advertise with standardized menus, serve food through drive-up windows and walk-up counters, and franchise their outlets in special ways.

From the vantage point of information entrepreneurialism, fast-food restaurant chains are especially competitive and successful when they have an infrastructure of skilled information professionals and technologies. The information component helps them to select restaurant sites, to alter their menus to match the changing tastes of their clienteles, to audit the services of each establishment, and to monitor costs, cash flow, inventory, and sales. Their operational efficiencies hinge on information technologies as much as on economies of scale— from the microphones and audio systems that make it easier for drive-through customers to order food to the simplified electronic cash registers that automatically calculate costs and change so that relatively unskilled teenage workers can be relied upon as high-speed labor. The skills of backstage professional analysts consuming bytes of data expedite the large-scale sale of bites of food. Fast-food restaurant chains have not shifted from selling bites of food to selling bytes of information, but their operations have become intensively informationalized. Information entrepreneurialism gives certain organizations greater leverage than their less technologically sophisticated precursors.

An interesting concrete example is the Mrs. Fields Cookies chain, which utilizes an expert system to guide store managers in several areas of business (Ostrofsky and Cash, 1992). Its database of historical sales for each store at various times during the day helps tailor advice about the quantities of different kinds of cookies to bake at specific times during the day. Other modules guide managers in sales strategies when sales are slow and prompt them with questions to ask prospective employees in employment interviews. Mrs. Fields Cookies employs young managers who usually have no previous experience in bakeries or in managing fast-food outlets. Although the company could send novice managers to a special school similar to McDonald's Hamburger U, it profited handily in the first few years of its growth by substituting its expert system for longer-term managerial training.

The fine-grained monitoring of sales in the Mrs. Fields system, however, has the potential to provide benchmarks for controlling managerial and employee performance as well. Of course, Mrs. Fields does not keep records on the customers who buy and eat the firm's cookies, but many sales systems do track information about customers, for differing reasons. Some organizations, such as automobile dealerships, are legally required to track specific sales. Others, such as home furnishing stores, want delivery addresses. Still others, such as insurance companies, need to maintain continuing relationships with their customers. The emerging technology of two-way interactive television will enable people to purchase numerous services and the telecommunications firms to collect rich data about home shopping (Kling, forthcoming b). In many sales tracking systems it is difficult to separate the surveillance of organizational performance from the potential surveillance of customers. An application designed for one purpose can easily spill over to the other. The appetite of information entrepreneurial practices for data-intensive marketing analysis is not respectful of organizational boundaries.

The way in which Mrs. Fields organizes work illustrates one trend that we believe advanced computing technologies may extend. Behind the company's expert systems is a group of diverse and highly skilled symbolic analysts at corporate headquarters who design, refine, and maintain them. The stores are operated by a much less sophisticated and less well paid cadre of workers who are very unlikely to join the symbolic analysts at the corporate headquarters in Utah. Mrs. Fields shares the same environmental conditions as other franchised cookie stores, but its institutional configuration differs significantly, leading it to pursue information entrepreneurial strategies more intensively.

Institutional explanations of surveillance technology adoption such as information entrepreneurialism place more weight on the internal configurations of organizations, and the strategies and interests pursued by coalitions within them, than on objective external "needs" for surveillance. The information entrepreneurial model would predict, for instance, that the number and kind of symbolic analysts would be a better predictor of usage patterns in individual organizations than would a measure of their environmental uncertainty. It would also place much greater importance on investigating how the values and strategies of information capitalist practice are transferred to commercial organizations through education, professional associations, consultants, popular literature, and specific production technologies such as computers.

Information entrepreneurialism, as a set of practices for organizing corporate production, has evolved in the context of important social transformations and technological advances that encourage and reward, but do not determine, information entrepreneurial strategies under certain conditions. We discuss some of these social transformations in the next two sections, along with the rise of quantitatively oriented professional management education that played a major role in bringing information entrepreneurialism into organizations.

Large Organizations, the Emergence of Information Entrepreneurialism, and the Intensification of Computer-Based Surveillance

Mobile Societies and Indirect Social Relationships

One of the major social transformations of the past hundred years in industrial societies has been the growth of a mobile population and the commensurate growth of organizations, with masses of shifting customers, clients, and other parties. Though these broader "environmental" shifts provide a sense of context, we have argued that linking these transformations to changes in social surveillance requires an institutional explanation of the organizational adoption and use of surveillance technologies. In this section we will sketch the links between these changes and the increasingly intensive use of data systems for surveillance through the emergence of information entrepreneurialism in the past few decades. Information entrepreneurialism has become more prevalent, we argue, with the support of a massive institutional matrix of analytic management education, job market, and career paths.

The difference between shopping in a small-town store and shopping in a store in a huge retail chain, such as Sears, is not in the logic of retail store-based sales, but in the relationship between customer and retailer. In the huge chain store, customers rarely deal with people who know them outside of these specific narrow business transactions. Small-town shopkeepers often know their clients in other ways: they or their children have gone to school together, they attend the same churches, and so on. Yet even in small-town societies, people sometimes find it necessary to deal with large and distant organizations, such as tax collectors and the military.

During the past one hundred years, there have been astounding transformations in the ways that life in industrial societies is organized. New means of transportation—trains, buses, cars, and airplanes—have enabled people to become very mobile. In the early nineteenth century, most people who were born in the United States lived and died within fifty miles of their birthplaces. Today, in a highly mobile society, a huge fraction of the urban population moves from city to city, following better jobs and better places to live. Adolescents often leave their hometowns to attend college, and may move even farther away for jobs. Further, more than 130 metropolitan areas in the United States now have populations of more than 250,000, so that even moving "across town" in one of these cities can bring a person into an entirely new network of friends, employers, and service providers. The combination of mobility and urban development means that many people seek jobs, goods, and services from businesses whose proprietors and staffs do not have much firsthand knowledge about them.

In the past hundred years the scale of businesses and the number of government agencies with huge clienteles have also increased. In the nineteenth century few businesses had thousands of clients, and a smaller fraction of the public interacted frequently with the larger businesses of the day. Similarly, government agencies were smaller. Overall, most business was conducted through face-to-face (direct) relations, and only very specific government activities, such as taxation and the military draft, were carried out between people who did not know each other at all. Craig Calhoun (1992) characterizes contemporary industrial societies as ones in which a significant fraction of people's important activities are carried out with the mediation of people whom they do not see and may not even know exist. Today, banks can readily extend credit to people who come from anywhere in the country, and they can do so with relative safety because of large-scale credit record systems that track the credit histories of more than a hundred million people. The credit check brings together a credit seeker and employees of the credit bureau who are related *indirectly*.

Other private firms, such as insurance companies and mail-order companies, also extend services to tens of thousands of people whom local agents do not—and could not—personally know. In these transactions, judgments about insurability and creditworthiness are made through indirect social relationships, and are often mediated by computerized information systems. Furthermore, many new government agencies responsible for accounting for the activities of millions of people have been created in the twentieth century: the Federal Bureau of Investigation (1908), the Internal Revenue Service (1913), and the Social Security Administration (1935), along with various state departments of motor vehicles and so on. The sheer scale of these services creates "environmental conditions" that give organizations incentive to use computerized record systems to help routinize the maintenance of indirect social relationships. However, organizations of similar kinds and sizes, such as banks or police agencies, differ in their aggressiveness in using new technologies and management practices.

The Rise of Information Entrepreneurialism

What explains the difference between the more and less information-intensive organizations when many of their environmental conditions are similar? We believe that informational entrepreneurial styles of management are an important part of the answer. But information entrepreneurialism is a relatively recent phenomenon, developing only after managerial capitalism. In *The Visible Hand*, Alfred Chandler (1977) documents the way that certain large enterprises in the late nineteenth century helped foster professional management jobs. U.S. railroads were among the first firms to organize enterprise on a such a huge scale that families were too small to staff all of the key management positions; other larger industrial and commercial enterprises followed suit by the first decades of the twentieth century. Schools of professional management also developed to train young men for these new positions, and by mid-century, the M.B.A. was a popular degree in the United States.

After World War II, management schools began to shift from the case study approach, identified with the Harvard Business School, to more mathematical approaches to management. These curricula emphasized more quantitative skills based on microeconomics, managerial finance, and management science. By the 1970s, most U.S. schools of business had organized their curricula to emphasize analytic techniques in most areas of instruction.

In the 1980s, business schools were caught up in "PC fever." Some schools computerized their curricula with significant support from computer firms such as IBM and Hewlett Packard, and once the leading schools set the style, many other schools followed rapidly with ubiquitous computer labs. In addition, business schools developed a new academic specialty in the 1970s, "information systems." Today, a majority of business schools offer both required and elective courses in information systems. Although information systems courses teach business students diverse ways to computerize to help gain economic advantage, they very rarely teach about privacy issues and the problematic side of some information systems. The shift in the education of M.B.A.s from the traditional case-based approach to grounding in quantitative analyses resulted in a cadre of M.B.A.s trained in an approach that supports information capitalism.

It is instructive to see how two leading textbooks designed to teach M.B.A. students diverse approaches to information technology address privacy issues. *Management Information Systems,* by Kenneth Laudon and Jane Laudon (1994), devotes about 4 out of 776 pages to privacy issues. The text lists five core privacy principles from a very influential federal report, but does not examine how these principles can apply to any specific case, including any of the dozens of cases the authors use to illustrate many other practices of information management. Nor does the text provide any cases that examine privacy issues directly. *Corporate Information Systems Management,* edited by James Cash Jr., Warren F. McFarland, James McKenney, and Linda Applegate (1992), is more generous in devoting 5 out of 702 pages to the examination of privacy issues. Cash and his colleagues begin their short privacy section with three brief illustrations of how the practices of credit bureaus and marketing managers can intrude on personal privacy. The text also gives students several additional concrete examples about ways that managers can compromise or protect their customers' privacy while practicing information capitalism. Cash and his colleagues make a serious effort to sensitize their student readers to privacy issues, although one might wish they had provided analyses of privacy issues in other sections of the book that advance the development of new information systems with personal data. At any rate, their account is probably the best in any of the popular information systems texts for M.B.A. students. Information systems texts written before the late 1980s completely ignored privacy issues.

In a similar way, texts about marketing teach business students to create more comprehensive information systems to identify potential customers more efficiently and to improve sales and service by retaining and analyzing more data about customers' behavior. Overall, business schools teach their students to be clever and opportunistic information entrepreneurs, without paying much attention to the ways that routine business practices can create problems in public life, such as by intruding on personal privacy. In fact, Smith (1994) found that many managers are relatively casual about how they handle personally sensitive records about their companies' clients.

By 1989, U.S. colleges and universities conferred almost 250,000 bachelor's degrees in business and almost 75,000 M.B.A.s each year (U.S. Department of Commerce, Bureau of the Census, 1992). The popularity of business degrees rose rapidly in the United States between 1970 and 1989, with the number of B.A.s in business awarded annually more than doubling and the number of M.B.A. degrees almost tripling in this twenty-year period. During the 1980s alone, U.S. businesses hired almost 2.5 million people with B.S. degrees in business and almost 600,000 with M.B.A.s.

In a parallel, but less intensive, way, public agencies were increasingly staffed by people who also studied quantitative methods and computing in their educations in public administration, social science, law enforcement, and so on. About 11 million of 117 million people in the U.S. workforce in 1991 were managers (U.S. Department of Commerce, Bureau of the Census, 1992, table 629). Although the majority of employed managers do not have M.B.A. degrees, we suspect that M.B.A.s and professionals with similar training disproportionately populate the most aggressively information entrepreneurial organizations. These numbers are crude indicators, rather than rigid parameters, of a mechanistic process of social change. For example, only a small portion of graduates stimulate innovation in their organizations, but a large fraction of the college-educated management cadre employed since the 1970s understand key aspects of information entrepreneurialism, even when they follow rather than lead.

Schooling is, however, just the beginning for many managers who seek to innovate. The business press publishes (and exaggerates) stories of computerization efforts that promise better markets and profits. Magazines such as *Harvard Business Review* and *Business Week* publish stories about using information technology, including data systems the use of which has implications for privacy issues, for competitive advantage. However, they rarely highlight the privacy issues in their enthusiasm to excite managerial readers about new ways of conceiving of business opportunities. In addition, professional associations help managers learn diverse approaches to their trades. In some professions, such as marketing, finance, and operations management, computerization strategies play an important role, and professional associations in these fields offer talks, workshops, and publications for their members that also help popularize key aspects of information entrepreneurialism.

In practice, it is difficult to separate institutional explanations of surveillance technology use, such as the professionalization of symbolic analysts within organizations, from the larger environmental conditions that encourage these strategies, such as increasingly large clienteles. In any era, organizations use available technologies for keeping records; papyrus and paper were used for centuries. In modern societies, where computers and telecommunications are common tools for storing and accessing organizational records, the opportunities for operating enterprises that have millions of customers or clients, the ability to tighten social control over dispersed and mobile populations, and the nature of potential problems have changed a great deal.

There is significant potential payoff to organizations that can effectively exploit the informational resources that this systematic record keeping entails for identifying potential customers, assessing credit risks, and so on. Further, third-party data brokers such as TRW Information Services, Trans Union, and Equifax have developed lively businesses by catering to these markets—by offering custom search services, passing information to client firms, and devising new information products to facilitate precision electronic marketing.

Society within an Electronic Cage?

There is a risk of distortion in writing about information technology and surveillance from the viewpoint of organizations. Organizations seem to expand existing information systems, use existing systems for new purposes, and invent new systems much more rapidly than they remove old systems. Consequently, it is easy to portray organizations as relentless in building their element of a larger electronic cage in which to ensnare their publics.

From the viewpoint of any particular organization, or the managers within it, only a few aspects of a person's behavior are readily known. An insurance company can use its own records or the Medical Information Bureau to gather selected medical data about a person. A bank has its own records and reports from credit bureaus to assess the creditworthiness of a person seeking a car loan, but it rarely seeks medical data. Police organizations may have some criminal history information about suspects in a robbery case, but they rarely seek detailed financial or medical records on those persons; when they do seek such records for a specific investigation, the information is not routinely shared through the police data networks. In short, the myriad data systems in existence are highly segmented. Some data systems can be linked in practice; in the United States, it is very common for people to be asked for their social security numbers when they apply for diverse services, including driver's licenses, bank accounts, health insurance, and even library cards. But many "matching systems" use more diverse information, such as combinations of names and addresses (Kusserow, 1991; Shattuck, 1991).

Unfortunately, we know very little about how ordinary people perceive the information webs into which diverse organizations weave them. At the extremes, we know that many people seem relatively indifferent, some are deeply worried, and some work hard to remain relatively unknown and unlinkable. In the United States, some surveys of public attitudes have shown high levels of concern about reductions in privacy and strong perceptions that laissez-faire computerization reduces personal privacy (see, e.g., Harris and Westin, 1991: 13; 1992:

15). But privacy issues are not politically explosive in the United States in comparison with such issues as levels of taxation, abortion rights, and homelessness. Sometimes specific technology families, such as Caller ID, can mobilize many people; the announcement of Lotus MarketPlace:Household led to thirty thousand protest letters. But these are exceptions rather than the rule.

Database Technology, Information Entrepreneurialism, and Changing Patterns of Social Control

Faster computing hardware platforms and interlocking technologies, such as computer networks, database management systems, and graphics, can play key roles in increasing the scale of data that firms can manage and analyze. The know-how involved is not primarily computer expertise, but deep expertise in some domain, such as finance or marketing, and sufficient computer expertise to bring computational power to bear on the problem framed by the analyst. Organizations that take advantage of such technologies manage and analyze data in three major domains:

1. changes in production, with greater emphasis upon managing data as a strategic resource and leading to slow but important changes in the structure of (information) labor markets;

2. improvement of control over relationships with customers and clients, especially the elaboration of indirect social relationships; and

3. development of more information products.

We are most concerned in this essay with the second strategy, the elaboration of indirect social relationships, but it is difficult to separate these domains in practice. The drive for new information products can lead to technologies that further enable the surveillance of indirect social relationships, as can reorganizations of production that place greater emphasis on surveillance data.

The growth of technologies that support large-scale databases has some key ramifications for ways that organizations function, the kinds of services that business sell, and changes in the relationships between organizations and their clients. In our introduction to information entrepreneurialism above, we discussed the rise of organizations with huge clienteles and the growing prominence of indirect social relations when people interact with organizations. A society in which social relationships are often indirect can give people a greater sense of freedom than they might have in a different kind of society. One can move from job to job, from house to house, and from loan to loan and selectively leave some of one's past behind. The managers in organizations that provide long-term services, such as banks, insurance companies, and apartment houses, often want to reduce their business risks by reconstructing what they believe are relevant parts of a person's history.

These patterns encouraged very large organizations, such as some of the biggest banks, insurance companies, and public agencies, to take an early lead in adapting mainframe computing to support their huge personal record systems in the 1950s and 1960s. In the 1970s and 1980s, these organizations enhanced their computer systems and developed networks to communicate data more effectively, regionally, nationally, and internationally. Many of those organizations have massive appetites for "affordable" high-speed transaction processing and tools to help them manage gigabytes and even terabytes of data.[3] Some of these kinds of organizations have been experimenting with exotic technologies such as supercomputing, and they have cadres of professionals who are eager to exploit new technologies to track and manage their customers and clients more efficiently. Large-scale database technology supports finer-grained analyses of indirect social relationships, such as precision marketing to improve a firm's ability to target customers for a new product, or the ability of a taxing agency to prowl multiple large databases in search of tax cheaters.

Managers and professionals in business organizations and public agencies characterize their searches for information about people in limited and pragmatic terms—such searches, they say, improve their rationality in making specific decisions about whom to hire, to whom to extend a loan, to whom to rent an apartment, and whom to arrest (Kusserow, 1991). From the viewpoint of individuals, these searches for personal information are sometimes fair and sometimes invasive of their privacy (Shattuck, 1991; Laudon, 1986b). Information entrepreneurs, like other entrepreneurs in a capitalist economy, are sensitive to the costs of their services. When there is no price on goods, as on clean air or personal privacy, they are usually ignored, except when protective regulations are enacted to compensate for market failures.

Some of the key policy debates about computerization and privacy reveal conflicting values, not just conflicting interests. There are at least five major value orientations that influence the terms of key debates

(Kling, 1978, 1991, forthcoming a). These values can also help us understand the social repercussions of computer-based surveillance technologies:

Private enterprise model: The preeminent consideration is profitability of financial systems, with the highest social good being the profitability of both the firms providing and the firms utilizing the systems. Other social goods, such as consumers' privacy or the desires of government agencies for data, are secondary concerns.

Statist model: The strength and efficiency of government institutions is the highest goal—government needs for access to personal data on citizens. The need for mechanisms to enforce citizens' obligations to the state will always prevail over other considerations.

Libertarian model: Civil liberties, such as those specified by the U.S. Bill of Rights, are to be maximized in any social choice. Other social purposes, such as profitability or welfare of the state, are secondary when they conflict with the prerogatives of the individual.

Neopopulist model: The practices of public agencies and private enterprises should be easily intelligible to ordinary citizens and should be responsive to their needs. Societal institutions should emphasize serving the "ordinary person."

Systems model: Financial systems must be technically well organized, efficient, reliable, and aesthetically pleasing.

In different instances, policies and developments may support, conflict with, or be independent of these five value models. Each of them, except the systems model, has a large number of supporters and a long tradition of support within the United States. Thus, computing developments that are congruent with any of these positions might be argued to be in "the public interest." Information entrepreneurialism is most directly aligned with the private enterprise value model for guiding social action, but the information capitalist approach can also support statist values in cases where public agencies use computerized information systems to model and explore alternative revenue-generating programs, to assess the effectiveness of social programs, or to track scofflaws through networks of records systems. It is conceivable that information entrepreneurialism could support neopopulist consumer control, by constructing databases that report on the quality of commercial products and services or by enhancing access to government records systems. However, such uses are extremely rare, and they are not accessible to the majority of people, who are not computer savvy. It is difficult to imagine that many new computerized systems would, on balance, support libertarian values; however, enhanced privacy regulations reduce the extent to which computerized systems that support statist or private enterprise values can further erode personal privacy in the United States.

Computer-based information systems can be used in myriad ways that help organizations with huge clienteles better manage those relationships. For example, in 1991, American Express announced the purchase of two CM-5 parallel supercomputers from Thinking Machines, Inc., which it will probably use to analyze cardholders' purchasing patterns (Markoff, 1991). American Express's purchase of these two multimillion-dollar computers illustrates how the conjunction of large-scale database technology and information entrepreneurialism tilts the social system to emphasize private enterprise values over libertarian values. Whereas American Express is an innovator in experimenting with parallel supercomputing for market research, other firms that manage huge numbers of indirect social relationships with their customers will follow suit as the price/performance of these computers, the quality of the systems software, and the technical know-how for using them all improve in the next decades. These styles of computer use systematically advance private enterprise values at the expense of libertarian values.

In order to help manage their often indirect social relationships with large populations of clients, organizations increasingly rely upon formal record systems. Today's computerized systems provide much finer-grained information about people's lifestyles and whereabouts than was readily available in earlier record systems. Although these data systems primarily serve the specific transaction for which the customer provides information, it is increasingly common for computerized systems with personal data to serve multiple secondary uses, such as marketing and policing.

Organizations using information entrepreneurial strategies are increasingly going to outside entrepreneurs who are able to supply personal data for secondary uses. The emergence of "data brokers" is the most obvious example of this trend. Large health maintenance organizations seeking to cut costs by obtaining fine-grained information about potential clients turn to data brokers such as the Medical Information Bureau to fill their data appetites. Many other organizations that collect personal information as a by-product of their core activities, such as phone companies and airlines, have the ability to offer profitable data collection services for other information entrepreneurial enterprises.

During the past two decades, direct-mail marketing and precision marketing have gotten big boosts through new techniques for identifying potential customers (Culnan, 1992). As we have noted, in the early 1990s, Lotus Development Corporation was planning to sell a CD-based database, MarketPlace:Households, which contained household marketing data provided by Equifax Marketing Decision Systems Inc., which is affiliated with a large credit agency, Equifax Inc. The database would have given anyone with a Macintosh access to data on more than 120 million Americans. Lotus MarketPlace:Household would provide marketers with detailed portraits of households so that it would be easier for them to ascertain where to send direct mail and what places would be best for telemarketing. All names would come encrypted on the disk, and users would be required to purchase access codes and to use a "metering" system to pay for new groups of addresses to search (Levy, 1991). Lotus attempted to reduce privacy problems by omitting phone numbers and credit ratings from MarketPlace:Household and by selling the data only to those who could prove they ran legitimate businesses. The street addresses could be printed only on paper and not on a computer screen. These measures did not adequately assure many people, however.

Lotus withdrew MarketPlace:Household in 1991 after it received more than thirty thousand complaints from consumers. Some industry observers speculated that Lotus withdrew MarketPlace:Household because the company's upper managers feared that bad publicity and consumer backlash could harm sales of other Lotus software. Lotus did, however, release a companion product, MarketPlace:Business, which characterizes business purchasing patterns, through a licensing arrangement.

Lotus MarketPlace:Household is an interesting kind of information product that illustrates another face of information entrepreneurialism, because it was to be sold to small businesses, which could more readily afford microcomputing. These users of Lotus MarketPlace: Household would have had a new resource to help expand their own use of information capitalist marketing strategies. The particular computer platform for a product like Lotus MarketPlace:Household has some consequences for personal privacy. For example, it would be much easier to remove records of objecting consumers rapidly and consistently from a centralized database than from hundreds of thousands of CDs of various vintages scattered throughout thousands of offices around the country. Consequently, a firm providing a mainframe-based version of MarketPlace:Household might face less resistance. Further, if the firm does not risk loss of business from consumer complaints, it might tough out a wave of initial complaints. Thus, a credit reporting firm such as Equifax or TRW might offer a variant mainframe-based version of MarketPlace:Household.

Debates about whether certain computerized systems should be implemented typically reveal major conflicts between civil libertarians on the one hand and those who value the preeminence of private enterprise or statist values on the other. Any particular computerized system is likely to advance some of these values at the expense of others. Many socially complex information systems are enmeshed in a matrix of competing social values, and none is value free.

Problems for the people about whom records are kept arise under a variety of circumstances; for example, when the records about people are inaccurate and they are unfairly denied loans, jobs, or housing. In large-scale record systems (with millions of records) there are bound to be inaccuracies, but people have few rights to inspect or correct records about them—except for credit records. During the past thirty years, people have consistently lost significant control over records about them. Increasingly, courts have ruled that records about a person belong to the organization that collects the data, and the person to whom they apply cannot restrict their use. Consequently, inaccurate police records, medical records, and employment histories can harm people without their explicit knowledge about why they are having trouble getting jobs, loans, or medical insurance.

New ways of doing business—taken together with computer systems—have reduced people's control over their personal affairs. On the other hand, representatives of those private firms and government agencies that have an interest in expanding their computerized information systems frequently argue hard against legal limits or substantial accountability to people about whom records are kept. They deny that problems exist, or they argue that the reported problems are exaggerated in importance. They further argue that proposed regulations are either too vague or too burdensome, and that new regulations about information systems would do more harm than good. The pro-

ponents of unregulated computerization are generally wealthy, organized, and aligned with the antiregulatory sentiments that have dominated U.S. federal politics during the past fifteen years. Consequently,
they have effectively blocked many attempts to preserve personal privacy through regulation.

In this way, many representatives of the computer industry and of
firms with massive personal record systems behave much as the representatives of automobile firms did when they first were asked to face
questions about air pollution. As smog became increasingly visible in
major U.S. cities in the 1940s and 1950s, the automobile industry worked
hard to argue that there is no link between cars and smog (Krier and
Ursin, 1977). First, industry spokespersons argued that smog is not a
systematic phenomenon; then, they argued that smog comes primarily
from other sources, such as factories. After increases in smog were
unequivocally linked to the use of cars, they spent a good deal of energy fighting any regulations that would require them to reduce the
pollution emitted by cars. Overall, the automobile industry slowly
conceded to reducing smog in a foot-dragging pattern that Krier and
Ursin (1977) characterize as "regulation by least steps." In a similar
way, the organizations that develop or use personal record-keeping
systems have been systematically fighting enhanced public protections.

The increasing importance of indirect social relationships that we
described earlier gives many organizations legitimate interests in using
computerized personal record systems to learn about potential or
actual clients. These organizations usually act in ways designed to
maintain the largest possible zone of free action for themselves while
downplaying their clients' interests. The spread of larger and more
interlinked personal data systems will not automatically provide people
with corresponding protections to reduce the risks of these systems in
cases of error, inappropriate disclosure, or other problems (Dunlop and
Kling, 1991). Information entrepreneurial practices are closely implicated in these policy issues.

The history of federal privacy protections in the United States is
likely to continue without a new level of political mobilization that
supports new protections. The Privacy Act of 1974 established the Privacy Protection Study Commission, which in 1977 issued a substantial
report on its findings and made 155 recommendations for the development of "fair information practices." Among these were that people
should have the right to know what records are kept about them, the

right to inspect records for accuracy, the right to correct (or contest) inaccuracies, and the right to be informed when records are transferred from one organization to another. Fewer than a handful of these proposals were subsequently enacted into federal law.

Leaders of the computing movements that enable large-scale databases and their associated industries could help lessen the possible reductions of privacy that their applications foster by initiating relevant and responsible privacy protections. However, expecting them to take such initiatives would be naive, given that they work within social arrangements that do not reward the reduction of their own market opportunities. The commercial firms and public agencies that will utilize surveillance technologies in the next decades face their own contests with their clients and data subjects, and they fight for legal and technological help, rather than hindrance. As a consequence, we do not expect privacy regulations in the next two decades to become significantly more restrictive. Although the public is becoming sensitized to privacy as a mobilizing issue, at present it does not have the salience and energizing quality of such issues as tax reduction, abortion, or even environmental pollution. This does not mean that there will not be any new privacy protections for private persons. Regulation by least steps, in the case of personal privacy, can take the form of very bounded regulations, such as the Video Privacy Protection Act, which regulates access to video store rental records, and the Electronic Communications Privacy Act of 1986, which protects communications on wires between organizations but not within buildings.

Conclusions

We opened this chapter with a simple but fundamental question: Why is the continuing development of information technologies that impinge on personal privacy a continuing struggle in contemporary advanced industrial societies? Few analysts have tried to answer this question directly, although some answers are implicit. Gandy, for example, discusses the panoptic sort as a social architecture for processing information about people. He implicitly views extensions of personal record-keeping systems and various precision marketing and surveillance systems in terms of an Ellulian logic of a self-completing system. Laudon and Laudon (1994:702–3) focus on rapid improvements in the absolute capabilities and the cost/performance of information technologies. They also identify "advances in data mining techniques" used for precision marketing by firms such as Wal-Mart and Hallmark. This last item relates to information entrepreneurialism, but Laudon and Laudon mention supercomputing technology and analytic technique without further discussions of shifting context.

Our answer is quite different, and focuses upon the micropractices of those who build such systems and their incentive systems, as well as the institutional structures in which they work—that is, information capitalism. *Information entrepreneurialism* is our term for a set of social practices that encourage the use of data-intensive techniques and computerization as key strategic resources of corporate production. Information entrepreneurialism thrives within an information capitalist economic order, and it has been stimulated by some of the major social transformations of the past one hundred years in industrialized society: the increasing mobility of populations, the growth of nationwide organizations, and the increasing importance of indirect social relationships. The key link between information entrepreneurialism and the new technologies that support large-scale databases lies in the possibilities for enhanced information processing that it provides to analysts whose managerial strategies profit from significant advances in the capacity to analyze records of an organization's (potential) clients and operations.

We find it especially important to examine the institutional aspects of the use of surveillance technologies. The information entrepreneurial model argues that coalitions within organizations actively pursuing data-intensive strategies are a key driver of our society's increasing surveillance of indirect social relationships. Attempts to introduce products such as Lotus MarketPlace:Household are difficult to understand only as methods for improving bureaucratic efficiency. Information entrepreneurs actively pursue organizational strategies that take advantage of broader changes in society and surveillance technology. The creation of strong institutional support for data-intensive management techniques, education, professional mobilization, and career paths is an important driver of information entrepreneurialism.

The growing importance of indirect social relationships in North American society leads many organizations to seek data about potential and actual clients. Some organizations collect their own data, and some rely upon specialized data brokers to help them construct specialized personal histories pertinent to their specific concerns, such as creditworthiness, insurability, employability, and criminal culpability. The positive side of these informational strategies includes improved organizational efficiencies, novel products, and interesting analytic jobs. However, as a collection, these strategies reduce the privacy of many citizens and can result in excruciating foul-ups when record-keeping errors are perpetuated from one computer system to another with little or no accountability to the persons concerned.

These social changes can be influenced by the policies and practices of commercial firms and public agencies. They are not inevitable social trends. For instance, the public might insist upon stronger fair information practices to reduce the risks inherent in expanding record systems. Laudon (1993) has proposed an elaborate scheme to reduce casual privacy intrusions that would enable people to be paid when personally sensitive data about them are used outside of direct client-service provider relationships. In short, society can and should change some key rules, rights, and responsibilities that characterize the current form of information capitalism. In practice, relatively few such restraints have been imposed upon the unfettered exchange of personal information between organizations, both public and private.

We are not optimistic that there will be any substantial shift toward more privacy protections over the next two decades, and without such changes that are exogenous to the direct use of specific computer applications, the trends we have discussed are likely to continue. These trends clearly merit systematic empirical inquiry.[4]

Notes

This essay has benefited from discussions about information capitalism that Rob Kling had with Vijay Gurbaxani, James Katz, Abbe Mowshowitz, and Jeffrey Smith. Mary Culnan and Jeff Smith also provided important insights into the importance of direct-mail marketing organizations. Our colleague John King has been a continual partner in provocative discussions about technology and social change.

1. Examples include Laudon's (1986a) study of police records systems and Lyon's (1991) study of British identity cards.

2. Today there are important debates about the extent to which information collected by government agencies should be made available at low cost to the public—or given to private firms that then resell it at higher costs.

3. A terabyte is equivalent to 10^{12} bytes.

4. For example, it may be worthwhile to study organizations that adopt large-scale database computing technology in order to understand the applica-

tions these firms automate as well as the changes computerization may bring about in their relationships with their clients.

References

Burnham, David. (1983). *The Rise of the Computer State.* New York: Random House.
Calhoun, Craig. (1992). "The Infrastructure of Modernity: Indirect Social Relationships, Information Technology, and Social Integration." In H. Haferkamp and N. Smelser (eds.), *Social Change and Modernity.* Berkeley: University of California Press.
Cash, James, Jr., Warren F. McFarland, James McKenney, and Linda Applegate (eds.). (1992). *Corporate Information Systems Management: Text and Cases,* 3rd ed. Boston: Irwin.
Chandler, Alfred D. (1977). *The Visible Hand: The Managerial Revolution in American Business.* Cambridge, Mass.: Harvard University Press.
———. (1984). "The Emergence of Managerial Capitalism." *Business History Review* 58 (Winter): 473–503.
Culnan, Mary. (1992). "How Did They Get My Name? An Exploratory Investigation of Consumer Attitudes toward Secondary Information Use." Unpublished manuscript, Georgetown University.
Dunlop, Charles, and Rob Kling. (eds.). (1991). *Computerization and Controversy: Value Conflicts and Social Choices.* Boston: Academic Press.
Flaherty, David. (1989). *Protecting Privacy in Surveillance Societies: The Federal Republic of Germany, Sweden, France, Canada and the United States.* Chapel Hill: University of North Carolina Press.
Gandy, Oscar H., Jr. (1993). *The Panoptic Sort: A Political Economy of Personal Information.* Boulder, Colo.: Westview.
Louis Harris & Associates and Alan F. Westin. (1991). *Harris-Equifax Consumer Privacy Survey.* Atlanta, Ga.: Equifax.
———. (1992). *Harris-Equifax Consumer Privacy Survey.* Atlanta, Ga.: Equifax.
Ives, Blake, and G. P. Learmouth. (1984). "The Information System as a Competitive Weapon." *Communications of the ACM* 27: 1193–1201.
Kling, Rob. (1978). "Value Conflicts and Social Choice in Electronic Funds Transfer Systems Developments." *Communications of the ACM* 21 (August): 642–57
———. (1991). "Value Conflicts in New Computing Developments." In Charles Dunlop and Rob Kling (eds.), *Computerization and Controversy: Value Conflicts and Social Choices.* Boston: Academic Press.
———. (forthcoming a). "Information Technologies and the Shifting Balance between Privacy and Social Control." In Rob Kling (ed.), *Computerization and Controversy: Value Conflicts and Social Choices* (2d ed.). San Diego, Calif.: Academic Press.
———. (forthcoming b). "Institutional Processes in the Diffusion, Use and

Impacts of Information Technology." In Russell W. Belk and Nikhilesh Dohlakia (eds.), *Consumption and Marketing: Macro Dimensions.* Boston: PWS-Kent.

Kling, Rob, Mark Ackerman, and Jonathan P. Allen. (forthcoming). "Information Entrepreneurialism: Information Technologies and the Continuing Vulnerability to Privacy." In Rob Kling (ed.), *Computerization and Controversy: Value Conflicts and Social Choices* (2d ed.). San Diego, Calif.: Academic Press.

Kling, Rob, Spencer Olin, and Mark Poster. (1991). "Emergence of Postsuburbia." In Rob Kling, Spencer Olin, and Mark Poster (eds.), *Postsuburban California: The Transformation of Postwar Orange County.* Berkeley: University of California Press.

Kling, Rob, Isaac Scherson, and John Allen. (1992). "Massively Parallel Computing and Information Capitalism." In W. Daniel Hillis and James Bailey (eds.), *A New Era of Computing.* Cambridge: MIT Press.

Krier, James, and Edmund Ursin. (1977). *Pollution and Policy: A Case Essay on California and Federal Experience with Motor Vehicle Air Pollution, 1940–1975.* Berkeley: University of California Press.

Kusserow, Robert P. (1991). "The Government Needs Computer Matching to Root Out Waste and Fraud." In Charles Dunlop and Rob Kling (eds.), *Computerization and Controversy: Value Conflicts and Social Choices.* Boston: Academic Press.

Laudon, Kenneth. (1986a). "Data Quality and Due Process in Large Interorganizational Record Systems." *Communications of the ACM* 29 (January): 4–11.

———. (1986b). *Dossier Society: Value Choices in the Design of National Information Systems.* New York: Columbia University Press.

———. (1993). "Markets and Privacy." In *Proceedings of the International Conference on Information Systems.* Orlando, Fla.

Laudon, Kenneth, and Jane Laudon. (1994). *Management Information Systems: A Contemporary Perspective* (3rd ed.). New York: Macmillan.

Levy, Steven. (1991). "How the Good Guys Finally Won: Keeping Lotus MarketPlace Off the Market." *Macworld,* June, 69–74.

Luke, Timothy, and Stephen White. (1985). "Critical Theory, the Informational Revolution, and an Ecological Path to Modernity." In J. Forester (ed.), *Critical Theory and Public Life.* Cambridge: MIT Press, 22–53.

Lyon, David. (1991). "British Identity Cards: The Unpalatable Logic of European Membership?" *Political Quarterly* 62, no. 3: 377–85.

McFarland, F. W. (1984). "Information Technology Changes the Way You Compete." *Harvard Business Review* 61, no. 4: 91–99.

Markoff, John. (1991). "American Express to Buy 2 Top Supercomputers from Thinking Machines Corp." *New York Times,* October 30, C7(N), D9(L).

Ostrofsky, Kerry, and James Cash. (1992). "Mrs. Fields' Cookies." In James Cash Jr., Warren F. McFarland, James McKenney, and Linda Applegate (eds.), *Corporate Information Systems Management: Text and Cases* (3rd ed.). Boston: Irwin.

Reich, Robert. (1992). *The Work of Nations: Preparing Ourselves for 21st Century Capitalism.* New York: Vintage.

Rule, James B. (1974). *Private Lives and Public Surveillance: Social Control in the Computer Age.* New York: Schocken.

Rule, James B., David McAdam, Linda Stearns, and David Uglow. (1980). *The Politics of Privacy: Planning for Personal Data Systems as Powerful Technologies.* New York: Mentor.

Shattuck, John. (1991). "Computer Matching Is a Serious Threat to Individual Rights." In Charles Dunlop and Rob Kling (eds.), *Computerization and Controversy: Value Conflicts and Social Choices.* Boston: Academic Press.

Smith, H. Jeff. (1994). *Managing Privacy: Information Technology and Corporate America.* Chapel Hill: University of North Carolina Press.

U.S. Department of Commerce, Bureau of the Census. (1992). *Statistical Abstract of the United States.* Washington, D.C.: U.S. Government Printing Office.

7

Coming to Terms with the Panoptic Sort

Oscar H. Gandy Jr.

Recently, I received what most people would consider a rather curious bit of mail. The Strub Media Group sent me a flyer that asked a bold question: Have you tried gay lists? The letter inside addressed me, incorrectly of course, as "Dear Direct Marketer," because I was on the subscription list of *DM News,* one of several publications that serve this large and growing segment of the information industry. The letter described gay men and lesbians as "the affluent and responsive market for the '90's," noting that readers of gay publications have household incomes nearly twice the national average, reflecting an even more striking disparity in educational attainment. The lists that Strub was offering to rent had been derived from periodical subscriptions, catalog and other mail-order purchases, records of donations, recent housing changes, vacations at Provincetown resorts, and even records of attendance at plays. Although the promotion did not also indicate that other names, addresses, and telephone numbers may have been derived from inquiries to AIDS hot lines or calls to 976 or other audiotext information services, I will wager that not a single person volunteered to have his or her name included in these lists, and many would be outraged if they were to find themselves so listed. Yet there is very little preventing the collection and use of the information that makes these and similar lists possible.

Part of the difficulty with the collection and use of personal information to support the marketing and sale of a variety of goods and services rests in the fact that personal information is not only used to *include* individuals within the marketing scan, but may also be used to *exclude* them from other life chances linked to employment, insurance, housing, education, and credit.

Each week *DM News* provides readers with a service card through which they can order information about the new lists and databases that have recently become available on the market. This service is in addition to the regular classified and display ads for lists and list management services that make up the key auxiliaries of the direct-response marketing industry (Novek, Sinha, and Gandy, 1990). These lists and databases represent the traces of value individuals unknowingly provide each time they interact with the market system and the administrative state. These interactions include records of purchases as well as records of inquiries regarding purchases or investments under consideration. Because information about nonmarket behaviors is also believed to be relevant to estimates of an individual's economic potential or risk, data about almost any other transaction that involves the generation of a machine-readable trace may be made available for sale. In this essay, I explore the ways in which this personal information finds use within the market system as an instrument of social control.

Background

The collection and use of personal information are critical to the operation of what I have called the *panoptic sort*. The panoptic sort is a complex discriminatory technology. It is panoptic in that it considers *all* information about individual status and behavior to be potentially useful in the production of intelligence about a person's economic value. It is a discriminatory technology because it is used to sort people into categories based upon these estimates.

The conceptual heritage of my theoretical work includes many sources whose epistemological and political stance at some level may be seen to be incompatible. I have not allowed these tensions to prevent me from combining insights from Michel Foucault, Karl Marx, Max Weber, Anthony Giddens, and Jacques Ellul into the fabric of my research and theory. Although none of these authors has focused his critical and analytic lenses on marketing and the sphere of circulation to the extent that I believe is warranted, each has had much to say about the critical role that information plays in the development and reproduction of systems of power.

The contribution of Foucault is apparent in my embrace of panopticism as an apt description of the role of surveillance in the technology of power (Foucault, 1979). I do not make the critical error that many make by suggesting that surveillance is complete, or that it is even capable of being complete. Ien Ang (1991) notes that the continuing pressure to define audiences (and markets) in narrower slices generates requirements for larger and more costly samples at the same time the intrusiveness of measurement technology generates an increased level of resistance within the subject population. However, the presence of contradictions and counterforces in no way serves to deny the rationalist goals that lead organizations to gather more and more information about marketing targets.

Foucault's contribution is not limited to the metaphoric anchor of the panopticon as prison. His discussion of disciplinary surveillance in the service of correct training has been extended to broad areas of social practice in the critical analyses of Frank Webster and Kevin Robins (1986; Robins and Webster, 1988). Weber's contributions are also broad, but for the purposes of this essay, they primarily inform my discussion regarding the role of information in the rationalization of an organization's efforts to maintain predictability in its operations.

Ellul (1964), of course, is the source of much contemporary thinking about technological systems. His expansion of the definition of technology to include the philosophy and ideology of efficiency as well as the hardware, software, and expertise necessary to realize the goals of progress and the reduction of uncertainty is reflected in my definition of the panoptic sort. The panoptic sort, as a complex technology, includes not only the computers and telecommunication systems that facilitate the collection, storage, processing, and sharing of personal information, but also the analytic approaches that differentiate, classify, segment, and target individuals and groups upon the basis of models, assumptions, and strategic orientations that demand the maximization of profit and the minimization of risk.

The Logic of the Sort

The panoptic sort is the outcome of an evolutionary or dialectical process that has transformed the personal relationship between buyers and sellers into an impersonal transaction that is controlled by a cybernetic intelligence. As examined by James Beniger (1986), the effort to control mass consumption has involved the development and use of communications and information technology to provide marketplace feedback. This feedback serves not only to coordinate the production process so as to avoid the crisis of overproduction, but also to provide critical information about the extent to which advertising and promotional efforts have produced their desired effects on consumers. In Beniger's view, scientific advertising in the control of mass consumption is equivalent to Frederick Winslow Taylor's scientific management in the control of mass production (p. 355).

We might see personal information performing three distinct, but related, functions within the panoptic system: identification, classification, and assessment. *Identification* refers to the need for reliable evidence of the identities of individuals with whom one does business. James Rule and his colleagues (1983) have examined the variety of tokens that have been developed over the years to provide the level of identification that different kinds of commercial transactions seem to require. The most frequent, and the most readily understandable, request for identification is in the context of purchases that are made on the basis of something other than cash. Identification is required for personal checks, but it is not usually required when payment is in the form of legal tender. Identification is frequently required when one picks up or receives goods or services from a site or agent different from the one where payment or promise was made. Identification tokens provide some level of confidence that consumers are who they claim to be.

Increasingly, however, the call for personal identification is not derived from a concern with authentication. Instead, the capture of identifying information (name, address, telephone number, social security, mother's maiden name) is motivated by the desire to establish, or to enhance, a consumer record. This is information that contributes to the second panoptic function, that of *classification.*

As Foucault (1979, 1973) and others make clear, classification is a process intimately involved in the exercise of power. Personal information facilitates the assignment of individuals to groups that are seen as "types" on the basis of shared characteristics. This sorting, or assignment to groups, is akin to the disciplinary isolation that Foucault observes in the pursuit of correct training in schools, prisons, hospitals, and military brigades. Classification and sorting are thought to increase the efficiency and effectiveness with which rewards and punishments can be applied in order to reduce uncertainty about the future behavior of disciplinary subjects. Classification serves the same function within the marketplace, where commercial firms seek to improve, or at least maintain, their market shares and rates of profit.

In addition to linking identifying information to evidence of a person's ability to pay, the process of classification may also provide information about the potential value of the consumer as a target for future commercial appeals. Information about purchases, inquiries, resources, and responses to offers facilitates the assignment of individuals to market segments. It allows marketers to estimate the probability that a particular offer will generate an appropriate affirmative response.

Although the current mode of theorizing privileges the assumption of personal agency, there is heuristic value in thinking of consumers as products. Such a view supports the use of the production function as a metaphoric representation of marketing technology. In this view, the consumer's decision to buy is the product of the careful application of strategic resources that are under the control of the vendor. As with Beniger's expansive definition of control, this production function approach recognizes that much remains beyond the control of the marketer.[1] The resources generally under the marketer's control include the fixed attributes of the product or service. Those beyond complete control, but subject to influence, are the resources, tastes, and preferences of potential consumers. Of course, not all attributes are equally productive of an affirmative response in all consumers. Because of this, promotional materials may emphasize some product attributes and ignore others (including price). Information about potential consumers helps the supplier decide on the optimal combination of price and promise. This knowledge about consumers may also suggest that the level of expenditure necessary to turn *some* individuals into consumers may in fact exceed the revenues that those sales might produce. Once identification has determined that consumers are who they say they are, and classification has guided decisions about what kinds of people they are, it is the process of *assessment* that determines whether they should be included in or excluded from the stream of promotional information.

Assessment makes explicit the evaluative potential that is inherent in each act of classification. Classification involves differentiation, and the value of any difference within the panoptic sort is frequently based on its predictive utility. That is, classification is an element of instrumental rationality. Beniger describes classification in the context of a control strategy he calls "preprocessing" (1986:15-16), which involves the reduction of complexity through the elimination of unnecessary or irrelevant information. The process that assigns a complex individual to a group on the basis of race, gender, or neighborhood ignores the myriad other facts that make up that person's uniqueness in preference for the efficient predictability in this narrower classification. Race, gender, age, and education work as markers for classification because of their empirical associations with other behaviors or statuses. Thus, these markers reduce the uncertainty experienced by suppliers of goods and services and increase their confidence in their estimates of each person's value as the target of a commercial appeal. In the next section, I examine the variety of ways in which information about individuals is used to facilitate the operation of the panoptic sort.

The Operation of the Sort

We should avoid, of course, the confusion about technological systems that assigns them intelligence and needs or some kind of integrative reality akin to biological systems. The criticism with which Giddens (1984:293–97; 1987:17–18) assails functionalist theories might also be applied to the vision with which Ellul (1964) develops his perspective on technology. The panoptic sort can be seen to be part of a panoptic system, but it is only our critical and analytic glance that makes this system appear to be an operational whole.

Of course, there is a telecommunications network, and several interconnected networks can be seen to be part of a telecommunications system. But no physical network, even a network infrastructure defined broadly enough to include personnel, skills, and formal rules of procedure, stands as a model for the more complex system that I refer to as the panoptic sort.[2] This network/system only facilitates the decisions by individuals in organizations to contribute to, and comply with, rules and regulations in ways that reinforce and reproduce the marketing system that I describe as panoptic.

As a complex technology, the panoptic sort involves the hardware and software used to process transactions and to store the information that is the by-product of those transactions. This technology includes the routines that result in the transformation of this information into standardized forms that thereby facilitate its combination in ways that we recognize as knowledge or intelligence. In addition, it includes the systems and rules of access and authorization that allow this information and intelligence to be shared with others. Thus, of necessity, this system must include the market for personal information that has developed to coordinate the accretion and flow of vital intellectual resources. I am persuaded by Giddens's theory of structuration to include also within this system the routine patterns of interaction between consumers and commercial institutions that develop over time and generate a kind of naive acceptance, or banalization, of surveillance.

Information Gathering

In understanding the operation of the panoptic sort, it is important to understand the great variety of ways in which information becomes available for use in making decisions and in modifying decision systems. If we think of every interaction with a bureaucratic organization as a transaction, there is an increasing likelihood that each transaction is recorded in machine-readable form. Table 7.1 provides a glance at the variety of data records or files that may be associated with identifiable individuals and that may also be updated with each new interaction with an organization. Gary Marx (1985) has noted that the collection of this information is increasingly automated, in that its collection does not depend upon a person's interaction with another individual. He argues that this modern form of surveillance differs from earlier forms in that the target of surveillance increasingly initiates the cycle of observation through his or her own actions, for example, by placing a card in a reading device, signing on to a database service, calling a toll-free phone number, or mailing a response card or form.

It is the happy marriage of the computer with high-speed telecommunications that makes the collection of personal information quick, efficient, and distance insensitive. Thomas McManus (1990) has coined the acronym TTGI (for telephone transaction-generated information) to focus our attention on market systems that process millions of transactions per hour, with each transaction generating information of potential value. The point-of-purchase terminals in gas stations and at grocery checkout counters, ATMs, and self-service video rental kiosks are all part of a commercial service network. This network provides for identification, authorization, and transfer of value claims all within a matter of seconds. Generally, the consumer receives goods or services and a paper record of the transaction. Additional copies of transaction data may be received and captured by the store, the bank, and the transaction processor. If the goods and services are to be delivered, another series of transaction-generated records is produced. Each record provides information of potential use within the panoptic sort. Each record also raises questions of access, ownership, and control.

Table 7.1. Personal contributions to machine-readable, network-linked data files

1. *Personal information for identification and qualification*
   Includes birth certificate, driver's license, passport, voter registration, automobile registration, school records, marriage certification

2. *Financial information*
   Includes bank records, savings passbooks, ATM cards, credit cards, credit reports/files, tax returns, stock/brokerage accounts, traveler's checks

3. *Insurance information*
   Includes insurance for health, automobile, home, business, general and specific liability, group and individual policies

4. *Social services information*
   Includes social security, health care, employment benefits, unemployment benefits, disability, pensions, food stamps and other government assistance, veterans' benefits, senior citizens' benefits/subsidies

5. *Utility services information*
   Includes telephone, electricity, gas, cable television, sanitation, heating, garbage, security, delivery

6. *Real estate information*
   Involved with purchase, sale, rental, lease

7. *Entertainment/leisure information*
   Includes travel itineraries, recreational profiles, automobile and other rentals/leases, lodging reservations, airplane reservations, ship reservations, train reservations, entertainment tickets/reservations, newspaper and other periodical subscriptions, television/cable rating

8. *Consumer information*
   Includes store credit cards, other accounts, layaway, leases and rentals, purchases, purchase inquiries, subscriber lists, clothing and shoe sizes

9. *Employment information*
   Includes application, medical examination, references, performance assessments, employment history, employment agency applications

10. *Educational information*
    Includes school applications, academic records, references, extracurricular activities/memberships, awards and sanctions, rankings

11. *Legal information*
    Includes records of the court, attorney's records, newspaper reports, index and abstract services

The Production of Intelligence

As I have suggested, the panoptic sort operates by transforming transaction information into intelligence that guides the presentation of inducements and offers to some, but not all, who might come to consume goods and services through the market. This intelligence is produced in a variety of ways, but nearly all share a common dependence upon personal information. In most cases where the information being gathered is about persons with whom the organization already has a prior relationship, a file has already been established. Data gathered from any future transactions with the firm, or from transactions with other organizations that share or provide information about the individual, may be used to sharpen the stored image or profile of an identifiable person. The organization uses this enhanced profile to maintain a level of service as well as to develop cross-marketing approaches that aid in selling other services available within the corporate family. American Express, for example, is reported to maintain and regularly update information about its cardholders in upward of 450 categories (Chofras and Steinman, 1990). This extensive profile supports authentication and security requirements of a nonbank "credit" card, but it also supports the corporation's extensive publishing and direct-response marketing activities.

It should be clear, however, that in the production of intelligence, personal information is not synonymous with the legalistic specification of "individually identifiable information." That is, when personal information about individuals is combined with similar information about other individuals, the goal is frequently the generation of information about countless others whose behavior has not been directly measured. The panoptic technology is an *inferential* difference machine. Its predictions are based on information gathered from samples of persons and samples of their behaviors. Information gathered from particular individuals is frequently most useful in developing approaches to *other* individuals who may remain unknown to the organization until they respond to a promotional appeal.

At the simplest level, the compilation of lists based on transactions, the analytic assumption is that people who have recently made purchases of one kind are more likely to respond favorably to offers of a similar kind than are people who have not actively demonstrated such an interest in the recent past. Thus we find the offerings of list vendors filled with names and addresses and other personal identifiers derived from recent purchases, subscriptions, and donations. For increments in costs-per-thousand names, these lists can be further subdivided into finer segments on the bases of gender, ethnicity, geography, level of creditworthiness, and other attributes that marketing models (formal or "seat of the pants") suggest will improve the efficiency of sales production.

As just one of dozens of readily available examples, TRW Target

Marketing Services fall 1992 catalog offers a consumer database with a count of more than 164 million identifiable individuals. The information that allows TRW to offer demographic "selects" at prices ranging from $2.50/thousand (gender) to $10/thousand (ethnic markets) is supposed to be derived from public records. Public driver's license records allow TRW to offer more expensive selects of those who wear corrective lenses at a rate of $20/thousand. Other TRW consumer databases come from subscriptions and directories, and make estimates of ethnicity from consumer surname and confirming data sources. TRW's special status as a leader in the consumer credit reporting industry allows it (until the attorneys general of a number of states suggested otherwise) to offer special financial lifestyle databases that include selects for "active credit shoppers" and "elite retail shoppers."[3]

TRW's "Highly Affluent Consumer Database" is described as a list of individuals with incomes in excess of $100,000. The list has been generated through a proprietary statistical model using census and other broadly available information in combination with TRW's proprietary consumer data. TRW's "Smart Consumer Clusters" database is based upon a statistical model that TRW claims is superior to traditional clustering models. The end result is a classification of consumers by lifestyles that is used to characterize neighborhoods, similar to the earlier geodemographic clustering technology developed by Jonathan Robbin for his Claritas Corporation.[4]

Just as within the traditions of "normal science," there are different approaches within marketing science to generating intelligence about classes and types of consumers and their responsiveness to particular kinds of appeals made within particular information environments. Although the bulk of this marketing intelligence is derived from secondary analysis of data gathered from public and private sources, a substantial amount of industry- and product-specific information is generated by tightly controlled experiments.

Advances in telecommunications facilitate the realization of almost laboratory-quality control through the random assignment of individuals to experimental treatment conditions. The attributes of addressability and verifiability (Gandy and Simmons, 1986) that characterize modern telecommunications allow marketers to send different promotional messages to different consumers such that they are seen at different times and within different programs. When this exposure information is linked with the assistance of supermarket or home-based scanning of universal product identifiers (UPC codes), it becomes possible to estimate the productivity of particular appeals, presented to particular kinds of consumers, in the context of particular program fare.

Of course, these experiments are not limited to the specialized environment of electronic mass media. Advances in printing technology facilitate the delivery of personalized appeals in magazines, by direct mail, and, most productively, through promotional coupons. Coupons can be mailed to consumers directly, made available to segments of the local market through specialized inserts in zoned editions of local Sunday newspapers, or delivered to the home by hand. Coupons may be systematically varied in terms of their redemption value. Coupons sent to particular households may even be imprinted with information about the household, and this information may be linked automatically with additional information about purchases made for that household when the coupon is scanned for redemption at the supermarket.[5]

Creative approaches to linking persons with purchases include devices that generate discount coupons for competing products when a substitute or complement is purchased. Depending upon the relationship between participants, some or all of the information generated, or enabled through the use of scanning technology, may be sold, rented, or exchanged in the market for personal information.

Thus, intelligence about consumers and potential consumers is produced through the operation of predictive models of varying degrees of sophistication. The information used to operate these models is gathered from surveys, investigations, experiments, public records, and records of transactions. This information is produced or gathered directly by organizations as a by-product of interactions with individuals, or it is purchased on the relatively open market for personal information.

The Market for Personal Information

There is no readily available estimate of the size of the market for personal information. Indeed, there is no list of the firms that are in the business of selling information about identifiable individuals. The larger firms in the business are really agents and consolidators, selling lists or managing their rental on behalf of the smaller firms that are in other lines of business but that have come to recognize the economic value of their customer list.

Late in 1992, the U.S. Supreme Court announced its willingness to examine a case involving the IRS and its refusal to recognize the value of mailing lists as nontangible assets. A publisher, the Herald Company, claimed that more than 20 percent of its net worth was based on the estimated value of its 460,000-name list of subscribers. The company valued these assets at $68 million. In the petition before the court, the value of all customer, mailing, and subscriber lists worldwide was estimated to exceed $10.5 billion.[6] Of course, the value of assets is not related in any clear way to the value of transactions involving those assets in any given year. This is due in part to the fact that considerable value added may be involved in transforming raw transaction data into knowledge or intelligence that can be used in marketing, commercial siting, or other investment decisions that might come to rely upon the use of personal information.

Estimates of the size of the market in personal information vary considerably depending upon how one specifies the boundaries of this market. It seems clear that an estimate based on the sale or rental of personal information should include the fees that are charged for the production of a credit report, including the fees that are charged to the subject of the report. Because under the Fair Credit Reporting Act the credit record can legitimately be used for employment decisions, as well as for decisions about the granting of credit, the demand for this information is quite high. The difficulties involved in the estimation of the annual value of rentals and enhanced services regarding personal information in lists and electronic databases are exacerbated by the fact that many of the transfers are unrecorded because they are of questionable legal status.

Estimates of this market should also consider the fees that are paid for access to public records. Fees paid to states and municipal governments vary considerably. Journalists and their newspapers have taken some states to court because they have been charged fees for access to data in electronic form that were the same as rates common to the supply of the data in the form of photocopies.[7]

A Question of Value

Estimates of the dollar value of the market for personal information bear no satisfactory relationship to what we might consider to be the true value of that information. The classical perspective on value, which has been largely overturned, emphasized the sphere of production as the site of value determination. Value was determined on the basis of the value of the resources, primarily labor time, that were used up in the production of commodities. The neoclassical perspective seeks to find the index of value in the market price, which, under optimal conditions, reflects the subjective estimations of value to both consumers and producers. Part of the unsettled status of neoclassical economic theory is associated with an illogical and contradictory set of assumptions at the base of claims regarding the subjective estimation of value.

Institutionalists and other behavioral economists have challenged the assumptions of omniscience and rationality of consumers in the face of logic, experience, and experimental evidence (Earl, 1983). Consumers cannot know the present value of future benefits derived from particular choices because they cannot know the future. More problematic is the recognition that the individual tastes and preferences upon which these choices are to be made, even in the state of uncertainty about the future, are based on guidance systems that are subject to strategic influence. Tastes and preferences are not given, as neoclassical economics seems doomed to assume, but instead are influenced by advertising, marketing, example, and experience, and reflect the operation of systems of power.

Although neoclassical economics has succeeded in pushing aside the classical and Marxist position on the nature of value (Burkitt, 1984; Gandy, 1992b; King, Roderen, and Olsen, 1983; Machlup, 1979; Marx, 1971), we cannot agree that the value determined in markets is a true measure of value when the markets are flawed. The markets in personal information are flawed primarily because the goods that are exchanged in this market have not been freely supplied. Neoclassical and radical economists recognize that distortions in the markets for labor power, or for the commodities it can be used to produce, would result in prices that depart from the true value of those commodities. In both mainstream and critical perspectives on market failure, the existence and operation of disproportionate power are generally recognized as determinative of market prices.

Randall Bartlett (1989) has provided a masterful explication of the importance of different forms of power that have been undertheorized and largely ignored within mainstream economics. Several of the forms of power that he describes have particular relevance for our consideration of the value of personal information. Bartlett asserts that power is the "ability of one actor to alter the decisions made and/or welfare experienced by another actor relative to the choices that would have been made and/or the welfare that would have been experienced had the first actor not existed or acted" (p. 30). When individuals must supply personal information in order to acquire goods and services in the market, they are responding to a form of power.

It is not critical to our understanding of distortions in the market for personal information that we know whether this power is granted or ungranted.[8] It is important only that we recognize that the information ordinarily would not been supplied if it were not required. However, in general I would suggest that the provision of information in commercial interactions represents a transaction cost that has been assigned to a consumer who is a contract taker, rather than a contract maker.

Generally, the collection of personal information is incidental to the exchange. It is an externality—a cost that is assigned at will, and for which there is no effective recourse. Indeed, frequently individuals are unaware that their transactions generate information that can and will be used as a commodity and traded in the marketplace. Consumers are generally unaware that their calls to toll-free phone numbers for information generate records that are supplied to the firms by the carriers as an enhancement to the value of the service. Similarly, consumers were unaware, and many were greatly disturbed to learn, that American Express was making use of the information generated by their behavior as "members" to sell and to allow others to sell items to the kinds of persons their profiles suggested they were. Indeed, the Direct Marketing Association's efforts to respond to public anxiety and concern about the use of personal information reflect this widespread public ignorance through the title of its popular educational pamphlet, "How Did They Get My Name?"

Consumers seem to feel that it is their right to determine whether transaction-generated information should be shared. In a national telephone survey conducted in 1989, nearly 90 percent of the respondents agreed somewhat or agreed strongly that "companies should seek your permission before they tell anyone else about products you buy, or the services you use."[9]

More recent surveys financed by Equifax and, I would suggest, driven by a desire to demonstrate broad public acceptance of the use of personal information for credit, insurance, and direct marketing purposes, also have revealed broad resistance to the marketing of transaction-generated information.[10] Equifax's 1992 survey reported that it was "not all right" or was a "cause of concern" for 67 percent of consumers if companies obtain "*public record lists* in order to mail people information about products and services" (Harris and Westin, 1992: 11; emphasis added). In 1991, in contrast, only 31 percent of the public indicated that it was unacceptable for organizations to gather names and addresses based on age, income, neighborhood, and shopping patterns for the purposes of direct marketing (Harris and Westin, 1991).

A Regime of Rights

One response to the problems involved in the commercial use of personal information is to establish formal restrictions on its collection and use. The development of a body of statutory regulation is problematic, however, for a number of reasons, not the least of which is the substantial power of business interests who have been successful in turning back many of the efforts of privacy advocates to establish broad limits on data collection and use.

The industry has generally been successful in establishing a legislative "benefit of the doubt" in favor of an assumed grant of the right to collect, share, or sell personal information for marketing purposes. Individuals are presumed to have given their implied consent for this use of personal information. Recognizing that individuals do not agree, the corporate community has promoted the possibility that consumers can "opt out" as the solution to whatever problems firms might encounter in their dealings with the small number of consumers who want to avoid direct marketing appeals.

The opt-out, or negative, option has long been a standard business practice for mail-order businesses such as book and record clubs, which would send the "club member" the next selection automatically unless the consumer mailed back a card "opting out," or indicating that he or she did not want to receive the selection. As the process was automatic, the consumer generally had a rather limited amount of time in which to invoke the negative option. This negative option was firmly established as the appropriate response to privacy concerns in the battle over the use of customer video rental records.

The Video Privacy Protection Act of 1988, which originally would have required "clearly expressed written, informed consent" before information about video rentals could be shared, was signed into law in a much transformed version by President Reagan. Having convinced the Congress that direct marketing is a legitimate business purpose that would be needlessly burdened by the requirement of affirmative consent, the industry succeeded in having the bill modified so as to allow the sharing of this transaction-generated information for the purposes of marketing so long as the consumer has the opportunity to "prohibit such disclosures" (Gandy, 1993: chap. 7).

Since then, the opt-out solution has been represented as being responsive to public opinion, as evidenced in the 1991 Equifax report in which 89 percent of respondents indicated that it is somewhat or very important to be able to opt out (Harris and Westin, 1991). Of course, consumers were not asked in these surveys to evaluate the alternative of acquiring affirmative consent, or an "opt-in" requirement.

The opt-out solution places the onus on the individual to choose, either by responding on a form to a question in small print or by requesting a blanket removal or an identifying annotation indicating that he or she does not want to be called or to receive direct-marketing mail. The blanket option is inefficient and unresponsive for several reasons. The first, and most obvious, is that many individuals would not want their names removed from *all* lists that they might be on. When asked in 1991, only 22 percent of respondents indicated that they would like their names removed from all lists (Harris and Westin, 1991). Indeed, when asked in 1990, only 38 percent of the respondents to an Equifax survey indicated that they would *not* be upset at all if they could not receive at home "mail offers or catalogs geared to their interests" (Harris and Westin, 1990). Of course, as asked, the question says nothing about how they might come to receive those offers. The fact is, those who would be upset might include those who have been buying from the same catalog for years and would interpret the question to suggest that catalog sales would be banned entirely, making them worse off then they had been in the past.

A larger group, 56 percent, said they would not be at all upset if they no longer received offers of credit at home, by mail or by phone. As the form of this question was varied to include use of the phone, we cannot conclude that the smaller sense of loss is associated primarily with the nature of the offer rather than with the means through which it might be offered. The point to be made here, however, is that *some* lists, and some appeals, might be welcomed more readily than others; thus a blanket exclusion would not serve most people very well.

Beyond the problem of the inefficiency of a blanket bar to the use of personal information for the purpose of direct marketing is the fact that even this restriction would not exclude some of the more troublesome and annoying uses of personal information. First of all, not all organizations that might make mail or telephone appeals are members of the Direct Marketing Association. Not all members follow the organization's guidelines to the letter or the spirit of the organization's code. Exceptions within the evolving policies usually allow for communications where there is a prior "relationship" with the consumer. A prior relationship may be considered to have been established if the individual has sent in a product warrantee card, assuming, incorrectly, that the information he or she has provided on the card is required for the warrantee to be in effect.

Fraudulent and deceptive practices are common. For example, even though members of an association of Yellow Pages information providers have agreed that they will not use information about callers unless those callers provide affirmative consent, as through the use of the star sign key on a Touch-Tone phone, some radio ads for the service include the star key in the number they suggest people call when they use the service. Thus, unknowingly, individuals grant permission under a system of self-regulation that seems on its face to be responsive to public concerns about privacy and the use of personal transaction information.

The Marketplace Solution

Because of the difficulties inherent in the development and use of a regulatory regime (Flaherty, 1989), many argue for the establishment of a more explicit market for personal information. Even Alan Westin (1991), a scholar who is well known for his development of the concept of informational privacy, has suggested that individual freedom might best be served when property rights in personal information are formally established, and then individuals might trade these rights against goods and services. Presumably, in such a market data subjects would be able to sell rights to use personal information to the highest bidder.

As I have noted in the earlier discussion of the problems involved in establishing a value for personal information, the differences in power that exist between individuals and most bureaucratic organizations with which they must make decisions about the exercise of their rights in personal information guarantee that most individuals will be price takers in most transactions (Jussawalla and Cheah, 1987). Because they are price takers, and because the price that is established reflects the value to the organization more than any measure of value to an informed data subject, individuals will nearly always be underpaid (Novek et al., 1990).

These same differences in power that generate price distortions in the market for personal information also operate on that market from the legal sphere. The process through which rights are established and then guaranteed in law is a process that is distorted by power. It is, or it should be, clear that individuals and organizations use their political power to establish, maintain, or extend their market or economic power. The legislative and judicial arenas in which battles over a regime of information rights will be fought cannot be expected to guarantee a fair fight when the combatants are so unevenly matched. Flaherty (1989) reminds us that those who fight on the side of privacy interests are little more than a ragtag band. The American Civil Liberties Union is one of the primary groups pursuing a privacy agenda. However, the ACLU in recent years has demonstrated a willingness to settle for the politically expedient over the fundamentally correct position on personal privacy.[11]

Because personal information is at the very least a joint product when it is generated through a commercial transaction, differences in power over the definition of property claims are bound to result in greater support for corporate interests. After all, the data reside in the firms' computers and were entered through keystrokes or point-of-purchase terminals owned or leased by the corporations. Legal arguments may find parallels in copyright regimes that assign rights to the corporation when intellectual property is produced under contract.

Transaction-generated information is produced as a by-product, an externality. In the case of pollution, firms that generate noise and smoke would like to deny responsibility for their by-products; however, firms actually pursue ownership rights to the data that are produced as by-products of their sales activities. This positive externality represents the generation of value for which some actors are denied a share. Other examples lead to different arguments and conclusions. Although we might accept that the negative that the photographer produces as a by-product of the process involved in the production of a portrait might actually be the property of the photographer, we would like to believe we can limit his or her use of that negative to produce other images for other uses for which we have not provided a release or other formal consent. On what basis should these claims be determined? As Thomas McManus (1990) has demonstrated with regard to telephone transaction-generated information, there are a great many claimants whose voices need to be heard. The power and resources that they can bring to bear on the determination of these rights provide little room for optimism that the interests of consumers will come to dominate the outcome of this struggle.

In the earlier discussion of the problems in markets in general and in markets for personal information in particular, I noted that individuals do not, and cannot, fully understand the value of the commodities they acquire, or the resources they exchange against other goods, services, or opportunities. Whereas goods and resources, including time, might be considered in terms of value forgone—an economist's construction of personal estimates of the values that could be generated, or utilities served, if the resources were put to other uses—we find special problems emerge when the resource in question is personal information. It is not the use to which the data subject might put the information that generates meaningful consequences, but the use to which it might be put by others.

Although personal information can be seen to be linked to economically valuable, if intangible, assets such as reputation, its use by others is frequently more determinative than its use by the person to whom the information refers. Thus, the value of the information an individual supplies to another is linked to uses to which that information might be put by others to enhance or degrade their reputational assets. Such use is beyond the individual's control, unless there are formal or informal "understandings" that have a binding force due to the influence of law or custom.

Efforts to establish formal limits, or standards of fair treatment, to classes of information generally held to be "sensitive" in terms of the consequentiality of the information have not been entirely successful. Raymond Wacks (1989) has made some of the most useful inroads into the problem of sensitivity. He has attempted to specify an a priori index of sensitivity, on which various kinds of personal information are assigned scores reflecting their assignment to classes based upon his estimate of their "potential for harm" to the individual. Wacks admits that his list is highly subjective, and I cannot help but agree. For example, Wacks's classificatory scheme includes medical information, information about sexual activity, and information about voting frequency within the category he has assigned the highest level of sensitivity. He does not classify leisure activities, including travel or the use of information products or services, as being particularly sensitive. Indeed, he assigns the lowest level of sensitivity to information about a person's membership in clubs. Yet we can see from the example of the gay lists described above that what a person reads provides information that is treated as an index of sexuality, sexual activity, and medical status. As many politicians have discovered, information about membership in clubs that discriminate against blacks, Jews, and women can have quite serious political consequences.

As with all measures of value, estimates of consequentiality are inherently subjective. Estimates of negative value may be standardized in terms of some cultural criteria, but such criteria will always be distorted by the influence of power. Bartlett's (1989) notion of value power should be extended to include the moral influence aspects of subjective value that socioeconomists such as Amitai Etzioni (1988) argue play a role in the calculus of choice. Shame, as well as economic loss, can be associated with the disclosure of private facts. And, although authorities can make claims about what the average, or reasonable, person might consider to be private or potentially embarrassing, such a standard must, by definition, assign costs to those who depart from the norm.

In Conclusion

This chapter has examined the operation of a discriminatory technology that I refer to as the panoptic sort. This technology supports the rationalization of the marketing function by identifying individuals who share attributes that make them particularly attractive as potential consumers. This technology is dynamic in that feedback, or knowledge of results, can be used to improve the precision with which segmentation and targeting proceed in subsequent rounds of the game.

I have also suggested that the panoptic sort is a discriminatory technology that discards at the same time it skims off the high-quality targets of opportunity. This process can be seen to generate a self-perpetuating, deviation-amplifying system of inequality. Individuals become dependent upon others to assist them in making choices. The illusion of choice is sustained even as the reality of a continually narrowing range of options is easy to see. The options differ in quality and in their potential to modify the life chances of those who choose.

I have suggested that efforts to control the use of this technology through regime of rights or a formalized market in personal information cannot be anything but unsatisfactory, or suboptimal, because of the influence of power within markets and within the rule-making environment. As Giddens (and Marx) suggests, although the action of knowledgeable agents produces and reproduces the world in which we must continually struggle, this world is never faithful to our design. Eternal vigilance, activism, and communication with others are required to increase the odds that the worlds we do create are worlds in which we can survive as the kinds of people we would like to be.

Notes

1. Beniger suggests that "*control* encompasses the entire range from absolute control to the weakest and most probabilistic form, that is, any purposive influence on behavior, *however slight*" (1986:8).

2. See my discussion of the problems in defining a telecommunications infrastructure in Gandy (1992a).

3. The U.S. Federal Trade Commission recently succeeded in pressuring TRW to stop using its credit data in its mailing list business, although a competitor, Trans Union Corp., reportedly refused to bend to FTC pressure, claiming its use of credit data is permissible under the law. See Miller (1993).

4. Robbin's approach is explored in some detail by Michael J. Weiss (1988).

5. Cauzin Systems, Inc., of Waterbury, Connecticut, provided me with a marketing package in 1989 that described the use of its "softstrip" technology to encode and print comprehensive information about households and consumers on coupons. The promotional flyer also identified several color overlays that could be used to make the softstrip "invisible" to the consumer.

6. In a five to four majority vote, the Court ruled that firms acquiring other firms could include as depreciable assets the customer lists they acquired. Unsatisfied with the conclusions of the Court, some members of Congress began congressional efforts to establish a statutory basis for the treatment of these intangible assets. Representative Dan Rostenkowski was reported to be developing a bill to submit to Congress. See Alberta (1993).

7. For stories of the trials and tribulations surrounding journalistic use of electronic databases, see Koch (1991).

8. The power to collect personal information may be granted when an individual signs a contract, fills out an application, or enters an establishment where the request for personal information is a matter of established policy and entering represents the granting of implied consent.

9. This national telephone survey was conducted as part of the Telecommunications and Privacy Project, on which I served as the principal investigator. The project was funded primarily by a grant from AT&T. A total of 1,250 adults participated in the survey.

10. Equifax is a major provider of credit, medical, and other personal information to the business sector. It recently "withdrew" from the marketing of consumer "targeting" services, perhaps in response to the warnings about public backlash that its surveys had revealed. It was also a partner with Lotus, the computer software company that reportedly lost several millions of dollars when its CD-ROM consumer database product Lotus MarketPlace:Household was withdrawn from the market under a barrage of critical consumer mail.

11. ACLU specialists on privacy suggested that they had to support the final version of the Video Privacy Act, even though it firmly established the negative option, because no other option was politically viable.

References

Alberta, Paul. (1993). "Aftermath of High Court Decision on List Depreciation: Bill Mulled." *DM News,* May 10, 3.

Ang, Ien. (1991). *Desperately Seeking the Audience.* New York: Routledge.

Bartlett, Randall. (1989). *Economics and Power: An Inquiry into Human Relations and Markets.* New York: Cambridge University Press.

Beniger, James. (1986). *The Control Revolution.* Cambridge, Mass.: Harvard University Press.

Burkitt, Brian. (1984). *Radical Political Economy: An Introduction to the Alternative Economics.* New York: New York University Press.

Chofras, Dimitris N., and Heinreich Steinman. (1990). *Expert Systems in Banking.* New York: New York University Press.

Earl, Peter. (1983). *The Economic Imagination: Towards a Behavioral Analysis of Choice.* Armonk, N.Y.: M. E. Sharpe.

Ellul, Jacques. (1964). *The Technological Society.* New York: Alfred A. Knopf.

Etzioni, Amitai. (1988). *The Moral Dimension: Toward a New Economics.* New York: Free Press.

Flaherty, David. (1989). *Protecting Privacy in Surveillance Societies.* Chapel Hill: University of North Carolina Press.

Foucault, Michel. (1973). *The Order of Things.* New York: Vintage.

———. (1979). *Discipline and Punish: The Birth of the Prison,* trans. Alan Sheridan. New York: Vintage.

Gandy, Oscar H., Jr. (1992a). "Infrastruction: A Chaotic Disturbance in the Policy Discourse." In Institute for Information Studies, *A National Information Network*. Queenstown, Md.: Institute for Information Studies, Aspen Institute, ix-xxxiv.

———. (1992b). "The Political Economy Approach: A Critical Challenge." *Journal of Media Economics* (Summer): 23–42.

———. (1993). *The Panoptic Sort: A Political Economy of Personal Information*. Boulder, Colo.: Westview.

Gandy, Oscar H., Jr., and Charles E. Simmons. (1986). "Technology, Privacy and the Democratic Process." *Critical Studies in Mass Communication* 3 (June): 155–68.

Giddens, Anthony. (1984). *The Constitution of Society*. Cambridge: Polity.

———. (1987). *A Contemporary Critique of Historical Materialism*. Berkeley: University of California Press.

Louis Harris & Associates and Alan F. Westin. (1990). *The Equifax Report on Consumers in the Information Age*. Atlanta, Ga.: Equifax.

———. (1991). *Harris-Equifax Consumer Privacy Survey 1991*. Atlanta, Ga.: Equifax.

———. (1992). *Harris-Equifax Consumer Privacy Survey 1992*. Atlanta, Ga.: Equifax.

Jussawalla, Meheroo, and Chee-wah Cheah. (1987). "Economic Analysis of the Legal and Policy Aspects of Information Privacy." In *The Calculus of International Communications*. Littleton, Colo.: Libraries Unlimited.

King, Donald, N. Roderen, and H. Olsen (eds.). (1983). *Key Papers in the Economics of Information*. White Plains, N.Y.: Knowledge Industry.

Koch, Tom. (1991). *Journalism for the 21st Century*. New York: Praeger.

Machlup, Fritz. (1979). "Uses, Value, and Benefits of Knowledge." *Knowledge: Creation, Diffusion, Utilization* 1, no. 1: 62–81.

Marx, Gary. (1985). "I'll Be Watching You." *Dissent* (Winter): 26–34.

Marx, Karl. (1971). *Value, Price and Profit*, ed. Eleanor Marx Aveling. New York: International.

McManus, Thomas E. (1990). *Telephone Transaction-Generated Information: Rights and Restrictions*. Cambridge, Mass.: Harvard University, Program on Information Resources Policy, May.

Miller, Michael. (1993). "FTC Takes Aim at Trans Union, TRW Mail Lists." *Wall Street Journal*, January 13, B1.

Novek, Eleanor, Nikhil Sinha, and Oscar Gandy. (1990). "The Value of Your Name." *Media, Culture & Society* 12: 525–43.

Robins, Kevin, and Frank Webster. (1988). "Cybernetic Capitalism: Information, Technology, Everyday Life." In V. Mosco and J. Wasko (eds.), *The Political Economy of Information*. Madison: University of Wisconsin Press, 44–75.

Rule, James B., Douglas McAdam, Linda Stearns, and David Uglow. (1983). "Documentary Identification and Mass Surveillance in the United States." *Social Problems* 31, no. 2: 222–34.

TRW Target Marketing Services. (1992). *Datacard Catalog* (Fall). Richardson, Tex.: TRW.

Wacks, Raymond. (1989). *Personal Information, Privacy and the Law.* Oxford: Oxford University Press.

Webster, Frank, and Kevin Robins. (1986). *Information Technology: A Luddite Analysis.* Norwood, N.J.: Ablex.

Weiss, Michael J. (1988). *The Clustering of America.* New York: Harper & Row.

Westin, Alan F. (1991). "How the American Public Views Consumer Privacy Issues in the Early 90's and Why." Testimony before the Subcommittee on Government Information, Justice and Agriculture, House Committee on Government Operations, Washington, D.C., April 10.

Privacy: A Concept Whose Time Has Come and Gone

Calvin C. Gotlieb

Privacy, Confidentiality, and Security

For many years now, in a course I teach on computers and society, I have started the section on privacy and freedom of information by emphasizing the distinctions among privacy, confidentiality, and data security. Privacy is a social, cultural, and legal concept, all three aspects of which vary from country to country. Confidentiality is a managerial responsibility; it concerns the problems of how to manage data by rules that are satisfactory to both the managers of data banks and the persons about whom the data pertain. Security is a technical issue. It focuses on how the rules of data access established by management can be enforced, through the use of passwords, cryptography, and like techniques. In the course, I go on for some half dozen lectures to talk about privacy, particularly the laws in Canada compared with those in other countries. I then present about three lectures on software protection, data security, and related topics.

I have now come to the conclusion that the emphasis on privacy is wrong. This in spite of all the laws that have already been passed and are even now being formulated about privacy, in spite of the never-failing interest of the media in the subject, in spite of the by-now-venerable institutions such as the provincial and federal offices of the Privacy Commissioner, and in spite of almost everyone's professed concern about the continual erosion of privacy, as witnessed by the very conference that gave rise to this volume. The reason I think the emphasis is wrong is that, all protestations to the contrary, most people, when other interests are at stake, do not care enough about privacy to value it. The thesis of this presentation is that the trade-offs where privacy has been sacrificed are now so common that, for all practical purposes, privacy no longer exists. This is particularly true for those aspects of privacy that are captured in computerized data banks. But it is also true, more or less, for anonymity, reserve, and the right to be left alone, those near definitions of privacy that are given whenever the legal implications of it are being explained. Sometimes privacy is traded off under coercion or with regret, but often the surrender is made quite willingly—so often that it is time, I think, to look at the whole subject in a more realistic manner.

Privacy of Personal Information in Data Banks

In the United States, the issue of privacy, first seriously addressed in a seminal paper by Warren and Brandeis (1890), resurfaced in 1968 when hearings were held on a proposal to gather demographic and other social science data from many agencies into a single national data bank. Fears about how government might misuse a comprehensive data collection were compounded by evidence presented in congressional hearings on how companies gathered and used data for such purposes as reporting on consumer creditworthiness and underwriting insurance. Years of intense public debate culminated in the passage of the 1974 Privacy Act, which regulated the use of federal government data banks. In all of the discussions and debates, much emphasis was placed on the need to balance the right to privacy against the right of individuals, the press, and others to have assured freedom of access to information—especially government-held information. Thus in the United States the 1974 Privacy Act was accompanied by amendments to the 1966 Freedom of Information Act, to make sure that act really could do its work. This pattern of dual legislation on privacy and freedom of information was followed in other jurisdictions—for example, in many of the fifty U.S. states, in our Canadian Bill C-43, the Federal Privacy Act and the Access to Information Act passed in 1982, and in similar legislation enacted for most Canadian provinces.

Behind all such legislation there is a sense of a principal trade-off that is always present. There is a need to ensure privacy about personal records, which have to be collected for government, industry, and individuals to make good decisions on almost anything, versus an interest in maintaining openness in both government and private industry and in being able to protect against secret decisions that affect individuals without giving them an opportunity to be involved in the decision making. But in spite of more and more legislation about privacy in government-held data banks, and the trend for many businesses and organizations to announce voluntary codes or guidelines about privacy, there is near unanimity that the erosion of personal privacy has continued with little or no abatement. The reason for this steady erosion, everyone is convinced, is that the technology of gathering, disseminating, and accessing personal data easily and at little cost has become nearly universal, and nearly irresistible. The problem, then, is how to deal with a rampant technology.

I agree that there has been a steady diminution in both the sense and the reality of privacy. But I suggest to you that the reason has *not* been that new technologies are being deployed without regard to the consequences. In fact, there are many reasons, but they are all variations on the theme that we wanted or needed something that was worth *more* than a little extra privacy. And only in a few cases has that something been better access to information. In fact, we have given away privacy for many reasons, sometimes willingly, sometimes reluctantly, but almost always saying—or at least thinking in the backs of our minds—"It really isn't worth trying to save it today." I offer some examples below.

The first and easiest example is the case of credit cards. When you apply for a credit card, you most certainly give up some privacy about your personal finances. The more credit cards you carry, the more you give up. Nothing *forces* us to use credit cards. We could instead, for example, carry traveler's checks, which are equally acceptable in most situations.[1] But few people who can qualify for a credit card fail to carry at least one. We tend to regard the odd person who refuses to have one as just that—odd. Now in every province or state there are laws regulating the use of data banks carrying information about personal credit and expenditures. One good aspect of the laws is that they usually make it possible for us to see our own credit ratings, if we wish to do so. But these laws do nothing to slow the spread of credit cards. In fact, they were not *designed* for that, because people *want* credit cards. And we get them, voluntarily giving away a little of our privacy in doing so. Most of us have little confidence that the laws about limiting access to our credit records, or the assurances of bankers and merchants that our spending secrets are safe with them, offer genuine protection. We go for the credit cards anyway, because we do not see that aspect of our privacy as very important.

The next example is just as old—use of the social insurance number

(SIN) or, in the United States, the social security number. We are told that giving a social insurance or social security number freely to any agency or organization that asks for it is a bad thing, because it makes it easier for governments to tie one data bank with another, and the first thing you know there will be that big data bank in the sky ready to make doomsday judgments. So there have been serious reports commissioned on use of the SIN, and whenever an organization issues a new form asking for it, you can be sure that some journalist will make a story out of it. But in Scandinavian countries, the equivalent of the SIN is routinely expected every time one interacts with a government agency at any level. Scandinavian countries *do* have more and bigger government data banks with personal data, and we may be inclined to think that this is just what one would expect of socialist states, which all of them are, to greater or lesser degree. But everyone knows that today it is almost as easy to link data banks *without* using the SIN as it is to connect them through the SIN. In many situations it is possible, with a little inconvenience, to obtain a service without stating the SIN, or even to get it and only note that you do not wish to fill out the space where it is requested. How many of us bother to withhold the SIN even when we can do so? Not many of us, I suspect, because we have come to feel that there is not much privacy attached to the SIN. We have given up that part of our privacy for the convenience of dealing easily with agencies. Maybe there were protests for a while, and some of them continue to be heard, but the truth is that by now not many of us care about whether we give out our SINs or not. I predict that before long there will be no news value at all in any story involving the SIN.

The next example is meant to show that in spite of all the guidelines and laws on privacy that exist, we really do not expect our privacy to be protected. In the last analysis, we take it for granted, accept, and even approve that both government and private organizations will find ways to change the rules when they feel the need to do so.

Without fail, every code or guideline on the use of personal data banks contains a clause to the effect that data collected from an individual should be used only for the one purpose stated at the time of collection. For example, the guidelines on the protection of privacy created by the Organization for Economic Cooperation and Development (OECD) have two clauses as follows (in slightly abbreviated form):

Purpose Specification
The purpose for which data are collected shall be specified not later than the time of collection, and subsequent use shall be for that purpose or limited to purposes that are not incompatible with that.
Use Limitation
Data should not be used or disclosed for other purposes than indicated above except with the consent of the data subject or as required by law. (1980)

Canada officially approves of the OECD guidelines, and has urged their adoption by private industry as well as by government and its agencies. However, when it comes to *laws* on privacy, there are always escape clauses that makes it legal to disobey the use limitation whenever it is determined that there is good reason to do so. Thus the Privacy Act (sections 7 and 8) states:

Personal information under the control of a government institution shall not, without consent of the individual to whom it relates, be used by the institution except
   (a) for the purpose for which the information was obtained or compiled by the institution or for a use consistent with that purpose;
   or
   (b) for a purpose for which the information may be disclosed to the institution under subsection 8(2).

Subsection 8(2) lists the thirteen conditions under which information may be disclosed, and these include "for any purpose in accordance with any Act of Parliament or any regulation that authorizes its disclosure." In other words, information shall be kept secret, except when we determine by an act or regulation that it may be disclosed. This escape clause is used, too—very frequently. For example, employers regularly remit records of employee earnings so that the government can make the appropriate contribution to the employee's Canada Pension Plan (CPP), an earnings-based plan run by the government that covers a large fraction of the working population. An unemployed person, after a waiting period, and provided certain other conditions are met, can receive unemployment insurance compensation (UIC) for a specified period. It is government practice, openly admitted, to use the SIN to match the CPP contribution file against the UIC file, so as to find persons who are both working and receiving unemployment insurance benefits. Thus a government file created for one purpose, to record entitlements to the CPP, is used for another completely different purpose, namely, to identify those who might be receiving, knowingly or unknowingly, UIC benefits without entitlement to them. This exception to the general privacy rule of limiting use to which information is put is condoned by law, and by most people, because it is felt that a privacy principle should not be used to protect those who might be getting an unfair advantage. In the interest of fairness, we have relaxed the privacy rule. Computer matching of files is widespread in Canada, and in the United States, an inventory conducted in 1983 revealed more than five hundred state-conducted matches (U.S. General Accounting Office, 1986).

I am sure that some of you are ready to say, "These three examples are old hat—you are just giving a new twist to what we all know." My answer to that is, exactly so. Perhaps some others of you are thinking, "We had no choice as to whether we wanted to give up our privacy, chip by chip. The technology was forced on us, and that made us surrender our privacy." To that I say, not at all. In my opinion, most people have made the choice willingly. It is true that for some twenty-five years now there has been a steady flow of articles about the loss of privacy, about how the day of Big Brother is about to descend on us, or is in fact already here. But it is my opinion now that these complaints and protests have come mainly from journalists, lawyers, and academics like me. I now believe that most of the populace really does not care all that much about privacy, although, when prompted, many voice privacy concerns. The real reason that the trade-offs referred to above have been made, have been possible, is that they are in line with the wishes of the large majority of the population. How have I come to what, for me, is such a painful conclusion? It is from watching what happens to privacy issues in the political sphere, especially in Canada. What is true in Canada is also true, perhaps, but only perhaps, in lesser degrees in other countries. What is happening politically in Canada is—nothing! When did you last hear a cabinet member, or a member of Parliament, talk about privacy before an election? Admittedly, there may have been some privacy issue or initiative raised during times when constitutional or economic issues had subsided. But it is during elections that politicians talk about things that they believe really concern the electorate, and not during any election within my memory has *any* question even remotely related to privacy been debated. Another piece of evidence, somewhat different, but in the same vein—according to the terms of the Privacy Act and Freedom of Access to Information Act in Canada, the Justice Department was required, after five years, to review the acts, to see how they were working and to make recommendations for change. That review *did* take place; I expect that many of you are familiar with the ensuing report, *Open and Shut* (Committee of Justice, 1987). Beyond any question, that is an outstanding work. The committee really did its homework in preparing that report. There are 108 recommendations in it, all of them sensible, some important, and a few that really *must* be enacted into law. And what has happened in the eight years that have elapsed since that report was published? Approximately three of the committee's suggestions have been adopted, and then—dead silence. Is anybody now talking about the issues raised there? Is the opposition taking the government to task for failing to act on identified injustices? These are rhetorical questions. The answers are no, and the reason that they are no is that the politicians are very much aware that there is zero penalty for failing to take steps that might protect or recover privacy.[2] I believe that politicians know much better than academics, lawyers, and journalists what is important to people. And if they are not talking about privacy at election times, or when key reports on it appear, it is because privacy is not a serious political issue. Its time has gone.

Trends

The fact that governments pass laws to show their interest in protecting privacy but reserve the right to bypass the laws when they are inconvenienced by them contributes to a growing sense of cynicism about privacy protection. This sense is reinforced when a government tries to hide behind the privacy law because it is reluctant to reveal something that might embarrass it. An example of this latter could be seen in the flurry of news stories that took place at the end of March 1993 in connection with a Commission of Enquiry that was looking, on behalf of the government of Nova Scotia, into the causes of the Westray mine disaster, where twenty-six miners lost their lives. When the opposition asked, in the (federal) House of Parliament, why all the documents relating to an $85 million loan given to Curragh Inc., the owner of Westray, were not being made available to the Provincial Commission of Enquiry, the government response was that it was cooperating fully. This led to an extraordinary event the very next day, when a spokesman for the commission called a news conference to protest that key documents were being withheld in spite of repeated efforts to obtain them. The federal government then claimed that it could not release the documents because of the provisions of the Privacy Act. When the opposition and the press jumped on this secrecy as evidence of a cover-up ("Westray Papers," 1993), the government quickly back-pedaled and said that the documents in question were not being released because they had been presented to cabinet when the loan was being considered, and therefore were being withheld under the provision of the Privacy Act that allowed cabinet documents protection from release. And indeed the Privacy Act *does* allow such protection, but calling upon it in this way only increased the suspicion of a cover-up. Later the government promised to release *all* documents, but by that time the damage had been done in this cynical use of the Privacy Act.

Journalists, too, are often very eager to show that they are protecting the public interest by highlighting stories where they see privacy as being threatened, whether the threats are real or superficial.[3] An example of this can be seen in the headline "Privacy Threatened, 60 Per Cent Tell Poll," which was attached to a 1993 *Toronto Star* article on a report of a survey conducted by Ekos Research Associates on behalf of the federal government and a number of private financial institutions.[4] The two last points in the article state:

Only 18 per cent of those surveyed admitted to having experienced serious invasions of privacy.

The least acceptable information seekers are telemarketers, survey companies and telephone companies. (Vienneau, 1993)

Now, 18 percent is not all that large a fraction of the population to experience serious invasions of privacy. And if the next item is meant as an indication of what a serious threat is, all I can say is that lucky indeed is the country where telemarketers, survey companies, and telephone companies rate high on the list of those seriously invading personal privacy. After all, it is very easy to cut a telephone conversation short if one really wants to do so.[5] Whether the general public *really* sees the above as "the least acceptable information seekers" is difficult to say, but apparently that is the way it came out in this study. One can be pardoned for thinking that a less alarmist headline might have been given to the story.

Most of the examples I have been giving are drawn from Canadian sources, because this is the context in which this essay was first presented, and this is what I know best. But concerns about privacy and stories about it are to be found in the U.S. press just as frequently as in Canada, if not more so. In 1993, the *New York Times Magazine* devoted two important articles to the issue, separated by an interval of only six weeks. In the first of these, "Who Killed Privacy?" Roger Rosenblatt is puzzled that "privacy in our time has not only been invaded; it's been eagerly surrendered" (1993:24). He notes the pervasiveness of bugging devices, the readiness of people to discuss the most intimate details of their lives on the television shows of Oprah, Donahue, and Geraldo (to say nothing of Dr. Ruth, whom he doesn't mention), and that for a while Lotus Development was prepared to market a CD-ROM disk called MarketPlace:Household, containing such information as marital status, income, and buying habits on 120 million citizens. In the end, Lotus withdrew the product, but the fact that it was seriously considered is a clear indication of the direction of things.[6] In the second article, "Big Brother's Here: And—Alas—We Embrace Him," Floyd Abrams (1993) is much more rueful. He looks back with nostalgia to the time when it was possible to board an aircraft or approach the president without being searched, or to hold jobs that carried with them responsibility for people's lives without being tested for drugs. In the context of the argument being made here, it may be noted that in almost all of the examples quoted by the two journalists, people are making trade-offs against privacy. Sometimes these trade-offs are made necessary for safety and security reasons; sometimes the reasons are quite trivial. The *New York Times*'s preoccupation with privacy continues. An article by Jeffrey Rothfeder on the op-ed page of April 13, 1993, details the kinds of personal information that are easily and legally obtained from a variety of sources, not only for public figures such as Dan Rather, Dan Quayle, and Vanna White, but for almost anyone.

The techniques for surveillance in the workplace and elsewhere that are described in this volume also illustrate reductions in privacy. But the theme of this book suggests that these techniques are being adopted to exercise social control, and I do not see this view being challenged by the contributors. I am arguing here that they are being implemented because people want the benefits that flow from the techniques, and that their adoption should be viewed not as social control, but as responses to expressed needs and market forces. So far, the examples I have cited relate to situations that have existed for some decades in the past. Following are two examples of more current situations where privacy is being affected because of new technology. About these there have been some debates and protests about the privacy implications, but in the end the decision has been to ignore or accept the risks to privacy for the sake of perceived benefits that come with the technologies.

The communications industry offers numerous opportunities for us to trade away privacy for new capabilities. One only has to note the huge growth in the number of cellular phones, in spite of the well-known fact that it is very easy for someone to eavesdrop on a conversation originating from such a phone. The set of services offered by telephone companies under the rubric of call management services includes several that have privacy implications. Perhaps the most widely used is Call Display (also referred to as Caller ID), which makes it possible, for a monthly fee, for subscribers to identify the numbers from which incoming calls are made. When this service was introduced, there appeared in the *New York Times,* for example, many letters to the editor questioning the practice.[7] With Call Display, it is possible to see unlisted numbers, on which the callers have paid fees to avoid having listed in the telephone directory. Because of privacy concerns, in some jurisdictions (including Ontario) telephone companies have been required to provide, without charge, Call Blocking, whereby an incoming caller who has requested the service can precede his or her call by a key sequence that has the effect of preventing the number from being displayed. Whatever the considerations about privacy, it has to be noted that cellular phones and Call Display attract very large numbers of customers who, presumably, for the most part, have set the concerns aside.

For another example, several computer laboratories are experimenting with, or have actually put into place, techniques whereby workers carry badges that make it possible for management to keep track of them wherever they are on the premises, and to record any conversations they engage in. The technique differs from the familiar telephone beeper; here the badge identifies the worker, and infrared scanners and transceivers placed in strategic spots throughout the building detect the presence of the badge wearer and microphones pick up conversations. At the Xerox Palo Alto laboratory the technique is known as *ubiquitous computing,* and it is regarded as an extremely useful tool for those engaged in cooperative research projects (Weiser, 1991). At the DEC/Olivetti laboratory in Cambridge, England, the Active Badge

Project has been in place for some time, and, according to reports of senior researchers there, including Dr. Andrew Hopper and Professor Roger Needham, the benefits have been many ("Does Your Computer," 1991). They insist that there have been no problems about privacy because of the ease with which anyone can opt out of being monitored (for example, by pocketing the badge or turning it face down on a table), and because of the protocols that have evolved allowing anyone or any group to maintain privacy when they wish to do so, without negative consequences.

Some Problems with Privacy Laws

When the Charter of Rights and Freedoms was passed in Canada, it was widely believed that one result would be a trend toward "Americanization" of the Canadian justice system. This would happen because as more and more cases were decided in the Supreme Court of Canada on the basis of interpretations of the Charter, these would necessarily influence decisions in the lower courts. The Supreme Court, and appointments to it, would become increasingly important, because over the long term the views of the appointees would affect the political, social, and even the economic climate of the country. Also, there would be a trend to test whether the Charter could be used to win cases over a very wide range of issues.

These expectations have already been realized in significant measure, and one area where there has been some disconcerting fallout is that involving privacy. Supreme Court decisions, based upon interpretations of Section 8 of the Charter, which guarantees the right "to be secure against unreasonable search or seizure," have had the effect of making police work appreciably more difficult (Moon, 1992). Police, as "agents of the state," are being prohibited from using wiretaps, hidden cameras, listening, tracking, or other surveillance devices when someone who is a police officer or police informant is party to the use. The result is that undercover work is much more dangerous because backup cannot be brought in quickly enough should it become essential. So one effect of the Charter has been to protect the privacy of those the police might have good reason to suspect are committing crimes, making it harder to gather evidence from them. At the same time, there is nothing to stop journalists and private investigators from using cameras and listening devices. The right to use these when spying on public figures is clearly established in the argument by Warren and Brandeis (1890) cited earlier, and in the United Kingdom we have seen that right exercised to its full in the recent spate of stories about the royal family. So in this respect the privacy laws may be too weak. This weakness also came to light in a notorious way when, during negotiations on the constitutional plebiscite, some private remarks Quebec's Premier Bourassa made over a cellular telephone were intercepted and made public, much to his embarrassment.

In my final example I would like to turn to an area where I believe that progress is being inhibited because of privacy laws that pretend to be effective, but that are often circumvented and are really unnecessary in their current form because people are ready to see them relaxed. This is the domain of medical records. The law, in Ontario and in many other jurisdictions, is that these are the property of the physician, or of the institution that collected the data, and that they are passed from one entity to another only under very strictly controlled conditions. For this reason, patients do not even have the right to see their own records, although one of the principal recommendations of the Krever Commission regarding the confidentiality of health records was that they be given this right (Commission of Enquiry, 1980). In fact, most general practitioners will reveal records to a patient when approached to do so; hospitals routinely give patients their X rays to take to other departments or other doctors, and even the College of Physicians and Surgeons of Ontario has reversed its long-standing objection to allowing patients access to their own records.

But there is need to change the laws governing medical records beyond giving patients access rights to their own records; the laws governing transfer of records between third parties have to be changed, too. Right now, most of the medical records that exist in computerized form relate to patient billing. The technology exists, however, for all medical data and reports to be computerized, and the cost is low enough so that even a single family practitioner can afford to have the equipment. The benefits would be substantial. Reports from laboratories doing blood analyses, medical imaging, and other tests could be transmitted overnight by modem, complete with warnings that would alert physicians about unusual conditions that have been seen to be present.[8] I believe that most persons would be very pleased if the computerized records held by their family doctors were to contain a basic (but not necessarily complete) component that could be easily transmitted to any specialists to whom they are referred. This would save countless repetitions of filling out forms every time one goes to see a new doctor. It is true that consolidating records in machine-readable form in this way will result in a reduction of privacy, but I am convinced that most persons would readily give up some (but not all, of course) of their privacy about medical records if they were fully aware of the advantages—greater accuracy, prompter alerts and actions, cost savings, greater convenience—to be had. There is little doubt that the existence of privacy laws is a serious inhibition to this technology's being put in place, laws that are essentially ignored anyway when a company deems it necessary to test its employees for drug use or the presence of HIV. The privacy laws respecting medical records are already routinely ignored when it is convenient to do so, and they are an obstruction that prevents good things from happening.

The larger point I am trying to make is that the privacy laws are too weak at some times, and too strong at others. The Justice Department is struggling to produce laws that will allow police to use modern technology in its investigations, on one hand, and that will protect individuals from intrusions made possible by technology, on the other—a difficult problem, but it is my conviction that any approach that is based on a general principle of privacy of personal data is doomed to failure.

What Comes after Privacy?

Before I attempt to answer the question posed in this section's heading, I would like to point out that privacy as a legal concept is relatively recent. In common law the concept has to be inferred from a variety of precedents, starting with one in the United Kingdom on Peeping Toms. In earlier days, when most people lived in villages, privacy on almost any matter was not expected and was almost impossible to achieve, a condition that still exists in many small communities. In the civil law that holds in France and in most European countries where the legal system is descended from the Napoleonic Code (and beyond that, from Roman law), the concept of privacy is not to be found. Instead, there is systematic enumeration of situations in which people might be hurt by actions that, in other countries, would be regarded as invasions of privacy.

What must be assured in every civilized and free society is, of course, security of person. Even those called homeless strive mightily to achieve, at the very minimum, "a small secure room with a door that locks" (Brown, 1993:1). This aspect of privacy, however, is guaranteed in other ways, for example, through charters or bills of rights. Besides this bare minimum in security, we need other forms, including, in some situations, although far less often than is commonly assumed, security of personal data. But as I said at the beginning of this essay, data security is a very different thing from privacy.

At the beginning I also talked about confidentiality, the rules for managing access to and dissemination of data. And it is on these rules that I propose we concentrate, instead of on privacy. We need agreement on such rules in a vast number of cases, both in the public and private sectors, in institutional, organizational, and employment situations. It is possible to formulate *some* general guidelines on the rules, and these, for example, are just what we have in the OECD guidelines referred to previously. Guidelines are what they say they are—general rules that do not even *pretend* to cover all situations. It *may* be desirable to enact specific rules, governing the management of certain data gathered for particular purposes, into law. But when we try to enact comprehensive laws on a vague concept such as privacy, covering *all* personal data gathered by *all* the agencies of such a huge monster as the federal government, we get into trouble—deep trouble. We end up with laws that are contradictory, laws that cannot be upheld because in too many cases most people do not expect, or even want, to see them respected. This is just where we are with our general laws about data privacy.

If we talk about confidentiality, we are on much firmer ground. And as I have said so much about trade-offs, let us recognize confidentiality for what it has become—a *commodity*. When we accept a credit card, as well as pay the usual yearly fee, we also sign away permission for the credit giver to collect and release data about us. It would be well if this were highlighted in the agreement given to us along with the credit card. That agreement should be recognized for what it is—a contract. Perhaps we should be insisting on formal contracts, signed by *both* parties, about the management of data. The contracts might specify penalties for failure to live up to the agreement, and the ordinary laws of contracts would apply. If we do not want data given to third parties, that should be in the contract, along with the penalties for failure to comply, and this kind of credit card would undoubtedly come with a higher yearly fee. Surely such confidentiality laws would be better than the privacy laws we have now. Privacy laws don't work because people don't want them to work in far too many situations, so they can't be fixed and made to work. We *do* want to retain some kinds of privacy, but not those aspects that are captured by data that circulates. Data privacy is technologically obsolete.

Notes

1. Although they are *not* acceptable for car rentals, even if as much as $1,000 is offered as security, as I found out on one occasion when I had lost my credit card and not yet obtained a replacement.

2. An exception is when the opposition gleefully pounces on a minister who perchance has revealed somebody's personal information, but it is difficult to view this as anything other than a chance to score against the government.

3. The main complaints that newspapers have about the Privacy and Access to Information Acts are that government is frequently reluctant to give access to its documents, as it is obligated to do. In this the newspapers often have good reason to claim that they are being badly done by, but details and examples are not appropriate to this essay.

4. A slightly different version of this story appeared on March 29. The survey, titled "Privacy Revealed: The Canadian Privacy Survey," was carried out by telephoning three thousand households between October 28 and November 4, 1992.

5. Another annoyance situation that is often cited as an example of invsion of privacy is junk mail. Most anyone has a large wastepaper basket close by as an effective way of dealing with this threat. Surely the increasing cost of postage ensures that this particular problem will never get altogether out of hand.

6. Such data are available from TRW, a financial agency that keeps records on some 170 million Americans.

7. In the *New York Times* on February 23, 1990, five letters were printed under the heading "Caller ID Won't Screen the Pesky Sales Pitch." Some of these were follow-ups to earlier letters.

8. In fact, many commercial medical laboratories are highly automated, and the outcomes of tests on samples provided by patients are machine-readable documents.

References

Abrams, Floyd. (1993). "Big Brother's Here: And—Alas—We Embrace Him." *New York Times Magazine*, March 21, 36–38.

Bill C-43: An Act to Enact the Access to Information Act and the Privacy Act. (1982). Ottawa: Queen's Printer.

Brown, Patricia Leigh. (1993). "The Architecture of Those Called Homeless." *New York Times,* March 28, 1, 18.

Committee of Justice, Canadian Government Centre. (1987). *Open and Shut.* Ottawa: Queen's Printer.

Commission of Enquiry into the Confidentiality of Health Information, Honourable Justice Horace Krever, Commissioner. (1980). *Report,* 3 vols. Ontario: Queen's Printer.

"Does Your Computer Know Too Much?" (1991). *Toronto Globe and Mail,* December 18, "Report on Business" (reprinted from *The Economist*).

Moon, Peter. (1992). "Ottawa Wrestles with Changes to Electronic-Surveillance Law: Amendments Made Necessary by Recent Court Rulings." *Toronto Globe and Mail,* November 11.

Organization for Economic Cooperation and Development (OECD). (1980). *OECD Guidelines on the Protection of Privacy and Transborder Data Flows of Personal Data, Annex to the Recommendation of the Council of 23 September, 1980.* Paris: OECD.

Rosenblatt, Roger. (1993). "Who Killed Privacy?" *New York Times Magazine,* January 31, 24–28.

Rothfeder, Jeffrey. (1993). "What Happened to Privacy?" *New York Times,* April 13, A13.

U.S. General Accounting Office. (1986). *Computer Matching: Assessing Costs and Benefits* (GAO/PEMD-87-2, November). Washington, D.C.: U.S. Government Printing Office.

Vienneau, David. (1993). "Privacy Threatened, 60 Per Cent Tell Poll." *Toronto Star,* March 30, A9.

Warren, Samuel D., and Louis D. Brandeis. (1890). "The Right to Privacy." *Harvard Law Review* 4 (December 15).

Weiser, Mark. (1991). "The Computer for the 21st Century." *Scientific American,* September, 94–104.

"Westray Papers Show Cover-Up, Liberals Charge." (1993). *Toronto Star,* March 30, A9.

Part III

CULTURE

Databases as Discourse; or, Electronic Interpellations

Mark Poster

The Mode of Information and Databases

In this chapter I shall underscore the way computerized databases function as discourses in Foucault's sense of the term, that is, the way they constitute subjects outside the immediacy of consciousness.[1] This effort contrasts with other critical positions on databases that miss their discursive effects, treating databases with categories that overlook the decentering operations of language on the subject. Such, for example, is the case with Marxist writings, such as those of Herbert Schiller (1981) and Tim Luke and Stephen White (1985), in which databases are seen as contributions to the power of major institutions, especially corporations. Here databases are a new instrument through which capitalists can tighten their grip on the mode of production. Information in databases, Marxist critics advise, is not equally available to all, as the somewhat utopian proponents of this technology contend, but redound preponderantly to the benefit of the economic ruling class. Similarly, liberal writers on the subject, such as David Burnham (1983), James Rule (1974), and Gary Marx (1988), address in particular the appropriation of database technology by the state, warning of the considerable augmentation of centralized power it provides. Liberals are concerned in particular with the threats to privacy occasioned by databases in the hands of the government.

Although these perspectives certainly offer much to consider, they fail to expose the cultural innovations brought about by the integration of database technology into existing political, economic, and social institutions. In each case, Marxist and liberal perspectives incorporate the novel system of knowledge into their existing conceptual frameworks, revealing only that side of the phenomenon that fits within their grids of understanding. For Marxists, databases are comprehensible only to the extent they are a factor in the struggle over the means of production; for liberals, databases enter the field of politics as a component in the never-ending danger of autocratic central government. For both positions, the novelty of databases is reduced to a minimum and the social individual or class as configured by the theory remains unchanged with the advent of the new. I posit that critical social theory must explore, in addition to these offerings, the relation of databases to the cultural issue of the constitution of the subject, and that in doing so Foucault's theory of discourse provides a most compelling guide.

With respect to the problem of culture, the chief limitation of Marxist and liberal theories is that they configure the social field primarily as one of action, minimizing the importance of language. With respect to databases, the action in question for Marxists is the relation of power between capitalists and workers, whereas for liberals it is the fate of political domination. Both positions forget that databases are composed of symbols; they are in the first instance representations of something. One does not eat them, handle them, or kick them, at least one hopes not. Databases are configurations of language; the theoretical stance that engages them must at least take this ontological fact into account. A form of language, databases will have social effects that are appropriate to language, though certainly they will also have varied relations with forms of action.

The poststructuralist understanding of language is of special relevance to an analysis of databases that proceeds from critical social theory because of the connection it draws between language and the constitution of the subject. Poststructuralists make a number of salient claims about the interaction of language and subjects: (1) that subjects are always mediated by language, (2) that this mediation takes the form of "interpellation," and (3) that in this process the subject position that is a point of enunciation and of address is never sutured or closed, but remains unstable, excessive, multiple.

The first proposition is to be understood neither as tautological nor as innocent. A human being is configured as a subject, is given cultural significance, in the first instance through language. The kind of bearing that society imposes on individuals, the nature of the constraint and the empowerment it operates, takes its effect in language. The significance of the proposition may become more clear if we remember that in our culture the bearing of language on individuals tends to be systematically obscured by the privilege we give (in language) to the subject as a point of origin of motivation, consciousness, and intention. Since Descartes's articulation of the configuration of the subject, since the dissemination of this configuration in Enlightenment thought, since the inscription of this configuration in the major institutions of representative democracy, capitalist economics, bureaucratic social organization, and secular education, it has become the cultural foundation of the West. Once understood as a subject, the individual is fixed in the binary opposites of autonomy/heteronomy, rationality/irrationality, freedom/determinism. The linguistic level of the configuration is actively forgotten or naturalized as the subject faces these binaries from the vantage point of interior consciousness.

At the micrological level of daily life, the subject is continuously reconstituted as such through interpellation or "hailing."[2] In determinate linguistic acts the subject is addressed in a position and/or provoked to an enunciative stance in a manner that obscures the position or the stance. When a teacher calls upon an elementary school student to answer a question, the position of the student as an autonomous rational agent is presupposed, a position that student must "stand into" first in order to be able to answer, in order to be a student. The operation of linguistic interpellation requires that the addressee accept its configuration as a subject without direct reflection in order to carry on the conversation or practice at hand. Interpellation may be calibrated by gender, age, ethnicity, or class or may exclude any of these groups or parts of them. The issue is not that interpellation is an invasion of society upon the individual that ought to be avoided; that objection already falls within the binary freedom/determinism and presupposes the constitution of the individual as subject. Rather, what is important is that the process goes on at the level of language and that in our culture it takes the particular form of the subject.

The third proposition is that the interpellation of the subject is always partial, incomplete, riddled with gaps, and open to reconfiguration and resistance. The constitution of the subject in language is different from the Newtonian understanding of the world of material objects, in which matter is pushed and pulled into determinate positions by laws that are inexorable and unchanging. In the most trivial case, the subject is always multiple, interpellated into different positions: the student is also child, friend, pet master. But in each instance of interpellation, the subject is configured as fixed, determinate, closed. In adult circumstances of some social weight, interpellation appears to be—or better, is—structured as final, real, complete. The fixing of identities is not a matter of being pushed or pulled by gravity but of being invited to play a role in such a way that the invitation appears to have already been answered by the subject before it was proposed but at the same time the invitation could be refused.

Foucault's Concept of Discourse

An understanding of the poststructuralist sense of the relation of language to the subject is necessary if we are to gauge the stakes at play in Foucault's concept of discourse, a concept that in turn is crucial to a critical approach to databases. Foucault employs the term *discourse* in most of his writings, especially in his work of the 1960s, *The Order of Things* (1966) and *The Archeology of Knowledge* (1969). In these works, Foucault presents a critique of the human sciences and an alternative method of analysis. In these works the term *discourse* is introduced above all as a counterposition to those who understand writing as the expression of a subject—those who, in their search for meaning in acts of reading or listening, move from words back to consciousness. Here is one of Foucault's more lucid statements of this position:

> In the proposed analysis, instead of referring back to *the* synthesis or *the* unifying function of *a* subject, the various enunciative modalities manifest his dispersion. To the various statuses, the various sites, the various positions that he can occupy or be given when making a discourse. To the discontinuity of the planes from which he speaks. . . . I shall abandon any attempt, therefore, to see discourse as a phenomenon of expression—the verbal translation of a previously established synthesis; instead, I shall look for a field of regularity for various positions of subjectivity. Thus conceived, discourse is not the majestically unfolding manifestation of a thinking, knowing, speaking subject, but, on the contrary, a totality, in which the dispersion of the subject and his discontinuity with himself may be determined. It is a space of exteriority in which a network of distinct sites is deployed. (1966:54–55)

The relation of writing to the subject is sharply reconfigured in this passage. The term *discourse* is used primarily as a way to register the difference of Foucault's theory of writing from that of humanism. It designates a move toward an exteriorization of the analysis that is itself strategic. Foucault's claim is not that he has discovered the one, true way to understand knowledge or even that his way is somehow epistemologically superior to other, humanist ways. His claim is only that if one seeks a critique of knowledge in our culture, if one seeks to distance oneself from our culture's way of regarding its own knowledge, the term *discourse* indicates the path of that move.

Many critics of Foucault, who are usually themselves within the humanist way of knowing, complain that Foucault does not adequately specify the term *discourse* as a field, does not carefully indicate the boundaries of discourse, or its object. Manfred Frank, for example, even quotes Foucault as acknowledging this deficiency, except Frank takes it as an admission of failure rather than as an indication that the interest of the term *discourse* lies not in relation to a well-defined object but in relation to a level of analysis of any knowledge domain. Here is Frank's quote from Foucault:

> Finally, instead of making the rather hazy meaning of the word "discourse" more distinct, I think that I have multiplied its meanings: sometimes using it to mean a general domain of all statements [*énoncés*], sometimes as an individualisable group of statements [*énoncés*], and sometimes as an ordered practice which takes account of a certain number of statements [*énoncés*]. (1992:110)

Foucault appears to be suggesting that if the aim is a critique of knowledge in our society, then the effort of theorization need not so much focus on delimiting the object as on specifying the level of meaning one is attempting so that the relation of knowledge to the subject—in other words, the cultural construction of the subject—can be raised as a question.

Beginning with the essay "The Discourse on Language," first presented as his inaugural lecture at the Collège de France in 1970, Foucault introduced a connection between the terms *discourse* and *power*. From that point on, most effectively in *Discipline and Punish* (1977) and *The History of Sexuality* (1978), Foucault developed usages of the category "discourse" that were distinct from those in his earlier works. In the 1970s and 1980s, *discourse* was frequently used as a couplet, "discourse/practice," an indication that Foucault refused the separation of discourse from the "nondiscursive." He also introduced phrases such as "technology of power" and "micro-physics of power," in which discourse was subsumed into arrays and articulations of various kinds of practices—institutional, disciplinary, resistive, and so forth. The question of the relation of language to the subject was here considerably broadened, as language, discourse was configured as a form of power and power was understood as operating in part through language.

The Panopticon as Discourse

The question of discourse, with its imbrication to power, then, is about the cultural issue of the constitution of the subject. And in particular it is about the constitution of the subject as a rational, autonomous individual. Max Weber had also developed the thesis of the rational subject as a problem, as an index of domination rather than, as in liberalism and to a certain extent in Marx, as a sign of freedom. But Weber's understanding of rationality was burdened by its character as a universal principle. He was able to historicize the problem of reason and the subject only to a minimal extent. Foucault noted this difference in his position from that of Weber, attributing to him an understanding of rationality as "an anthropological invariant," whereas Foucault's own effort was to analyze reason as historically constructed (1991:79).

Foucault's problem, then, is to construct a theory of discourse that historicizes reason, reveals the way discourse functions as power, and spotlights the constitution of the subject. Strictly speaking, Foucault never provided such a theory because, he argued, theory reinscribes the rational subject at another epistemological level. Instead, he demonstrated such a theory of discourse in his histories of punishment and sexuality. The closest he approached such a theory is found in brief statements, mostly in his occasional writings, such as the following given in a late interview:

> I do indeed believe that there is no sovereign, founding subject, a universal form of subject to be found everywhere. I am very skeptical of this view of the subject and very hostile to it. I believe, on the contrary, that the subject is constituted through practices of subjection, or, in a more autonomous way, through practices of liberation, of liberty, . . . on the basis, of course, of a number of rules, styles, inventions to be found in the cultural environment. (1988:50–51)

Discourse is understood as having a power effect on the subject even in movements of "liberation."

The power effect of discourse is to position the subject in relation to structures of domination in such a way that those structures may *then* act upon him or her. The chief characteristic of the power effect of discourse is to disguise its constitutive function in relation to the subject, appearing only after the subject has been formed as an addressee of power. A classic example of this operation of discourse is, for Foucault, psychoanalysis. The discourse/practices of Freud produce in the subject an Oedipalized child, an understanding of one's childhood as, in the case of boys, a desire for one's mother. Once the child-subject is so constituted by psychoanalytic discourse, the child is then seen as being forbidden this desire, with the consequences of the Oedipal traumas and its deep effects on the personality. But the crucial point is that the effect of the discourse/practice is to name the child's desire, to configure the child as a libidinal subject with the particular aim of his or her mother (Foucault, 1978:129-31). Discourse has the same function in *Discipline and Punish*.

The modern system of punishment, incarceration, is first of all itself not the result of a rational subject. Against liberals and Marxists, Foucault argues for a Nietzschean genealogy of prisons in which the origins of the prison are found neither in the ideas of the Enlightenment nor in the workings of early industrial capitalism. Foucault traces the origins of the prison to a multiplicity of nonrelated pieces of earlier history: Enlightenment critiques of Old Regime forms of punishment, military training practices and schedules, procedures of examination in schools, Bentham's architectural ideas for prisons—none of which is understandable as a cause of the prison. Foucault attributes the origin of the prison to a kind of nonagency as follows:

> Small acts of cunning endowed with a great power of diffusion, subtle arrangements, apparently innocent, but profoundly suspicious, mechanisms that obeyed economies too shameful to be acknowledged, or pursued petty forms of coercion—it was nevertheless they that brought about the mutation of the punitive system, at the threshold of the contemporary period. (1977:139)

Having dethroned the rational subject from the agency of the establishment of prisons, Foucault goes on to analyze its operations as discourse.

The story is by now well-known. Prisoners reside in cells surrounding a central tower in which a guard is placed who can look into the cells but whom prisoners cannot see. An invisible authority is thereby instituted, one who is all-seeing (hence the term *panopticon*) but invisible. This instance is part of a complex articulation of discourse/practices that includes the juridical practices that sentenced the individual to prison, criminologists who study prisoners as individual cases, administrative schedules and routines for prisoner activities, evaluation procedures for possible parole, and so forth. Foucault characterizes the operation of the panopticon in these words:

> By means of surveillance, disciplinary power became an integrated system. . . . it also organized as a multiple, automatic and anonymous power; for although surveillance rests on the individual, its functioning is that of a network of relations from top to bottom . . . and laterally. . . . this network holds the whole together and traverses it in its entirety with effects of power that derive from one another: supervisor perpetually supervised. (1977:177).

Properly understood, the panopticon is not simply the guard in the tower but the entire discourse/practice that bears down on the prisoner, one that constitutes him or her as a criminal. The panopticon is the way the discourse/practice of the prison works to constitute the subject as a criminal and to normalize him or her to a process of transformation/rehabilitation. My argument is that with the advent of computerized databases, a new discourse/practice operates in the social field, a superpanopticon if you will, that reconfigures the constitution of the subject.[3]

Databases as a Superpanopticon

Databases are discourse, in the first instance, because they effect a constitution of the subject. They are a form of writing, of inscribing symbolic traces, that extends the basic principle of writing as *différance,* as making different and as distancing, differing, putting off to what must be its ultimate realization. In its electronic and digital form, the database is perfectly transferable in space, indefinitely preservable in time; it may last forever everywhere. Unlike spoken language, the database is not only remote from any authorial presence but is "authored" by so many hands that it makes a mockery of the principle of author as authority. As a meaningful text, the database is no one's and everyone's, yet it "belongs" to someone, to the social institution that "owns" it as property, to the corporation, the state, the military, the hospital, the library, the university. The database is a discourse of pure writing that directly amplifies the power of its owner/user.

And everyone knows this. Because they do know it, they resist it. A poll conducted by *Time* magazine in late 1991 revealed that between 70 percent and 80 percent were "very/somewhat concerned" about the amount of information being collected about them in databases, with the higher figure referring to the federal government, credit organizations, and insurance companies, and the lower figure referring to employers, banks, and marketing companies.[4] The population is now cognizant of being surveilled constantly by databases and apparently feels ill at ease as a result. Database anxiety has not as yet developed into an issue of national political prominence, but it is clearly a growing concern of many and bespeaks a new level of what Foucault calls the normalization of the population.

Examples of the politicization of databases multiply everyday. The U.S. federal government has developed FinCen (Financial Crimes Enforcement Network), with an awesome power that combines artificial intelligence programs with massive parallel processing, to monitor bank transactions for the purpose of detecting criminal activity (Kimery, 1993). In the economic sphere, retailers that sell by modem regard the information they accumulate about customers as their property, as a valuable asset gained as a by-product of the sale, which they may then sell to other retailers. But customers do not want such information about themselves traveling, beyond their control, from one vendor to another. Although an effort to sell customer information by Lotus Corporation was thwarted by consumers, their resistance to the use of these databases is sure to fail because it is based on the modern political distinction between the public and the private. Consumers regard their purchases as private, as part of the capitalist system that designates all economic transactions as "private." But databases are a postmodern discourse that traverses and cancels the public/private distinction.

Increasingly, economic transactions automatically enter databases and do so with the customer's assistance. Credit card sales are of course good examples. According to the conventional wisdom of political economy, the consumer buys something in a "private" act of rational choice. Yet when the credit card is extracted from the wallet or purse and submitted to the clerk for payment, that "private" act becomes part of a "public" record. The unwanted surveillance of a personal choice becomes a discursive reality through the willing participation of the surveilled individual. In this instance the play of power and discourse is uniquely configured. The one being surveilled provides the information necessary for the surveillance. No carefully designed edifice is needed, no science such as criminology is employed, no complex administrative apparatus is invoked, no bureaucratic organization need be formed. In the superpanopticon, surveillance is assured when the act of the individual is communicated by telephone line to the computerized database, with only a minimum of data being entered by the sales clerk. A gigantic and sleek operation is effected whose political force of surveillance is occluded in the willing participation of the victim.

Unlike the panopticon, then, the superpanopticon effects its workings almost without effort. What Foucault notices as the "capillary" extension of power throughout the space of disciplinary society is much more perfected today. The phone cables and electric circuitry that minutely crisscross and envelop our world are the extremities of the superpanopticon, transforming our acts into an extensive discourse of surveillance, our private behaviors into public announcements, our individual deeds into collective language. Individuals are plugged into the circuits of their own panoptic control, making a mockery of theories of social action, like Weber's, that privilege consciousness as the basis of self-interpretation, and liberals generally, who locate meaning in the intimate, subjective recesses behind the shield of the skin. The individual subject is interpellated by the superpanopticon through technologies of power, through the discourse of databases that have very little if anything to do with "modern" conceptions of rational autonomy. The superpanopticon, this perfect writing machine, constitutes subjects as decentered from their ideologically determined unity.

If we look at databases as an example of Foucault's notion of discourse, we see them as "exteriorities," not as constituted by agents, and we look for their "rules of formation" as the key to the way they constitute individuals. Databases in this sense are carefully arranged lists, digitalized to take advantage of the electronic speed of computers. The list is partitioned vertically into "fields" for items such as name, address, age, and sex and horizontally into "records" that designate each entry. A retailer's database has fields that record each purchase an individual makes so that in the course of time a rich portrait of buying habits is created, one that is instantaneously accessible and cross-referenced with other information such as the individual's location and possibly cross-referenced as well with other databases keyed to items such as social security number or driver's license. In effect, these electronic lists become additional social identities as each individual is constituted for the computer, depending on the database in question, as a social agent. Without referring the database back to its owner and his or her interests or forward to the individual in question as a model of its adequacy or accuracy, we comprehend the database as a discursive production that inscribes positionalities of subjects according to its rules of formation. In this way we see the database outside the dichotomy public/private and outside the dynamics of the mode of production. Instead, the discourse of the database is a cultural force that operates in a mechanism of subject constitution that refutes the hegemonic principle of the subject as centered, rational, and autonomous. Now, through the database alone, the subject has been multiplied and decentered, capable of being acted upon by computers at many social locations without the least awareness by the individual concerned yet just as surely as if the individual were present somehow inside the computer.

Some readers may object that databases cannot be characterized as discourses in Foucault's sense because for Foucault discourses are large collections of texts. The examples he gives are psychology, economics, grammar, and medicine, all of which include sentences and paragraphs strung together by arguments. The same can hardly be said of databases, which for the most part are not textual in this way but rather agglomerations of isolated words or numbers whose location in the "discourse" is paramount. The only places where sentences of any kind are found in databases is in the program or code language that constitutes them and in some types of fields that are textual. And yet the crucial features of discourse are indeed contained in databases even though they omit the standard features of prose. Databases are fully what Foucault calls "grids of specification," one of the three "rules of formation" of discourse. These grids are "the systems according to which the different kinds of [the object in question] are divided, contrasted, related, regrouped, classified, derived from one another as objects of . . . discourse" (1969:42). Nothing qualifies as a grid in this sense as well as databases; they are pure grids whose vertical fields and horizontal records divide and classify objects with a precision that more traditional forms of discourse, such as psychology, must surely envy.

But what is most important about discourses for Foucault is that they constitute their objects. His greatest concern is to avoid treating discourse as "groups of signs," as texts or as writing perhaps in Derrida's sense, "but as practices that systematically form the objects of which they speak" (1966:49). His emphasis is on the performative aspect of language, what language does rather than what it denotes or connotes. Computerized databases are nothing but performative machines, engines for producing retrievable identities. A feature of many databases that indicates their status as "practice" consists of their "relational" abilities. Two databases may function as one if one field in each is identical. Thus if a census database and an employee database both have fields for social security numbers (which is increasingly the identifier field of choice), employers may use the census to discover whatever they might about employees that is not in their own records but in the census. These kinds of linkages between databases have been used in the Parent Locator System, the effort to find divorced and separated men who do not support their children. Relational databases thus have built into their structure the ability to combine with other databases, forming vast stores of information that constitute as an object virtually every individual in society and in principle may contain virtually everything recorded about that individual—credit rating data, military records, census information, educational experience, telephone calls, and so forth.[5]

The most sophisticated examples of the use of relational databases are in market research firms, such as Claritas Corporation. This company boasts the use of "over 500 million individual consumer records from *several* leading databases" (Claritas Corporation, 1991).[6] The company combines and analyzes data from the following categories of databases: media and market research studies, newspaper research (including readership of newspapers, viewing of television, and listening to radio), customer research studies, car and truck registration data, mailing lists, and credit rating data. The company combines more than twelve hundred databases in both the private and public sectors. Claritas generates its own database, Compass, which it makes available to its customers for their own research. Its masterpiece, however, is a database called Prizm, which is an identity construction system. Prizm divides up the entire population into "clusters" that can be as fine grained as six households. Each cluster is then fit into forty types, such as "rank and file," "black enterprise," "single city blues," "furs and station wagons," and so forth. Each type is defined by income, percentage of the U.S. population, age, class, size of household, and "characteristics." In the case of the identity known as "bohemian mix," some 1.1 percent of the population, characteristics are, for example, "Buy, wine by the case, common stock; Drive, Alfa Romeos, Peugeots; Read, GQ, Harper's; Eat, whole-wheat bread, frozen waffles; TV, Nightline" (quoted in USA Today, March 16, 1989, 1B). The company then provides a few sample zip codes where this species may be found.

Databases such as Prizm constitute subjects in a manner that inscribes a new pattern of interpellation.[7] The "hailing" of the individual is here quite distinct from that of the teacher and the student, the police officer and the perpetrator, the boss and the worker, the parent and the child. In these cases there is often a direct message sent and received in a face-to-face situation. With databases, most often, the individual is constituted in absentia, only indirect evidence such as junk mail testifying to the event. Interpellation by database in this respect is closer to the instance of writing, with the reader-subject being hailed by an absent author. But here again there are important differences: from the standpoint of the person being interpellated, the writer is known, even if only as a writer, and is an individual or finite group of individuals. The reader very often intentionally selects to be interpellated by the particular author, whereas in the case of computer databases that is rarely if ever the case. Interpellation by database is a complicated configuration of unconsciousness, indirection, automation, and absentmindedness both on the part of the producer of the database and on the part of the individual subject being constituted by it. More research needs to be done to specify the configuration of interpellation in various types of databases, to answer the question of just how centered or dispersed subjects are in these cases, and to determine the characteristics of this dispersion or multiplicity. However, the above discussion suffices to indicate the importance of databases in complicating the concept of interpellation. The computer database inaugurates a new era of interpellation far different from that of modernity, with its discourses of print and its handwritten system of case files. The category of interpellation may serve as the leading thread in a critical interpretation of databases, one that specifies the attributes of subject constitution, reveals the domination inherent in the process, and indicates the path by which the positions of enunciation at which subjects are interpellated may be multiplied throughout social space, mollifying the noxious effects of the discourse.

Once the form of representation embodied in the database is under-

stood, it may be compared with other regions of the mode of information—television viewing, computer writing, telephone conversation,
video and audio recording, and so forth. Each of these cultural technologies also has discursive effects, the sum of which may be seen as
slowly erecting the basis of a culture that is decidedly different from
the modern. In each case the subject as coherent, stable, rational center is refuted by heterogeneity, dispersion, instability, multiplicity. The
database is part of a larger, massive cultural transformation that positions the subject outside the framework of visibility available to liberal
and Marxist theoretical orientations. No wonder Lyotard struck a
chord when he announced in *The Postmodern Condition* (1984) his
"incredulity toward metanarratives." As daily life is pervaded more
and more by the regions of the mode of information, the culture of
modernity enjoys less and less verisimilitude. Though the effects of the
mode of information are differential with respect to class, gender, and
ethnicity, they constitute a very general phenomenon that betokens a
new play of power, a new dialectics of resistance, and a new configuration of politics and its theorization.

Like television, music reproduction, computer writing, and video
art, databases generate discursive effects by simulating a reality or, better, to use Baudrillard's term, a hyperreality. The fields that compose
the database construct representations of individuals. The fields, often
consisting of a fixed amount of characters, are highly limited by the
imperative of the technology, its rule of formation in Foucault's sense,
which is retrieval speed. The database is effective only to the extent
that its information is instantaneously accessible, but at the same time
it must be large and comprehensive in relation to its referent population. Near-total coverage and instantaneous accessibility characterize
a good database. Yet this accessibility refers to the constructions within
the database, which function as simulacra of the population covered.
To the database, Jim Jones is the sum of the information in the fields of
the record that applies to that name. So the person Jim Jones now has
a new form of presence, a new subject position that defines him for all
those agencies and individuals who have access to the database. The
representation in the discourse of the database constitutes the subject,
Jim Jones, in highly caricatured yet immediately available form.

Another way of understanding the discursive nature of databases is
to relate them to what Foucault calls "governmentality." This is a
form of power characteristic of welfare states. It is neither the micro-

physics of power that characterizes local situations in everyday life nor the grand state power of monarchs and presidents. Governmentality is a kind of bureaucratic power, one that relies upon knowledge of the populace to police society and maintain order. Foucault in places calls it "biopower" and takes as its precursor the management of the family as in ancient Greece, the original meaning of economy (Foucault, 1991). He defines governmentality as follows: "To govern a state will there-fore mean to apply economy, to set up an economy at the level of the entire state, which means exercising towards its inhabitants, and the wealth and behaviour of each and all, a form of surveillance and con-trol as attentive as that of the head of a family over his household and goods" (p. 92). Governmentality, or the form of power of the welfare states of the advanced industrial societies of the late twentieth century, is inconceivable without databases. The vast populations of these soci-eties might well be ungovernable without databases. Databases pro-vide contemporary governments with vast stores of accessible infor-mation about the population that facilitates the fashioning of policies that maintain stability. An important political effect of databases, as they have been disseminated in our societies, is to promote the "gov-ernmental" form of power, to make knowledge of the population available to coercive institutions at every level.

To counter this stabilizing effect of databases, Jean-François Lyotard suggests that a new emancipatory politics would consist in giving everyone access to databases (1984:67). Certainly this policy, however utopian under present circumstances, would serve to democratize information. Each individual or group would have easy computer access to the same information as the government. Although such a prospect sounds utopian, given the increasing poverty in the United States, it is conceivable that at least in principle computer access to such databases could be widely extended to the vast majority of the population. A policy that worked in this direction would indeed con-stitute a "freedom of information act." The thought of government critics being able to race through the cyberspace of data even as those data are recorded is a counterfactual that gives one pause.

Yet as a strategy of resistance it does not take into account the performative effect of the discourse of databases, their ability to con-stitute subjects. The implication of Lyotard's position is that "real" subjects would recuperate the "power" inherent in the databases, enabling them to manipulate its knowledge for their own ends, a politics different from the current conservative restrictions on the use of databases to those who can foot the bill, usually large social organizations. The thesis of the liberation of the databases presupposes the social figure of the centered, autonomous subject that the databases preclude. Postmodern culture configures multiple, dispersed subject positions whose domination no longer is effected by alienated power but by entirely new articulations of technologies of power. The cultural function of databases is not so much the institution of dominant power structures against the individual as it is the restructuring of the nature of the individual. Lyotard's suggestion presumes that knowledge and power are separable, that increased availability of databases equals increased knowledge equals increased power. But the viewpoint that I am proposing posits a different relation of knowledge and power, one in which knowledge itself is a form of linguistic power, the culturally formative power of subject constitution.

The process of subject formation in the discourse of databases operates very differently from the panopticon. Foucault argues that the subject constituted by the panopticon was the modern, "interiorized" individual, the one who was conscious of his or her own self-determination. The process of subject constitution was one of "subjectification," of producing individuals with a (false) sense of their own interiority. With the superpanopticon, on the contrary, subject constitution takes an opposing course of "objectification," of producing individuals with dispersed identities, identities of which the individuals might not even be aware. The scandal, perhaps, of the superpanopticon is its flagrant violation of the great principle of the modern individual, of its centered, "subjectified" interiority.

A politics of databases then would respond to the cultural form of subjectification in postmodernity. Instead of developing a resistant politics of privacy to counter the alleged incursions of databases on the autonomous individual, we need to understand the forms of agency appropriate to a dispersed, multiple subject and to generate strategies of resistance appropriate to that identity formation. The issue is not that the new forms of subjectification are in themselves emancipatory, but that they are the new arena of contestation. A politics that circumscribes freedom around the skin of the individual, labeling everything inside private and untouchable, badly misconceives the present-day situation of digitized, electronic communications. Because our bodies are hooked into the networks, the databases, the information superhighways, they no longer provide a refuge from observation or a bastion around which one can draw a line of resistance. The road to greater emancipation must wend its way through the subject formations of the mode of information, not through those of an earlier era of modernity and its rapidly disappearing culture. The appeal for community, as Ernesto Laclau (1993) and Chantal Mouffe (1993) argue, must take into account the forms of identity and communication in the mode of information, and resist nostalgia for the face-to-face intimacy of the ancient Greek agora. In the era of cyborgs, cyberspace, and virtual realities, the face of community is not discerned easily through the mists of history, however materialist and dialectical it may be.

Notes

This essay will appear in Wolfgang Natter, ed., *Contemporary Theory and Democracy* (New York: Guilford, forthcoming).

1. I shall be concerned not with all databases, but only with those that have fields for individuals. Thus inventory databases, for example, are excluded from my discussion.

2. The concept of "interpellation" entered the arena of critical theory with Althusser's essay "Ideology and Ideological State Apparatuses" (1970/1971), where he presents the Marxist concept of ideology as the interpellating agent. See also Silverman (1983).

3. Along similar lines, Gilles Deleuze (1992) suggests that we have changed from a a disciplinary society to a society of control.

4. The poll results were presented in a graphic within the magazine's cover story for the week, by Richard Lacayo (1991). I am indebted to Carol Starcevic for showing me this article.

5. David Lyon moderates the totalizing vision that is often drawn from this analysis: "It is not so much that we are already enclosed in the cells of the electronic Panopticon, but that certain contemporary institutions display panoptic features. Panopticism is one tendency among others" (1991: 614).

6. I am grateful to Colin Fisher for showing me this text.

7. Colin Hay of Lancaster University suggested this line of inquiry to me. See his forthcoming essay "Mobilisation through Interpellation."

References

Althusser, Louis. (1971). "Ideology and Ideological State Apparatuses" (1970), trans. Ben Brewster. In *Lenin and Philosophy and Other Essays*. London: New Left.

Burnham, David. (1983). *The Rise of the Computer State*. New York: Random House.

Claritas Corporation. (1991). "Claritas Corporation—An Overview." Advertising material.

Deleuze, Gilles. (1992). "Postscript on the Societies of Control." *October 59* (Winter): 3–7.

Foucault, Michel. (1966). *The Order of Things: An Archeology of the Human Sciences*. New York: Pantheon.

———. (1969). *The Archaeology of Knowledge*, trans. A. M. Sheridan Smith. New York: Pantheon.

———. (1977). *Discipline and Punish: The Birth of the Prison*, trans. Alan Sheridan. New York: Pantheon.

———. (1978). *The History of Sexuality*, vol. 1, *An Introduction*, trans. Robert Hurley. New York: Pantheon.

———. (1988). "An Aesthetics of Existence." In Lawrence Kritzman (ed.), *Foucault: Politics, Philosophy, Culture*, trans. Alan Sheridan et al. New York: Routledge.

———. (1991). "The Question of Method." In Graham Burchell et al. (eds.), *The Foucault Effect: Studies in Governmentality*. Chicago: University of Chicago Press.

Frank, Manfred. (1992). "On Foucault's Concept of Discourse." In François Ewald (ed.), *Michel Foucault, Philosopher*, trans. Timothy Armstrong. New York: Routledge.

Hay, Colin. (forthcoming). "Mobilisation through Interpellation." *Media, Culture & Society*.

Kimery, Anthony. (1993). "Big Brother Wants to Look into Your Bank Account (Any Time It Pleases)." *Wired*, December, 91–93, 134.

Lacayo, Richard. (1991). "Nowhere to Hide." *Time*, November 11, 34–40.

Laclau, Ernesto. (1993). "Power and Representation." In Mark Poster (ed.), *Politics, Theory and Contemporary Culture*. New York: Columbia University Press, 277–96.

Luke, Timothy, and Stephen White. (1985). "Critical Theory, the Informational Revolution, and an Ecological Path to Modernity." In John Forester (ed.), *Critical Theory and Public Life*. Cambridge: MIT Press, 22–53.

Lyon, David. (1991). "Bentham's Panopticon: From Moral Architecture to Electronic Surveillance." *Queen's Quarterly* 98 (Fall).

Lyotard, Jean-François. (1984). *The Postmodern Condition*, trans. Geoff Bennington and Brian Massumi. Minneapolis: University of Minnesota Press.

Marx, Gary. (1988). *Undercover: Police Surveillance in America*. Berkeley: University of California Press.

Mouffe, Chantal. (1993). "Democracy, Pluralism and Uncertainty." Unpublished manuscript.

Rule, James B. (1974). *Private Lives and Public Surveillance: Social Control in the Computer Age*. New York: Schocken.

Schiller, Herbert. (1981). *Who Knows: Information in the Age of the Fortune 500*. Norwood, N.J.: Ablex.

Silverman, Kaja. (1983). *The Subject of Semiotics*. New York: Oxford University Press.

Electric Eye in the Sky: Some Reflections on the New Surveillance and Popular Culture

Gary T. Marx

> Stare. It is the way to educate your eye and more. Stare, pry, listen, eavesdrop. Die knowing something. You are not here long.
>
> Walker Evans, *Walker Evans at Work*

> The country doesn't give much of a shit about bugging . . . most people around the country think it's probably routine, everybody's trying to bug everybody else, it's politics.
>
> President Richard Nixon on Watergate

Most analysis of information technology uses printed words and numbers. As important as historical, social, philosophical, legal, and policy analyses are, they are not sufficient for a broad understanding. We also need cultural analysis. This essay considers elements of surveillance as they are treated in popular media. Attention to visual images and music can tell us about cultural themes and values. The images we hold of surveillance methods are incomplete and partially independent of the technology per se. Images are social fabrications (though not necessarily social deceptions). Images speak to (and may be intended to create or manipulate) needs, aspirations, and fears. They communicate meaning.

Surveillance technology is not simply applied, it is also *experienced* by users, subjects, and audiences. Cultural analysis can tell us something about the experience of being watched, or of being a watcher.

One may well ask whether the serious social questions raised by surveillance technologies (such as computer dossiers, video and audio monitoring, drug testing, satellites, and electronic location monitoring and undercover methods) are not trivialized by considering mass media depictions. But here Erving Goffman's admonition to look for big meanings in little things, as well as Shakespeare's to "by indirections find

193

directions out" apply. There are strong intellectual and political grounds for studying popular culture and information technology.

To understand the threats (as well as the opportunities) posed by these devices, we must look at their cultural backdrop and ask how culture supports or undermines our most cherished values. For example, as a result of surveillance devices for monitoring and surveillance toys, children are now raised to view being watched and watching others through sense-enhancing technologies as the normal order of things. As adults, how will they respond to requests for information that in the past might have been seen as inappropriate? Conversely, will they be more likely than their parents to use privacy-invading technologies? Will this mean changes in interaction and in the meaning of intimacy and trust?

If liberty is indeed at risk from these tools, we need to know how the public perceives them and what sense it makes of media depictions. Where are the soft spots? What are the contours of public resistance or support for technologies that cross boundaries that in the past were impenetrable and even sacrosanct? What themes and representations do the supporters and opponents of the new technologies offer or fail to offer? What is referred to only by innuendo or euphemism?

The various actors involved with the culture of surveillance are engaged (whether they realize it or not) in a struggle to shape popular images. Should social scientists choose to merge their science and politics, the right picture and/or sounds can be worth much more than words, or words alone, in bringing about or blocking the spread of invasive technologies.

Apart from any advocacy issues, as social scientists we can better understand the technologies by looking at the meanings and symbolism that surround them. The images are socially patterned, not random.

Popular culture, of course, reflects developments in technology. For example, contrast Paul Simon singing in 1967's "Mrs. Robinson," "We'd like to know a little bit about you for our [presumably manual] files"or about the spy in a gabardine suit whose "bow tie is really a camera" in the song "America" to his "lasers in the jungle" and "staccato signals of constant information" in the 1980s song "The Boy in the Bubble."

But this also works the other way as well. Art, science fiction, comic books, and films have anticipated and even inspired surveillance devices and applications to new areas. For example, the 1936 film *Modern Times,* in which Charlie Chaplin's private reverie in the bathroom at work smoking a cigarette is shattered by the sudden appearance of his boss on a wall-sized video screen gruffly saying, "Hey, quit stalling and get back to work." The boss has a two-way video camera. H. G. Wells, Dick Tracy, James Bond, and *Star Trek* are some other familiar examples. In another example, a Spider-Man comic inspired a New Mexico judge to implement the first judicial use of electronic location monitoring equipment.

I approach the popular media with many questions (only some of which are dealt with here): How have culture creators depicted the new technologies? What images, symbols, and themes appear most often? A more difficult question concerns the symbols and themes that are not used. Familiarity with materials from other times and cultures and from critical media can help us discover what these are. What kinds of symbols are used for new, unseen, and unfamiliar elements, such as DNA sequencing? What assumptions do the creators appear to be making about the technologies? Is there an art of glorification, as well as denigration? What shared understandings are these believed to communicate? How is the desire for security balanced with the desire to be free from intrusions? How do social factors affect the behavior and definition of the surveillant and the surveilled? What conclusions can be drawn about how characteristics such as gender or race of the artist (or of the intended audience) affect the work? Is there understandable variation across media and types of surveillance devices (e.g., visual versus auditory, physically invasive versus noninvasive techniques, self versus other surveillance)? How do depictions of surveillance technology intended to help one person watch another differ from depictions of technologies intended to protect the individual from the surveillance of others? What separates the more moving and enduring creations from the less? How have themes evolved as the power and potential of the techniques have become clearer in the past two decades? How much consistency is there across media? How do treatments relate to the written ideas of social scientists and critics? How are these treatments affecting popular conceptions and understandings?

A particular challenge lies in linking the cultural images of surveillance to social, political, economic, and technical factors. Rather than a reductionist model, stressing the causal primacy of any one of these factors, they are interactive. Culture both shapes and is shaped by the available technology.

Another important issue involves the connection between what individuals perceive and experience and what the creators and/or owners of the cultural form intend them to experience. There are two parts to this: (1) Do such depictions accurately reflect personal experiences with surveillance? (2) How are they perceived by the audience? These are not necessarily independent. Through their educational role, the media help prepare individuals for what they should experience as watchers or as the watched.

Artistic statements, unlike scientific statements, do not have to be defended verbally. But the social scientist can ask about their social antecedents and impacts. Do they move the individual? Do they convey the experience of being watched or of being a watcher? Do they create indignation or a desire for the product? Do they make the invisible visible?

I will consider depictions of surveillance technology in popular music, jokes and cartoons, illustrations, advertisements (whether for products or ideas), and art. Like the material it is based upon, this essay is intended to communicate immediately and viscerally. In offering examples, my initial goal is for the reader/viewer/listener to consume and experience the materials. The message is to be found directly in what the songwriter, cartoonist, illustrator, advertiser, or artist suggests to the audience. The materials can descriptively stand by themselves. But I seek to go beyond being a collector, even at the risk of treading in alien interpretive waters, by asking how these depictions can be organized and what they may tell us about society and surveillance.

Jürgen Habermas has stated that "my question is my method." My approach is driven by a desire to understand surveillance in a broad fashion, but I also seek to systematize. In the first instance I have simply observed. The material presented is an illustrative sampling from a larger collection of materials gathered over the past decade. Clearly, surveillance is *not* a theme in most popular songs, jokes, or art. Not having taken a representative sample, I cannot say how minimal it is. However, I am confident that the materials presented here represent the popular materials that *do* deal with surveillance.

There is, of course, a leap from impressions to meaning. Subjectivity must be a part of any broad understanding of human affairs. Yet it can mislead if we claim that our subjective experience is necessarily representative. Although what is offered here is primarily my personal experience and interpretation of the materials, I hope it is suggestive of questions for more systematic and quantitative research.

Popular Music

Surveillance themes are pervasive in popular culture, although we often do not think of them as such. Consider, for example, the familiar song "Santa Claus Is Coming to Town." The words to this religious panopticon song are well known—Santa "knows when you are sleeping, he knows when you're awake, he knows if you've been bad or good, so be good for goodness sake." The message here is not be good because it is right, but be good because you will be externally rewarded and you won't get away with bad behavior anyway. Someone is watching—consistent with computer dossiers, "He's making a list, he's checking it twice."

I was surprised at how many surveillance songs I could identify, once I started listening for this. One well-known genre represents the positive, protective side of surveillance as something an individual seeks. Many religious songs involve the theme of an appeal to, or statement about, an all-powerful and all-knowing God looking over humankind. Another type involves the yearning for a lover and/or protector by someone who feels weak or vulnerable. The familiar song "Someone to Watch over Me" is an example. Such songs (at least until recently) were much more likely to be sung (and perhaps written) by females than by males. They are the passive expression of a hope or a plea, rather than an active seeking out of the individual. In contrast, males have been more likely to write and sing about their prowess as active watchers and discoverers.

My concern here will be more with the process of actually being a watcher, or the experience of being watched, than with pleas for the latter, and with changes in the music as more powerful surveillance technologies have appeared. Popular songs in this genre tend to involve either a love-inspired male surveillant or a chronicle (often of protest or satire) of what a surveillant does to others. Some suggest the erotic fantasy of secret watching.

The love songs discussed below can be categorized with respect to whether they involve (1) an equation of watching and knowing with love, (2) a search for a true love, (3) the surveillant's power to discover deception, or (4) voyeurism. These songs all refer to extrasensory powers of cognition possessed by the male singer as he watches a female. As sophisticated surveillance technology came into wider use in the 1970s, there was a shift from magical, intuitive powers to sense-enhancing technologies. In most cases the power for surveillance is greatly overstated. The ability to know more than can be known with the senses is equated to the ability to know everything.

The film *Rear Window* appeared at the height of a Cold War–generated climate of suspicion and the availability of new imaging technologies such as the zoom lens. It contains the classic line spoken by Thelma Ritter, "We have become a nation of Peeping Toms." Its syrupy theme song, sung by Bing Crosby, "To See You Is to Love You," is a traditional ballad of adulation, attesting to the powers of the love object. Here the mere sight of the woman is sufficient to make the singer love her. This song has none of the hard-edged obsessive watching and/or covert surveillance of later decades, in which the woman must be watched because she cannot be trusted. The singer is infatuated: "To see you is to love you and you're never out of sight." She has invaded and colorized his mind. Her charm means that the male singer sees her "anyplace I look" and "I see you all the time." Real watching and fantasy merge. Director Alfred Hitchcock juxtaposes the professional surveillance of James Stewart as a photographer suspiciously watching a neighbor's window with the male gaze in which he watches his girlfriend, played by Grace Kelly, and a scantily clad female entertainer in another window.

The Clovers' 1954 song "I've Got My Eyes on You" contains the essential elements of the possessive, all-powerful male gaze typical of many such songs, including Sting's "Every Breath You Take," which appeared almost thirty years later. The Clovers song has a strategic goal: "I'm gonna make you mine." The singer can "see everything you do." He watches "you all day long. I watch you all night, too. Know everywhere you go." The song can also be seen as offering a public marker. In singing "I've got my eyes on you," the singer announces his intentions and choice. To say, "I have my eye on that" need not literally mean it is being intensively watched, but rather "I choose that." This song conveys the idea of the woman as an active stimulant of the singer's attention: "The way you wiggle when you walk, it'd make a hounddog talk." In most other songs the object of attention is passive or unknown, not realizing that she is "performing" or has behaved badly, thus calling forth the intense male surveillance.

The Doors sing about "a spy in the house of love" who "can see you and what you do" and who knows your dreams and fears, and "everywhere you go, everyone you know."

In their 1957 song "Searchin'," the Coasters express a common ballad theme—the search for true love. Unlike in later songs, this is not a threat, nor is it bragging. The actions sung about are not motivated by suspiciousness of a woman who cannot be trusted or by the desire to gratify a secret obsession. Instead, the song represents a statement of determination, optimism, and yearning in proclaiming that the singer will "find her"—the ideal woman.[1]

"Searchin'" links directly to the search of the detective who is like the Northwest Mountie and hopes to bring in the ideal woman "someday." Sherlock Holmes, Sam Spade, Sergeant Friday, Charlie Chan, and Boston Blackie have nothing on him. Unlike the song in the Hitchcock film mentioned above, here there is an explicit and easy link between the male gaze and the professional surveillant.

The surveillance in "On Every Street," recorded by Dire Straits, has as its theme an effort to locate a particular individual. The song refers to the tracks increasingly left by inhabitants of an electronically marked world: "There's gotta be a record of you someplace, you gotta be on somebody's books" and "somewhere your fingerprints remain concrete." This involves a sadder, less hopeful search than that of the Coasters; perhaps the yearning is deepened because the singer knows exactly what he has lost and is looking for.

Suspicion-Driven Surveillance

In 1956, in "Slippin' and Slidin'," Little Richard has been "peepin' and hidin'" to discover his baby's jive, and as a result he "won't be your fool no more." Bobby Vee sings that "the night has a thousand eyes" and that these eyes will see "if you aren't true to me." If he gets "put down for another" or told lies, he warns, "I'll know, believe me, I'll know." The Who more directly imply the possession of extrasensory powers when they sing, "There's magic in my eyes." The singer knows he has been deceived because "I can see for miles and miles and miles and miles and miles." Hall and Oates sing about the inability to escape my "Private Eyes," which, while "looking for lies," are "watching you. They see your every move."

In a more contemporary song, the Alan Parsons Project makes direct use of technology to discover lies and to tell the deceiving lover to "find another fool" because "I am the eye in the sky looking at you I can read your mind."

Perhaps surprisingly for a group called the Information Society, the emphasis in their song "What's on Your Mind?" is not on sophisticated communications technology but on traditional means, perhaps involving intuition, and a gentle plea to inform the singer. The song contains the lines "There are some things you can't hide" and "I can see behind your eyes," yet asks, "If you hide away from me, how can our love grow?"

The classic song of this type is "Every Breath You Take," written by Sting, who reports that it is about "the obsessiveness of ex-lovers, their maniacal possessiveness"—written after a divorce. It is about surveillance, ownership, and jealousy (*Rolling Stone*, March 1, 1984). Sting has expressed surprise that many people think of it as "a very sweet love song." Many listeners hear the affirmative, protective, and positive aspects of surveillance, as when parents look out for children or caretakers watch those who are ill. Although Sting reports that he reads critic Arthur Koestler, he says that his song is personal, not political. The female is warned that her faked smiles and broken bonds and vows will be observed by the singer. In a wonderful example of life imitating and using art, this song was popular when it was released with police doing surveillance (thus detectives in Boston, and likely elsewhere, played the song while they tailed organized crime figures).

Although the song does not mention technological supports for the omnipresent and omnipotent surveillance it promises, it is easy to connect it with contemporary tools. One can hear the song to suggest the following:

> Every breath you take [breath analyzer]
> Every move you make [motion detector]
> Every bond you break [polygraph]
> Every step you take [electronic monitoring]
>
> Every single day [continuous monitoring]
> Every word you say [bugs, wiretaps, mikes]
> Every night you stay [light amplifier]
>
> Every vow you break [voice stress analysis]
> Every smile you fake [brain wave analysis]
> Every claim you stake [computer matching]
>
> I'll be watching you [video]

In most of the songs mentioned above, we see surveillance as a means of protection and discovery and even prevention, often in a context of doubt. Yet in other songs we see the pleasure of watching as an end in itself. For example, consider Queensryche's unsettling (from a standpoint of the object of surveillance) song "Gonna Get Close to You." Here the singer is "outside your balcony I have a room with a view and I'm watching you." He knows "when you're alone, I know when you turn out the light." In "Voyeur," by Lizzy Borden, we hear a similar theme: "I'm watching you, you're in my sights. I know you so well, I know your every move." In this song there is an element of compulsiveness ("I can't stop watching you") and the singer is distraught "because you don't even know me."

Chronicles of Surveillance

Here the voice is not that of the surveillant, but of an individual subject to surveillance, or of a third party telling us about it, frequently in the form of a satirical warning. The songs are concerned with threats to liberty, the chilling effects of being spied upon and the loss of privacy. A central theme is "They are watching us." Here the voice is not that of the swaggering, boastful, omnipotent watcher who makes veiled threats about his power, but the voice of the subject, victim, or concerned chronicler warning us about surveillance.

One form deals with the negative impact on the watcher. The 1966 television theme song "Secret Agent Man" warns of threats to life ("Odds are you won't live to see tomorrow") and depersonalization ("They've given you a number, and taken away your name"). For Dire Straits, "Private Investigations" result in being "scarred for life—no compensation." At the end of the day you are left with whiskey and lies and a "pain behind the eyes."[2]

In "Framed," the Robbins offer a first-person account of victimization by an informer. The lead singer is put in a police lineup and realizes he is a victim of "someone's evil plan. When a stool pigeon walked in and said, 'That's the man.'"

Bob Dylan's "Subterranean Homesick Blues" expresses many themes. One is the threat of covert surveillance involving a "man in a trench coat" with "badge out," microphones planted in the bed, and telephone taps. As a result, youth are satirically warned to look out. The song suggests that youth are being watched, regardless of whether they have actually done anything wrong or not. To avoid surveillance, they should not wear sandals and should try to be a success.

In "Talkin' John Birch Paranoid Blues" Dylan parodies the search for Communist conspiracies. What is initially omnipresent here is not surveillance, but Communists. But to overcome the problem requires a search that satirizes in its breadth. Communists are looked for "under my bed," "in the sink and underneath the chair," "up my chimney hole" even "deep down inside my toilet bowl," "in my TV set," "the library," and among "all the people that I knowed."

Sy Kahn, in "Who's Watching the Man," poses a classic issue for social control theory, asking "Who is watching the man who's watching the man who's watching me?" He doesn't understand why he is a target, because he pays taxes and doesn't vote or criticize. He reports a truck with a telephone company sign next to his house, which has no phone, and new wires on his roof. Unrealistic paranoia toward the end of the song makes its satirical intent clear. He wonders about three men in his barn "trying to read my electric meter through a telescope" and about someone living in his TV set.

In Orwell's *1984,* a video device links mass surveillance with mass communication (Rule, 1984). Individuals have almost no control over being seen or over what they see, hence they are doubly controlled. There are allusions to either or both mass surveillance and mass communication in a number of songs.

XTC's 1979 song "Real by Reel" protests the secret "invading our privacy" as "we play for the ministry." The most mundane acts and private recesses are now subject to documentation. "They" can film you everywhere—in bed, in the bath, when you cry or laugh. The camera can distort "so you won't know what's 'real by reel.'" It can even record "everything you feel."

The television viewer as a manipulated voyeur is a theme in several songs. Siouxsie and the Banshees, in "Monitor," express discomfort at seeing a victim who "looked strangely at the screen." Something too personal has been communicated to a mass audience in the comfort of their living rooms. The singers suggest a double meaning in singing about a "monitor outside for the people inside." This could refer to outside leaders watching citizens, or to a TV monitor for citizens who are outside the system of power to watch and be conditioned by. The monitor offers both a "prevention of crime, [and] a passing of time."

Vigil Cliche, in "The Voyeur," deal with predictable themes such as "private lives up for auction," information overload, and living vicariously through the mass media. As in the Peter Sellers film *Being There*, in which the main character's persona is formed by reflecting back what he sees on television, the singer lacks a firm identity.

The song also directly suggests a rarely acknowledged aspect of being captured on video—narcissism and exhibitionism. Television permits the singer to identify with media stars and to fantasize that he too is a celebrity. More generally, negative reactions to video invasions of personal space are very much tempered by the allure of seeing oneself on the video and feeling important as a result.

"Spy in the Cab," recorded by Bauhaus, is a song protesting the meters that record the driving behavior of truckers. The electronic extension of the employer's vision is resented by the drivers. "Hidden in the dashboard the unseen mechanized eye" with "a set function to pry," brings a "coldly observing" twenty-four-hour "unblinking watch."

In their 1979 "Fingerprint File" the Rolling Stones complain about "feeling followed, feeling tagged." The fingerprint file, "it gets me down." In a rare direct attack: "There's some little jerk in the F.B.I. a' keepin' paper on me ten feet high." Concern is expressed over "listening to me on your satellite," informers who will sell out and testify, and "electric eyes." As in Dylan's "Subterranean Homesick Blues," listeners are urged to be suspicious, lay low, and watch out. The song ends in a whisper: "These days it's all secrecy, no privacy."

Rockwell begins "Somebody's Watching Me" with a synthesized voice asking, "Who's watching me?" Like Sy Kahn, he makes the point that he is just an average man who works "from nine to five" and all he wants "is to be left alone in my average home." The listener is led to ask, "Why would anyone want to monitor him?" The implied answer is that the surveillance is out of control. Even ordinary people there is no reason to suspect become targets, not simply those who "deserve" to be surveilled. We cannot be sure if this is an out-of-control system or a logic of random application to create deterrence through uncertainty.

The singer always feels "like somebody's watching me and I have no privacy." Unlike the singers of religious songs, he does not get a feeling of safety from this surveillance. He wonders "Who's watching me?" It might be neighbors, the mailman, or the IRS. Yet these realistic questions give way to satirical unreality. He wonders if the persons on TV can see him and he is afraid to wash his hair "'cause I might open my eyes and find someone standing there." The latter could also be interpreted as satirizing those who complain about the loss of privacy. It takes something serious to a ridiculous extreme.

Judas Priest, in "Electric Eye" (1982), offers us the bragging voice of an electronic surveillant "up here in space" that has truly awesome powers: it watches all the time; its "lasers trace everything you do"; it probes "all your secret moves"; it is always in focus; its subjects "don't even know I'm there"; it is accurate, offering "pictures that can prove." It correctly equates knowledge with power: "I feed up on your every thought and so my power grows." People think they have private lives, but they should "think nothing of the kind." Unlike some songs that encourage resistance, this one advises, "There is no true escape" and "There's nothing you can do about it."

Paul Simon's "The Boy in the Bubble" suggests ambivalence. Simon catches the power and frenetic rhythms of telecommunications with "lasers in the jungle" and "staccato signals of constant information." With heart transplants and the boy in the bubble, these are "days of miracle and wonder"—yet this appears to be sarcastic, as it comes with images of remote bombs in baby carriages.

Mojo Nixon applies Nancy Reagan's "Just say no" to his defiant "I Ain't Gonna Piss in No Jar" (1987). He can be fired from his job, but something more important can't be robbed "my freedom and my liberty." He urges everybody to go to Washington. If "they want our piss we ought to give it to 'em. Yeah, surround the White House with a urinary moat."

"California Uber Alles," sung by Disposable Heroes of Hiphoprisy, tells of a long series of perceived negative policies by the governor of California.

Although social control is a major theme in rap songs, in general (as with graffiti wall art), they do not deal with the more subtle forms of surveillance. The emphasis is on direct coercion, harassment, and arrest at the hands of uniformed patrol officers. One exception is a Public Enemy song about the FBI infiltration of the Black Panther Party.

Cartoons, Comics, and Jokes

A colleague of Samuel Johnson wrote to him in 1778, "I have tried too in my time to be a philosopher; but, I don't know how, cheerfulness was always breaking in" (quoted in Davis, 1993). The same sentiment applies to the analysis of some of these materials. I have tried in my time to be a serious analytic, systematic sociologist and a righteous social reformer, but in working with these materials cheerfulness was always breaking in.

I have identified four types of surveillance humor: (1) accommodation, (2) machine-human frame breaks, (3) dystopias, and (4) reversals. A given example may fit more than one category, and other categories could be added. I will illustrate the four types with examples from cartoons and comic strips.[3]

The accommodation or cultural assimilation theme involves routinizing and folding into everyday activities new (and sometimes shocking) devices. The technology is domesticated and made familiar through its association with commonplace activities. It may serve as a functional alternative to traditional means. Some illustrations of accommodation surveillance humor follow.

Two businessmen are in an office concluding a deal. The man behind the desk offers his hand and says, "A handshake's good enough for me, Jack. This whole meeting's on videotape anyway." The camera is not seen.

Just before going to bed, a small boy in pajamas says, "I'm clean, mommy." In successive frames the mother checks his hands, face, and ears. In the final frame, the child hands her a bottle as she says "Urinalysis!"

Two men are riding exercise bikes at a gym and one says, "I think we're getting serious—she's springing for a credit check *and* a surveillance on me."

A man visiting a bank's loan department is told, "That's right, sir, no collateral is necessary. However, we will have to chain this little electronic device around your neck."

Two couples are standing talking at a cocktail party and one of the women says, "Franklin can't discuss that—he's under constant electronic surveillance."

A man approaches a suburban house with a white picket fence and encounters a sign reading "Beware of the Technology."

In an office meeting at the IRS audit division a supervisor, accompanied by an employee, tells the director, "Good news! McDonald [the employee] broke into a taxpayer's home computer."

"A handshake's good enough for me, Jack.
This whole meeting's on videotape anyway."

Figure 10.1. By permission of Nick Hobart.

A sign in front of a building with a long line of cars waiting to enter identifies it as "Joe's Drive-Thru Testing Center" offering a variety of testing, including emissions, drugs, blood pressure, polygraph, stress, loyalty, and cholesterol.

A second type of surveillance humor involves an element central to much humor—the breaking of frames. In this case machines, humans, or animals act like each other and cross the boundaries of what is conventionally expected of the type in question. This type of humor is part of a broader genre of person/machine jokes in which the frames that keep these distinct are crossed and the juxtaposition of things we "know" don't go together is humorous. Examples of this type follow.

A man receiving money from an ATM hears the machine say, "Now, remember that this has to last all weekend, so don't spend it foolishly. And don't forget the phone bill." The caption beneath reads "Why the Automated Talking Teller Never Caught On."

In a national park a ranger wearing a bear costume (minus the head) is standing in front of a sign reading "Do Not Feed the Bears" and writing a citation to two tourists who had previously offered the fake bear food.

A sign on the floor of a hotel room reads "This Way Marion Barry." A woman sits seductively on the bed waiting to activate a large mouse

Figure 10.2. By permission of Doug Marlette and Creators Syndicate.

trap and a voice from a closet with hidden video equipment says, "Now remember, no entrapment."

A man puts his feet up on his desk and a sign appears on his computer monitor reading "Take your feet off the desk."

The computer screen of a data entry worker reads "Faster! Faster! You're working 12% slower than the person next to you." Next to her is a smoking robot also entering data into a terminal.

A boss cracking a whip inside a galley ship with data-entry personnel lined up in columns is yelling, "Keystroke! . . . Keystroke!"

Finally, four "Far Side" cartoons:

At night a cow is sitting with several cowboys around a campfire. The cow tells them, "A few cattle are going to stray off in the morning, and tomorrow night a stampede is planned around midnight. Look, I gotta get back. . . . Remember, when we reach Santa Fe, I ain't slaughtered."

A man walking past a dog's house is met by the dog pointing a device at him that reads "Fear-o-sensor."

A couple who are passed out in their backyard wearing electronic collars is captioned "Hours later, when they finally came to, Hal and

THE FAR SIDE   By GARY LARSON

"A few cattle are going to stray off
in the morning, and tomorrow night
a stampede is planned around midnight.
Look, I gotta get back. ... Remember,
when we reach Santa Fe, I ain't slaughtered."

Figure 10.3. Reprinted with permission. All rights reserved.

Ruby groggily returned to their yard work—unknowingly wearing the radio collars and ear tags of alien biologists."

From the inside of a house occupied by whales, a picture window opens onto humans with cameras. One whale is saying to the other, "Uh-oh, Norm. Across the street—whale-watchers."

The third type of surveillance humor is "1984 dystopia," in which the image maker intends to shock us through satire. This says, It's all-powerful, it's everywhere, it's inhuman, it's crazy, and this is what it could/will logically lead to. This also suggests the question, Where will it end? Examples include the following.

A classic "Doonesbury" strip shows a black congressional aide delivering a proposal to his employer in Palm Beach, Florida. At the entry to the town he is stopped by police and asked for his pass card. He responds, "My pass card? You guys are kidding, right?" (This was cartoonist Garry Trudeau's response to a proposed law requiring non-residents of Palm Beach to carry identification while in that city.)

A drawing of Manhattan is captioned "Under new zero-tolerance rules the entire island of Manhattan has been confiscated by federal agents after a marijuana seed was found on West 23rd St. (see detail). Entire island will be sold at auction soon. Includes Brooklyn Bridge."

A second-grade classroom in the midst of great student pandemonium shows FBI agents entering and the teacher saying to them, "Thank heaven you're here." The cartoon is captioned, "Following their orders to investigate domestic terrorist organizations, the FBI checks on Miss Toog's second grade."

Three men are in a restroom looking in (unbeknownst to them) a one-way mirror. One says, "Company lie detector tests, company urine tests, I swear, where's it all gonna end?" What they don't see is the man on the other side of the mirror taking notes on their conversation.

Two men are talking. The first says, "Your wife just gave you that beautiful gold watch a week ago—now she's divorcing you?" The second, holding up his wrist, says, "It has a surveillance camera in it."

The cartoon "Sylvia" shows SuperCop exhorting a couple in bed: "The national average is 2.5 times a week." The man says, "She's here again," and the woman responds, "Tell her we're doing the best we can."

The final form of surveillance humor involves "reversals." Here an action may backfire and machines go out of control or end up being used in unanticipated ways. Charlie Chaplin's *Modern Times* remains the classic example of this type of humor; in one sequence in the film, he is literally drawn into an assembly line. The hubris of humans in thinking they are in control is revealed, as is the latent threat involved in tampering with the unknown. Actors are hoist with their own petards. Unintended consequences and surprise accompany innovations. Mistakes occur. The reliability and validity of the machine's results are questioned. The last laugh or revenge may even be had by the subject of the surveillance. The usual power relations enhanced by the technology may be reversed, or a device may be so out of control that everything gets destroyed. Some illustrations follow:

In a "Bloom County" cartoon, police with drawn weapons break into a man's house, having been called by the man's young son, who told them his father was using drugs. The son, in obvious response to educational efforts at school, says, "I just couldn't stand by and watch you flush your life down the toilet, dad!!" The police officer next asks the son what drugs are involved. The boy replies, "Tobacco, caffeine, Schlitz . . . you name it."

A couple sitting on a sofa are about to kiss when suddenly a loud siren goes off. The man exclaims, "Damn! I forgot to disconnect my personal alarm system."

A couple are lying in bed and the man says, "Not tonight, hon. It'll just wreak havoc with the motion sensors again."

A couple at home are watching a politician on TV giving a campaign speech; a device of some kind is attached to their television set. The husband states, "According to the voice-stress analyzer, he is not going to lower taxes."

A barricade in the middle of a blocked-off street has written on it, "POLICE LINE—NO VIDEO CAMERAS BEYOND THIS POINT."

Illustrations

Newspaper and magazine articles, editorials, and professional, business, and social movement communications concerned with surveillance and technology are often accompanied by illustrations or political cartoons.

Given the continuous flow of social interaction and words in everyday life, the communication of meaning through a single frozen frame is an accomplishment. As Erving Goffman (1979) notes, this is accomplished by a variety of conventionalized cues. The best-known visual symbol of surveillance is the eye, followed by the ear. This reflects sight and hearing's centrality to surveillance relative to the other senses. It is also more difficult to depict visually the contents of smelling, tasting, and feeling, and even the activity of the last of these.

The emblem of the Pinkerton National Detective Agency—a simple

"Damn! I forgot to disconnect my personal alarm system."

Figure 10.4. Drawing by Mankoff; copyright 1991 The New Yorker Magazine, Inc.

eye with the slogan "We Never Sleep"—is a good illustration. It suggests the agency's dedication to duty and the threat in its omnipresence. A public service poster from the MIT Campus Police shows a large computer-drawn eye made up of many visible dots and includes this message: "Counting your eyes there are about 18,000 eyes on our campus. There are only 52 in the MIT Campus Police Department. If you see something suspicious give us a call." An article on databases uses for illustration the familiar cue of an eye looking through a keyhole. WAC, a social movement concerned with stopping violence against women, has as its symbol an eye surrounded by the words "WAC IS WATCHING WOMEN TAKE ACTION." These have a direct, literal quality. We immediately understand the implications of a watchful eye.

Yet literal visual representations of surveillance are not common. The medium of drawing offers creative possibilities beyond traditional photography or testimony in court, which is more bounded by the reality. Common to many illustrations is the breaking of frames, in which things that are not usually together, or could never be together, in the real world are joined. As in humor, breaking frames is attention getting and often is seen as "interesting." Many surveillance-themed illustrations involve the grafting of two discrete elements together with a transfer of meaning (whether reciprocal or one-way) between objects. As with much linguistic communication, something new comes to be understood by reference to something already known. The familiar serves to inform or to offer a new way to think about the unfamiliar.

As with surveillance jokes, a common frame break in illustrations involves the merging of the human and the nonhuman. Eyes, ears, and technologies for enhancing seeing and hearing (magnifying glasses, binoculars, telescopes, microphones) are joined to elements that they are not (and generally could not be) joined to in reality. We see human-like technology and humans as machines. Some examples include the following:

A drawing accompanying a story about Caller ID in which the telephone earpiece contains an eye behind a peephole

An eye coming out of a computer, monitoring a worker

A boss with X-ray vision peering at a worker

An eye in the center of a computer disk

The wings of the American eagle converted into elongated ears (in response to Watergate)

A microphone in the raised arm and binoculars to the eyes of the Statue of Liberty

A Superman-like figure coming out of the top of a telephone

A computer printout coming from a man's chest while he holds a shopping bag and TV set, illustrating marketing research that joins television ad watching with shopping

An illustration for a story titled "From G-Man to Cursor-Man" showing a large mainframe computer wearing a jacket and a hat

A phone following a man around as an illustration of personal mobile phones

An individual standing under the lens of a giant microscope or under a magnifying glass intended to illustrate DNA testing

A bar code half covering a face (the symbol of a Dutch social movement concerned with data protection)

Although the vast majority of the articles these illustrations accompany include at least implied warnings and some ambivalence about the technology, images of individuals as direct victims are not common. An example of such an illustration is one of a man holding up a hand to block a spotlight that is shining down on him. Other examples include a drawing of persons cowering inside their homes as an unfriendly surveillance eye shines down on the houses and one in which a roof is lifted off a house to permit a view of the interior from above.

The technique of helping us understand something new by reference to something old can be seen in an illustration depicting a DNA identification card. This shows a double helix and some numbers that would be meaningless to most people, yet when these are made part of a familiar ID card, the meaning is very clear.

The idea of the "data shadow" or "data image" has been illustrated by showing a person with a shadow or a head made up of the kinds of personal data stored in computer databases. This shows the person as visible and suggests new meanings of the self or personhood.

The use of visual metaphor can be seen in the case of the politician skewered on the antenna of his cordless phone. He was overheard talking to his mistress, and when this information became public, it damaged his political career. This illustration presents a literal rendering of the damage done.

The verbal cliché is sometimes the subject of an illustration, as in a drawing of a wall with eyes and ears ("the walls have ears") and a federal agent holding up a spider's web with a gun in the center. This illustrated a news story about a gun purchase sting that bordered on entrapment—a web was spun for the suspect and bait was offered.[4]

Exaggeration is also used to make a point. One story about parents using beepers to locate their teenagers was illustrated with a drawing of a youth wearing four different-colored beepers on a belt.

A final element in surveillance-themed illustrations involves the extent to which they are moving and memorable. Does a picture make one take notice and want to comment on it to others? Is it something that stays with the observer (much as most people who have seen Edvard Munch's *The Scream* or the last scenes in *Casablanca* are likely to remember them). There is of course variation, but this is likely patterned and related to the characteristics of the individual and the material. What are some of the characteristics of memorable images? To answer this question fully would require a phenomenological analysis of the materials in which one studies how individuals make sense of

Figure 10.5. By permission of Roy Peterson, *Maclean's*.

the material. Judging only from my own responses, the most memorable images are those that mix the sacred and the profane and that build upon the historical memory of the viewer. Images of the American eagle and the Statue of Liberty joined to the dirty tools of eavesdropping are memorable. A drawing of a wrist with a bar code (from a book of German political cartoons) is moving because viewers bring to it their knowledge about concentration camp victims with numbers on their wrists.

Advertisements

In contrast to the kinds of illustrations discussed above, images in ads generally show less creativity and frame breaking. They are more straightforward. They describe a product or service and make more use of words along with the images. This greater realism reflects their partisanship in the promotion of tangible products rather than abstract ideas, which may be illustrated in a more balanced, or at least broader, fashion. In showing only a representational photograph of a product, an ad lets it speak for itself, although assumptions are made about how the audience will fill in the blanks.

This direct approach is illustrated by one ad that shows a variety of devices and simply asks, "Where can you go to see and hear what your eyes and ears can't?" No explanations or justifications are offered. The ad implies that it is obvious why you would want to do this, and there is no lurking moral ambiguity. Even more minimalist are some of the handwritten signs I have seen on the University of Washington campus—"Seattle Surveillance Specialists the cheapest rates in town."

However, when ads are undertaken to promote political agendas or films—such as the ads included here for the American Newspaper Publishers Association and for the 1991 movie *Kafka*—we often see greater imagination and framebreaking.

Western culture, and in some ways particularly the United States, is ambivalent about surveillance as a reflection of its more general attitudes toward power. We seek to be protected by surveillance and welcome the watchful eye of the protector. Yet we also fear the invasive or evil eye that breaks the boundaries between self and others and the group and society.

Not surprisingly, ads tend to emphasize the positive and ignore the negative aspects of surveillance. They deal with volatile material and are as interesting for what they say as for what they fail to say. Ads may provide legitimations and deny the nasty potential and normative violations made possible by surveillance. A television ad for a directional microphone asks, "Are you a curious person?"; an ad for a device designed to allow one to hear sounds from the other side of a

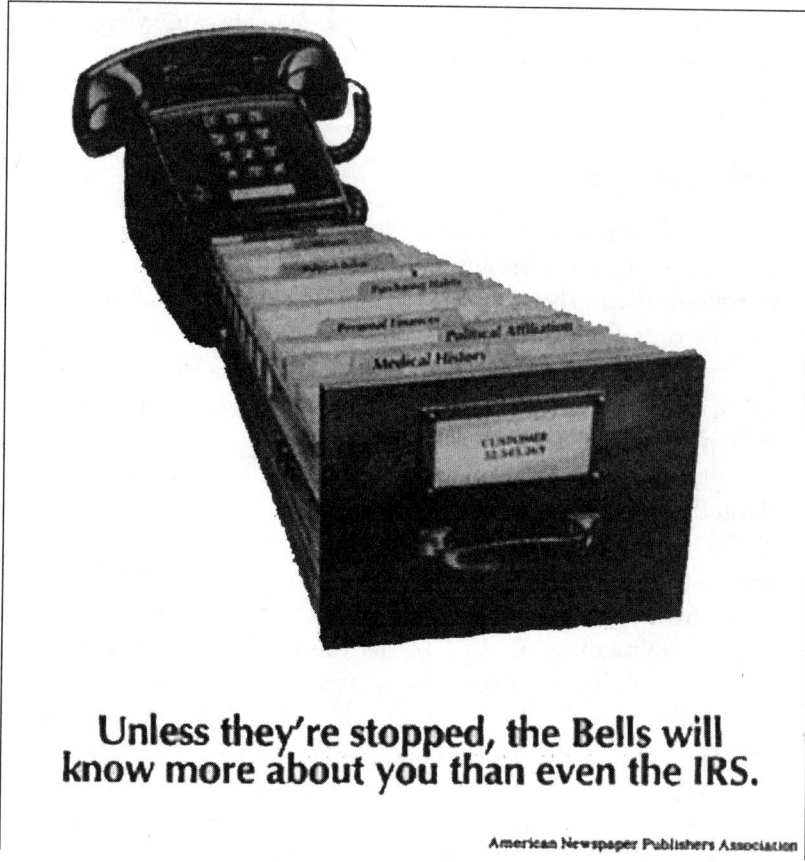

Unless they're stopped, the Bells will know more about you than even the IRS.

American Newspaper Publishers Association

Figure 10.6. Newspapers are conducting a blunt ad campaign against Bell telephone companies to keep them out of the information services business.

wall euphemistically invites the viewer to "diagnose sounds through a solid surface from any source"; an ad for an eavesdropping device that look like a radio "focuses ambient sounds onto a sensitive microphone"; a children's ad for "Super Ears" pushes the product's uses for listening to the sounds of nature. A Washington State appeal for motorists to report those driving illegally in special car pool lanes says, "Thanks for being a HERO" and invites them to call 764-HERO. A purveyor of surveillance technologies reports that his goods "empower the consumer."

Relatively few ads show the direct and honest appeal of one inviting you to "Eavesdrop for under $80!" And such a bargain! "You'd

Figure 10.7. Jeremy Irons in the title role of the Steven Soderbergh film *Kafka*.

expect to pay double for a mini-recorder . . . especially one that's voice-activated." Also straightforward is an ad for "electronic ears disguised as a radio," which shows a happy image of birthday domesticity and the caption, "People assume you're listening to a radio. In fact, you're hearing every word of their conversation . . . literally gives you super-hearing." It is also "fun for amateur spying."

An ad for a surveillance book shows a wolf's eyes peering out and asks, "Are you a hunter or the hunted?" The obvious implication is that it is better to be a hunter and to strike first. Consistent with the idea that the best defense is a good offense, some ads gloss over the potential for customers to use the products for aggressive gathering of information on others; instead, they redefine the technology as a defensive measure to protect oneself from snooping. There is line blurring with respect to the often morally suspect offensive uses and the more easily justified defensive uses of the technology.[5]

The name of a national chain that sells spying devices, Counter Spy Shop, suggests justification through the need for protection. One of its products, "the briefcase that sees everything," can be used to "capture theft, conspiracy or break-ins on tape!" Unstated is that it can just as easily be used as part of a theft or conspiracy and that, whatever its ostensible goal, its secret use in some states may constitute a felony.

Similarly, an ad for the widely publicized "secret connection briefcase" simply asks, "Bugged?" This implies a need to be protected. The first feature listed is a "pocket sized tape recorder detector [that] lets you know if someone is secretly recording your conversation." It also includes an "incredible 6 hour recorder—so small it fits in a cigarette pack." Although the ad does not say so, the latter is intended for use in secretly taping others, assuming they don't also have a detector.

Some of the largest security companies profit from this amoral mix by selling both surveillance and antisurveillance devices. Outside of specialized publications, there are few ads for devices designed for protecting oneself from the snooping of others. The public market for snooping seems much larger than that for protective devices.

Deception and lying may be defined in ads as "pretending." Thus an ad for a call-forwarding device reports that you can be at home and pretend to be at the office, and "best of all, the person calling never knows." Rather than words such as *secret, hidden, covert, snoop,* or *spy,* we see "discreet viewing," the possibility of "less conspicuous use," the ability to "unobtrusively snap a photo" or to gather information "unobserved."[6] A telephone conversation recorder "automatically records your conversations for replay so that you can concentrate on your call and later retrieve information without the bother of time-consuming note taking." Unstated are the advantages that a secret recording can offer "without the bother of having to ask permission."

Attention may be guided away from what the product is used for, or the conditions of its use, and toward its other attributes, such as design or materials. This offers other reasons for the purchase. For example, "The M3 is housed in a nice Parker knock off pen, so you not only get the best recording possible, the pen housing shows a bit of class as well." A camera hiding in a lighter has an "impressive enamel like finish and gold trim."

An osmosislike transfer of legitimacy may be suggested by reference to valued symbols. The aura of science, with its suggestion of modernity, power, efficiency, and certainty, is often drawn upon with terms such as "sophisticated technology," "high tech," "the scientific mea-

BUGGED?
THE SECRET CONNECTION BRIEFCASE

Pocket sized tape recorder detector lets you know if someone is secretly recording your conversation.

Micro-miniature hidden bug detection system lets you know if you're being bugged.

Ultra compact high powered portable communication system.

Miniature voice stress analyzer lets you know when someone is lying.

Siren alarm system alerts you if briefcase is stolen.

Built-in scrambler for total telephone privacy.

Super sensitive bomb sniffer warns you of hidden explosives.

Incredible 6 hour recorder—so small it fits in a cigarette pack.

Portable defense system gives you non-harmful protection against attackers.

Lined with bullet proof fabric that shields you against .357 Magnum.

World's first wireless telephone with an incredible 30 mile range.

Figure 10.8

sure of truth," "ultraminiaturized," "solid-state electronics," "integrated circuitry," "voice stress computer," "electronic analysis."

Hiding a video camera or an alarm in a warm cuddly object such as a teddy bear not only is intended to deceive but may make the transition to secret spying or alarms easier. A picture of a child hugging a big doll accompanies an ad for a baby monitor that permits you "to listen to what the children are up to."

The transference may involve esteemed sponsors or carriers whose use sanctifies or vouches for use by the ordinary person. The technology may be built to "military specifications" or may have been "originally designed for the DEA"; it may be "the same sophisticated technology used by professionals" or "used by U.S. government agencies." An ad for "electronic ears disguised as a radio" invites the user to "hear like a super hero."

The advertisements seek to show how the product is needed by, or serves the interests of, the consumer. In extreme cases this is even extended to the subject of the surveillance. For example, an ad regarding "new technology in the office" from United Technology informs us that it's all about "fun."

Some ads may attempt to create or manipulate fear. They may draw on a sense of responsibility or obligation. Ads for protective devices for children may imply that if you really love your child you have a duty to purchase the product.

The effort to generate anxiety and then to offer a means of coping with it is clearest in ads for defensive products and services. An ad for an intrusion detector shows a shadowy burglar breaking in, with the caption "Chances are that your home and both your vehicles don't have security alarms. Your daughter or son, away at college, are probably relatively defenseless as well." But not to worry, the simple Security Monitor will solve all problems. An ad for Child Guardian shows a smiling child wearing his electronic sensor on a belt but warns that "the number of child abductions each year grows increasingly alarming." But with Child Guardian, "your active youngster is under a 'watchful eye' every moment." An ad for Guardian Angel that includes an idyllic picture of a child playing warns, "It can happen anywhere: one moment your child is playing at your side. The next, he or she is gone." An ad for a drug testing system reports that "teen age drug abuse is our #1 problem" and shows a worried mom saying, "Something was wrong with my son but he'd insist things were O.K." Ordering the drug testing kit helped her "find the problem and helped put my family back together." An ad for a "memo muncher" asks, What is the cost of a memo seen by "a wrong person"? Is "your competition looking through your garbage at night?" Even absent that you can't be certain—"People are naturally inquisitive and you can never be quite sure that some private document doesn't end up in the wrong hands." Unless of course you spend $300 on their product. An ad in a computer magazine advises "GET DEFENSIVE! YOU CAN'T SEE THEM BUT YOU KNOW THEY'RE THERE. Hackers pose an invisible but serious threat to your information system."

The legal or ethical uses of a product may be mentioned, but with the understanding that other uses are possible. The choice, then, is the user's, and not in the product as such. Thus a voice stress computer "can sit on a desk or inside a drawer." The PB1 Mini Parabolic Mic System "should find application in situations from big game hunting to legal recording." An automatic telephone conversation recorder is "small enough to fit discretely underneath or next to your telephone."

Although much of the technology is new, the marketing of surveillance in work settings is not. A series of ads for "accounting and writing machines" from *Business Week* magazine in 1929, which by today's standards seem crude and even eerie in their directness, make visible verbal clichés such as "an eye for every angle of your business."

Computer programs called PEEK and SPY are more contemporary versions that let the employer do just that. To increase security, monitor production, and aid in training, the operator may peek at a "target" user's computer, but with the user's permission and he or she "may disallow watching at any time." The SPY program permits monitoring computer use without the user's knowledge or permission. In trying to convey the surveillance possibilities, an ad—intended to be humorous—shows a manager's neck stuck into a computer screen, a wire running to a workstation, and then a head coming out of the screen, watching.

The relative absence of actors makes these materials more difficult to analyze than the gender commercials studied by Erving Goffman (1979). Yet there is a clear gender component when humans are depicted. In most cases when a user is shown it is a man. Consistent with muting what actually goes on, and to avoid stimulating a sympathetic counterreaction, rarely is the object of the surveillance shown.

When it is, it is likely to be a subordinate, such as a child, worker, or prisoner. Women are more likely than men to serve as objects.

This illustrates what Foucault calls the male gaze and may reflect erotic curiosity and men's generally greater interest in technology. An implicit link between sex and violence may be seen in an ad that shows an attractive female within the viewfinder of a camera—which could equally be a rifle scope. For example, one ad for a book on surveillance shows an attractive woman in such a scope, and an ad for a nightscope frames a scantily clad woman in its lenses. It is captioned, "The dark holds no secrets with the night penetrator." This is "ideal for discreet viewing or map-reading, nocturnal wild life and astronomic observation, or maritime navigation." If that is so, one wonders why the ad shows a woman as the subject of surveillance. I have found only two ads that involve women as users, and no examples of the female gaze, in which a man is the object of technology applied by a woman.[7]

The ads reflect normative patterns in which it is more common for men to look at women than the reverse. Whether or not the male impetus to look is stronger, it is less socially inhibited.[8] Increased feminist consciousness and awareness of sexual harassment may further

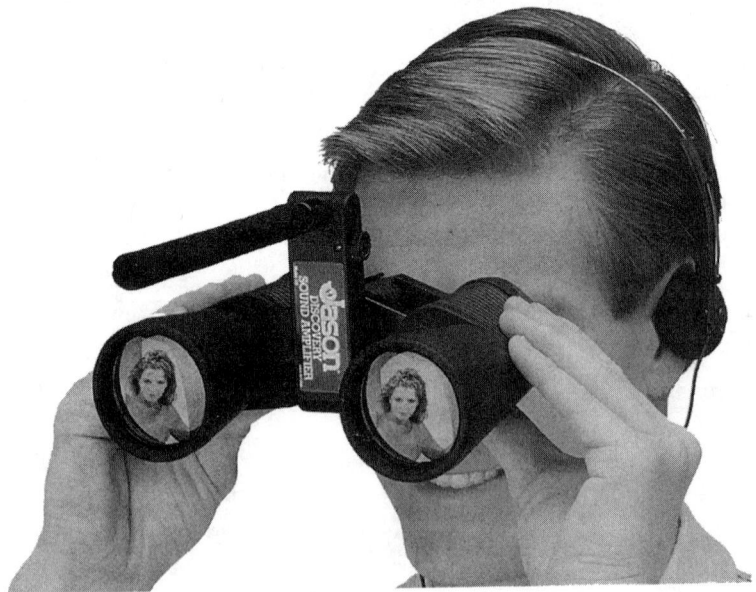

Figure 10.9

enhance the male market for covert surveillance devices, as the norma-tive boundaries become more restricted. But it may also mean greater equality in the gaze. We might expect more ads showing females as users, with males as objects of surveillance.[9]

Visual Art

Contemporary artists, in reflecting the material culture and cultural themes of their time, have turned to surveillance media and topics—using the technology to reveal unseen elements and to help us experience surveillance.

Although the inert eye, from Dalí and Magritte to the engraver of the U.S. dollar bill, has always been a theme, video and related tech-nologies offer new possibilities—particularly for performance art, which directly involves the audience and which merges, or at least breaks down, the conventional differences between subject and object. Video art, because of its real-time quality and mixing of images and sound, is an ideal medium for the artist concerned with surveillance themes. It offers temporal continuity and breadth and hence is more comprehensive than still photography.

Illustrative of the breakdown between art and reality is the work of artist Julia Scher.[10] Scher obtains loans and donations of equipment in order to reveal the conflict between the need for protection and the possibility of being victimized by the particular apparatus. Her art exemplifies what it seeks to communicate. Unlike fiction, it does not imitate reality. Rather, like cinema verité, it tries to capture something that is there. It reflects and creates reality. In a 1987 group exhibit in Los Angeles titled *Surveillance,* she placed the gallery itself under sur-veillance.[11] Viewers became part of the spectacle. The viewer's body heat tripped invisibly projected infrared beams at the entrance to the building. This caused flashing lights and an alarm (embedded in a rep-resentation of a human torso on the wall) to go off.

In another exhibit, Scher created a mock interrogation room in which subjects enter their names into a computer and then see their images on the screen along with a list of crimes they are (wrongly) accused of committing. Surveillance cameras are set up in various rooms permitting subjects to see themselves and others as they pass through the rooms. Reality and art fuse, as do target and agent. The surveillance cameras are not an invented form that mimics reality. This differs from "real" surveillance only because of its context and goals. The artist recontextualizes the technology in order to critique and even expose it. Her goal is to educate or entertain rather than to surveil. The viewer experiences video surveillance as both the object who is watched and the subject doing the watching.[12]

This self-monitoring is a form of biofeedback and illustrates one theme of contemporary surveillance societies: the voyeur and the exhibitionist may be merged. For those who are there, it is participatory art. It can be a mocking form and can involve playacting, as the participant chooses it and is aware of it. But it is not simply pretend. Further mixing elements is the fact that when Scher is not doing art, she runs a company named Safe and Secure, which installs surveillance systems.

Artist Richard Lowenberg uses contemporary military and industrial surveillance technology to reveal protected or unseen things—such as an air force satellite communications receiver or invisible heat patterns made by dancers. Absent technical supports, these are unseen because of distance, darkness, or barriers such as walls and skin.

Lowenberg's unobtrusive night work uses darkness-illuminating technologies. There are no telltale flashbulbs to give it away. Although his photographic art is hidden in darkness, the technology he uses pierces a barrier that for most of human history has protected information. The image intensifier (or nightscope) amplifies starlight twenty thousand times and FLIR (forward-looking infrared) systems need no light at all. The FLIR uses infrared sensors to provide a high-resolution thermal video display. It makes visible what we would experience (if we were aware of it at all) only as temperature variations, even though the infrared spectrum is omnipresent. The FLIR offers a shifting window into an ever-present thermodynamic world unaffected by light or darkness. This technology permits us to see in the dark and to see things that for normal communications purposes are not really (or at least practically) there.

For Lowenberg, thermal patterns serve as a kind of invisible ink. He produces temperature prints using a heat-reflective screen. We see variations in temperature rather than light—the darker the color, the warmer the area. In one example, using the FLIR imager he videotaped a dance performance that occurred in complete darkness. Dancers dipped their hands in water and finger-painted on a blank wall. As the temperature of the water gradually changes, amazing patterns are seen on the wall, even though neither the audience nor the dancers could see this absent the conversion of heat variations to light and dark hues.

In another example of using technologies to surface the unseen (but not purposefully hidden), Nina Sobel offers a visual representation of ever-present, but rarely seen, brain waves. Her *Encephalographic Video Drawings* records brain waves on video. In a unique example of self-monitoring, individuals confront their own previously unseen "mediated images." What is reflected is "real," even though the medium for showing it is not the phenomenon as such.

Given a free market and the double-edged, multiple-use potential of any technology, the usual workings of surveillance from the more to the less powerful can be highlighted and reversed. Paul Ryan and Michael Shamberg use video technology to watch the watchers—to catch them in the act, so to speak. In a 1969 video called *Supermarket,* they document a video surveillance system in a Safeway store—recording a large sign that says, "Smile, you are on photo-scan TV." The store manager tells them to stop and that it is illegal to shoot images in the store, to which they respond, "You're taking pictures of us, so why can't we take pictures of you?" This of course raises the first question of social analysis: Says who?

Another example of using technology to survey the surveyors can be seen in the film *Red Squad,* based on a New York collective following and interviewing police red squad members. This becomes reciprocal as they then become the subject of the red squad's gaze as well. Artist Lewis Stein takes pictures of surveillance equipment. Rick Preliner, in an audio scanning installation called *Listening Post,* permitted the gallerygoer to eavesdrop on airwaves used by federal agents and local police in the Los Angeles area.

Another form of artistic expression does not focus directly on surveillors as subjects, but intercepts their data on others. This represents an egalitarian sharing of the data or, in Susan Sontag's words, the "democratization of the evidence." Here the artist, like the control agent, invades the private space of the subject, but with a different purpose—to demythologize, authenticate, or question. We are shown what authorities see and hear about others.

Maria Kramer's video installation goes straight to the source. *Jean Seberg/The FBI/The Media* uses FBI documents to report on the U.S. countersurveillance activities directed at the actress. By enlarging and then displaying the documents, Kramer exposes (in both meanings of the term) the surveillance activities that may have shortened Seberg's life.

Michael Klier's Der Reece ("the giant") uses images from video surveillance cameras in a variety of urban settings to create a composite work. Louis Hock's *The Mexican Tapes: A Chronicle of Life Outside the Law* is a video narrative using night vision technology applied to three Mexican illegal immigrant families.

In *Abscam (Framed)*, Chip Lord mixes real surveillance data with fictional material. He plays a whispering newsman who returns to the scene and thus adds "fake" material. But given the fact that Abscam itself was, to a large degree, an artifact of the agents' intervention (creating a fake setting with some very attractive unrealistic inducements), such work raises deeper questions about just what *real* means. The ability to retouch or to create photo images digitally (e.g., as when *National Geographic* altered the size of a pyramid to fit its cover) raises related questions.

Gary Lloyd's *Radio Painting* (1983) is a canvas with a low-power FM radio transmitter embedded in it, so that anyone speaking within the presence of the work has his or her voice transmitted within a five-block range. Here the artist exercises some control over the "critic" by enforcing publicity and broadening the number of critics. The artist is in a position to hear the remarks made in front of the painting.

Artists also use more conventional tools to invade privacy and make public what is usually not recorded. Photographers traditionally have done this. Walker Evans used a concealed Leica camera for his famous series of New York subway photos.

French photographer and conceptual artist Sophie Calle has done a number of things along this line. She once randomly picked a man from a crowd and followed him to Venice, where she photographed him and kept notes of his activities. She took a job as a hotel maid and photographed the possessions and interiors of the same room over a three-week period as different persons stayed there. She invited strangers to her own apartment and photographed them while they slept. Once, she had her mother hire a private detective to follow and photograph her on a particular day. The detective did not know that the artist knew about and had arranged the surveillance. She recorded her feelings and imaginings as she went about the day—knowing she was being recorded and watched, but not when, where, or by whom. The resulting artwork juxtaposes the surveillance photos with her own conjectures and artificially manufactured emotions. This powerfully conveys her experiences of suspicion and paranoia, as the detective could have been anyone she saw that day.

In a variation of a Garfinkel or Goffman experiment, Calle has reported finding an address book and photocopying it, before returning it to its owner. She then called everyone in it and asked if she could interview them about the book's owner, without ever encountering him.

Some Implications

In the first instance, the materials discussed above literally or symbolically speak for themselves. As with a good meal, the value comes from the experience. Films such as *Rear Window*, the *Conversation*, and *Kafka*; songs such as "I Ain't Gonna Piss in No Jar"; and images of a robotic arm, with its hint of a skeleton cradling or crushing flowers, give us a jolt and a type of understanding that is otherwise unobtainable. This involves not only *Verstehen*, or understanding what another person experiences, but a nonreflective shock. These materials certainly can (and must) be considered on their own terms. There is wisdom in E. B. White's observation that "humor can be dissected as a frog can, but it dies in the process."

I would certainly not want to profane the sacred by connecting urine in a cup with the president's wife, nor would I have abstract emotionless analysis detract from the artistic experience. The broad exploratory approach taken here does not lend itself to a rigorous model of scientific hypothesis testing. Rather than deductively straining these materials through varieties of available theory, I will proceed inductively and indicate the theoretical implications that I find in the material.

Social scientists generally draw too rigid a line between their data and the offerings of the artist. Artistic creations can significantly inform us about surveillance and society. They can be approached from the standpoint of the sociology of knowledge and we can ask about the messages conveyed, how this has changed, and how it correlates with the characteristics of the creator and the context. Here art is treated as a dependent variable. But the materials can also inform us about broader societal issues, and we can speculate on their social impact.

I will consider below implications involving (1) education, (2) conflict, (3) power, (4) conflicting and uncertain values, (5) contextual meaning, (6) the need for research on the social impact of such material, and (7) comparisons between art and science as ways of knowing.

1. *These materials can help us see and understand (whether emotionally or cognitively) new developments in surveillance.* They offer an alternative language through visual metaphors. The meaning of authoritarianism, repression, domination, intolerance, and spying is likely to be different when experienced vicariously through seeing and hearing, rather than through reading and quantifying. The traditional role of the artist in making the unseen visible has a particularly appropriate meaning here. Such media can educate in a distinctive and perhaps more profound sense than can the exclusively verbal. They can help us see and experience in different ways, especially things that are new. For example, we can more readily understand electronic data and microscopic DNA sequences when they are transformed into images through artistic representations.

These new ways of seeing may include the idea of an alternative way of constructing the self, such as through the data image or shadow (Laudon, 1986; Clarke, 1994; Lyon, 1994). The meaning of personhood is changing. An image that shows a human form that is nothing more than credit card transactions and identifying numbers gives you the sense that there is another "you" out there, largely beyond your knowledge and control, that others have access to and even own.

The ease with which data can be distorted and manipulated is also illustrated by these materials. For example, computers make possible the distortion of a face or physical presence (the film *Rising Sun* gives a good example) and the mixture of real and nonexistent elements. When we actually see a "photograph" or image of something that has never existed (a horse's head on the body of a person, or an Egyptian pyramid of altered proportions, for instance) we can more easily come to appreciate the increased possibilities for deception and to question the validity of visual images. In this sense, "seeing is believing"—at least believing that we should not believe. This has major implications for courtroom evidence as well as for other presentations. Materials such as those discussed above can communicate the fragmented and movable quality of the "realities" we perceive, and may lead to a healthy skepticism—or an immobilizing paranoia.

The blurring line between human and nonhuman—robots, cyborgs, implants—is more easily grasped when we see the results through artists' imaginary creations. And finally, materials such as those addressed in this essay can help us grasp the scale, totality, comprehensiveness, and simultaneity of the new forms of surveillance across multiple dimensions. We can literally more easily see the big picture. The cartoon described above regarding the "drive-in testing service" is a good example of this, as are video pastiches made from far-flung surveillance cameras.

Artistic materials can educate and politicize by telling us what is happening and by offering warnings. They can bring the news to broader audiences (e.g., the cartoon about Palm Beach and the one featuring a computer telling an employee to work faster), in that they may have a wider audience and may use potentially more powerful and poignant means of conveying their messages.

2. *A struggle is going on over what surveillance technology means and how it ought to be viewed.* While we must be skeptical of simplistic determinisms, image and interest are often linked. To oversimplify, this involves conflicts over symbols and words, with vendors and dominants on one side (e.g., security companies, managers, various guardians) and subordinates, civil libertarians, skeptics, and resisting social movements on the other. Each side has allies in culture production. For the former, these tend to be manufacturers, advertising agencies, and their glorification of surveillance. For the latter, these tend to be cartoonists, popular songwriters, and artists who demystify, expose, and delegitimate. Reduced to essentials, the artists tend to view technology as the enemy or the problem, and the advertisers view it as the savior or the solution. The sides are mirror opposites. It is an interesting exercise to fill in the other half of the story. Such work is as revealing for what it says as for what it does not say.

Art and politics are often treated as if they are more independent than is the case. Scottish poet Ernest Fletcher said, "Let me write poems, I care not who writes the laws." Plato, on the other hand, wanted poets to be controlled by the state—and with good reason, from an establishment perspective.

3. *A related point is that these materials remind us that surveillance is often about power.* Many of the visual and textual messages make it clear that there are those in the role of controller and those who are controlled (managers and workers, men and women, parents and children, guards and prisoners, merchants and consumers). The notion of the all-powerful, all-knowing entity—whether involving God, super-

heroes, government, bosses, or parents—is so embedded in our culture as to be commonplace, and we rarely take note of it. It is against this backdrop that many of these materials are offered. As subordinates in some or many of the roles we play, we are in a position to understand this and can readily identify with the subject's experience.

4. *The materials also suggest that our relatively democratic and egalitarian society is uncomfortable with the naked facts and brute force of power.* Hence many of the messages are subtle, use euphemisms (bugging devices as "diagnostic tools"), deal only with the positive aspects of surveillance technology (nightscopes as great for watching nocturnal animals), and seek to transfer warm feelings from one type of object (e.g., a teddy bear) to another, unpleasant, type (e.g., a hidden camera).

Such treatment indicates the value conflicts and resulting profound ambivalence of our culture toward surveillance. These materials may convey the omnipresent, omnipotent, omniscient character of surveillance and, in so doing, its similarity to an all-knowing God. We are both fascinated (especially in North America) and repelled by it. It honors fantasies of omnipotence and desire for control and reinforces our fears of the inhuman and inhumane mechanistic. This ambivalence can be seen more generally in the contrasting views of the evil eye and the eye of God. The technology can both protect and violate. An important issue for study is whether this ambivalence has lessened in recent decades as concerns about security, productivity, and health have increased.

The ambivalence one can read into this material also reflects *value uncertainty* beyond value conflicts, in which meaning is unclear and still being negotiated as new products and uses continually appear. Conflicting laws, policies, and public opinion data also suggest this.

In this sense, culture is not a perfectly integrated system, but an ever-changing crazy quilt made of bits and pieces that are barely held together by weak threads, which often pull in opposing directions. Whether in physics or morality, this results in tension.

5. *We see that the meaning is not in the object, but in the context and how it is interpreted.* Thus electronic location monitoring technology used to confine those under judicial supervision may be presented and viewed as different from the same technology used to protect abused spouses, children, and those with Alzheimer's disease.

6. *This material calls attention to areas for social research.* It is

important to study the social functions and consequences of this material. How do audiences fill in the blanks? Like paint-by-number kits, these materials are often unfinished, and they rely on our bringing the connecting lines and colors to them. We need a better ecology of perceptions and values that will tell us what people see, or hear, when given a vague surveillance stimulus. The creators and owners of culture think they know (especially advertisers). But what images and assumptions do they hold, and are they correct? To what extent do they lead or follow? Do they reflect or create?

On balance, what is the net effect of popular media in creating an environment that welcomes, tolerates, or opposes the new surveillance? Does it educate for citizenship in a democratic society and create a healthy skepticism and even indignation? Does it demoralize and depress and create an immobilizing paranoia and beliefs that the technology is more powerful than it really is, and that we are in the iron grasp of an unstoppable technological determinism? Does this material subtly prepare us, prime the pump, create a receptive (if not necessarily overly welcoming) public, softening us up, much as long-range artillery does, before an assault? As social fictions and reality are blurred, what happens? What is the impact of songs such as "Secret Agent Man" and the television programs associated with them? What was the impact of *Candid Camera* in making a joke out of video invasions and deception, or of today's home video shows that treat these as entertainment or merely as the means of creating entries for competitions to win prizes? Does constant media exposure normalize, routinize, domesticate, and trivialize surveillance?

7. *Finally, this material reminds us of the parallel between science and art, as both may seek to go beneath surface realities and to question conventions.* For example, Richard Lowenberg's unmasking of the electromagnetic environment shares the goal of some researchers in mapping and making visible the invisible world. The sociologist does this when he or she analyzes latent functions and unintended consequences, demystifies social practices, and identifies the obfuscatory role that ideology and words can play (Marx, 1972). It would be useful to compare the work of artists and scientists discussed here with respect to subjects, presentation, and audience response, as well as to understand reciprocal influences among these two somewhat different, if overlapping, ways of knowing.

Notes

This essay draws from my forthcoming publication, *Windows into the Soul: Surveillance and Society in an Age of High Technology,* ASA-Duke University Jensen Lectures. I am grateful to Ann-Marie Wood, Jen Owen, Deborah Irmas, Mathieu Deflem, and Eve Darian-Smith for their help.

1. It is of course possible that the search is for a particular individual who does not want to be found, but given our notions of choice, that would put the singer in a negative light—pursuing someone who has rejected him. By the 1990s, antistalking laws criminalized such actions.

2. Of course, the adventure, bravery, self-sacrifice, and patriotism this song suggests can also be viewed positively.

3. Copyright and resource restrictions prevent my reproducing here more than a fraction of the materials discussed. However, I will provide them to readers who contact me c/o Department of Sociology, University of Colorado, Boulder, CO 80309.

4. Comprehending some illustrations fully requires effort, as most people respond to images directly and—initially at least—literally, rather than looking for linguistic and other referents and symbols. I had the ears and eyes in the walls image for several years before I "saw" the artist's intent. Where there are levels of meaning, as with this illustration, differences in our individual styles of perception and knowledge condition how much we see.

5. With respect to offensive and defensive uses, we need to differentiate defensive devices such as bug detectors, which have only one use, from more neutral tools such as bugs, which can be used defensively (e.g., in response to a perceived threat) or offensively.

6. An ad for the M2 fountain pen is an exception to the neutered language of most ads. This device is "small enough to be secreted in a coat sleeve" and is designed for "surreptitious" recording. However, this ad appears to be directed toward security professionals.

7. One illustration does involve a woman looking at a man, but the observed man is himself calling a hot line to report a tip.

8. This may be turned around and exploited. Consider the marketing of "Anne Droid," an attractive department store surveillance mannequin with a camera in her eye and a microphone in her nose. This has something of a last-laugh quality to it, as the leering male may himself be observed. The culture of surveillance may also be transferred back to ads for more conventional products, such as lingerie.

9. There are, however, advice manuals specifically directed toward women; see Culligan (1993) and Moers (1992).

10. On this breakdown, see Baudrillard (1983) as well as Mark Poster's contribution to this volume.

11. A copy of the catalog containing many of the works discussed in this section may be obtained from LACE, 1804 Industrial St., Los Angeles, CA 90021.

12. A nice cartoon rendering of this by Toos shows a man in his living

room with a video camera pointed at him as he sits and watches himself on his television set. It is captioned "Andrew has his own show on cable."

References

Baudrillard, J. (1983). *Simulations,* trans. P. Foss, P. Patton, and P. Beitchman. New York: Semiotext(e).

Clarke, J. (1994). "The Digital Persona and Its Application to Data Surveillance." *Information Society* 10 (June).

Culligan, J. (1993). *When in Doubt Check Him Out.* Miami, FL: Hallmark.

Davis, M. (1993). *What's So Funny?* Chicago: University of Chicago Press.

Goffman, E. (1979). *Gender Advertisements.* Cambridge, Mass.: Harvard University Press.

Laudon, K. (1986). *Dossier Society: Value Choices in the Design of National Information Systems.* New York: Columbia University Press.

Lyon, D. (1994). *The Electronic Eye: The Rise of Surveillance Society.* Minneapolis: University of Minnesota Press.

Marx, G. T. (1972). *Muckraking Sociology.* New York: E. P. Dutton.

Moers, G. (1992). *How and Why Lovers Cheat and What You Can Do about It.* New York: Shapolsky.

Rule, J. (1984). "1984—The Ingredients of Totalitarianism." In I. Howe (ed.), *1984: Totalitarianism in Our Century.* New York: Harper & Row.

Part IV

Regulation

11

The Public Surveillance of Personal Data: A Cross-National Analysis

Colin J. Bennett

The word *surveillance* typically implies the direct and physical monitoring of the behavior and communications of one or more persons. In the popular mind, it conjures up images of a variety of spying and listening devices that are becoming ever more sophisticated, remote, and intrusive. We tend not to think of computers as surveillance tools, yet in all advanced industrial states, the capacity of computer technology, in conjunction with new communications media, has recently facilitated a variety of different practices for the analysis of personal data that may have exactly the same impact on the individual as more physical and direct surveillance techniques.

The term *dataveillance* has been coined to describe the surveillance practices that the massive collection and storage of vast quantities of personal data have facilitated (Clarke, 1988, 1991). These practices emerged during the 1970s and 1980s and have been especially eagerly embraced by governments with neoconservative agendas. My first contention in this chapter is that the analysis, understanding, and ultimate regulation of dataveillance require a far more sophisticated and finely tuned appreciation of the different kinds of practices pursued, and of the various functions they may perform, than has been applied up to this point.

The body of the chapter is devoted to a comparative analysis of official responses (and nonresponses) to dataveillance in four English-speaking countries: the United States, Canada, Australia, and the United Kingdom. I present a broad comparison of the kind of risks recognized and of the options for regulation that have been proposed or implemented in the four countries. This cross-national analysis leads to some general conclusions about the comparative structural conditions that promote dataveillance techniques, and that will affect the abilities of different states to control their worst effects.

A Typology of Dataveillance

The spread of dataveillance has resulted from the complex interplay of technological structure and bureaucratic agency. At some points, computers have been instruments of strategic choice or reflections of existing organizational culture. At others, their potential has expanded the options and functions available without conscious intervention from human agents. Dataveillance has emerged through the coincidence of technological power and rationalist bureaucratic goals. In Weberian terms, dataveillance continues and extends the logic of rationalization inherent in any bureaucratic organization.

The various functions that dataveillance may perform for an organization demonstrate how information technology may bolster bureaucracy's capacity for social control. A recent report from the Ontario Information and Privacy Commissioner (1991) lists eleven different functions of the practice known as "data matching": the detection of fraud in government benefit programs; the reduction of duplicate benefits or billing; the verification of continuing eligibility for a benefit program; the recoupment of incorrect payments or delinquent debts; the monitoring of grant and contract awards; the identification of corruption; the identification of program mismanagement; the monitoring of information such as audits, verifications, and cost comparisons; the improvement of program procedures and controls; the identification of those eligible for benefits but not currently claiming; and the construction of comprehensive databases intended for research purposes.

We should, however, define these techniques on the basis of the functions they are held to perform rather than based on the motives of the organization. The problem is that there are a variety of practices that may vary across five different factors: their scope, their proximity to the transaction in question, their timing, the number of factors analyzed, and the impact on the data subject.

Personal versus Mass Dataveillance

The initial distinction made by Clarke in his typology of "techniques of dataveillance" (1991) is that between personal and mass dataveillance. Personal dataveillance involves the analysis of the records of individuals who have already identified themselves or have attracted attention for some prior reason. In most cases, this involves the analysis of transactional information provided by a client of, or applicant to, an organization for some service (a social benefit, a license, a grant, or the like). The screening or front-end verification of such transactions is a form of personal dataveillance, as of course are the less benign investigations of a data subject's record prompted by suspicion of a crime or misdemeanor.

Mass dataveillance begins with no a priori knowledge of the individual(s) who may warrant attention. Its aim is to screen groups of people with a view to finding those worth subjecting to personal dataveillance. It is based on a general rather than particular suspicion, but also tries to deter or constrain behavior. All forms of computer matching are mass dataveillance techniques. They all involve the aggregate comparison of different personal data systems to identify those "hits" that prima facie warrant further investigation.

Internal versus External Dataveillance

The search for records on an individual or class of individuals can take place at various levels of proximity to the transaction in question. The most routine, and probably most innocuous, kind of search is internal to the personal data system to which the transaction relates. For example, a tax authority may want to identify all income tax returns that claim deductions above a certain amount. Thus the data analysis is prompted by "either legal or other a priori norms that have been set down in advance by some authority" (Clarke, 1991:506).

Under other circumstances, comparisons may be made against other personal data systems, internal to the organization but gathered and stored for other reasons. A typical example would be the matching of applications for social security, either individually or in batch form, against pensions data. When drivers are stopped for traffic offenses, it is becoming standard practice for officers to do on-line checks against stolen vehicle registration records. Clarke calls this the "front-end audit," in which the "detection of an exceptional transaction [is used] as an opportunity to further investigate other matters relating to the individual" (1991:505).

Increasingly, comparisons of individual or aggregate personal data may be made against records kept by organizations other than those involved in a given transaction. This is the typical form of interagency data matching that has prompted the most concern in different countries. Matching may be used to detect individuals who incorrectly appear in two sets of records, such as government employees above a certain salary level who claim social assistance benefits. It may also be used to locate individuals who *should* appear in two systems of records but do not, such as American males with driver's licenses (over the age of eighteen) who have not registered for the draft (U.S. Congress, Office of Technology Assessment [OTA], 1986:38). On an individual level, interorganizational data sharing can be used for "cross-system enforcement," where an individual's relationship with one organization is dependent on his or her performance with another (e.g., the renewal of a driver's license is contingent on the payment of parking fines) (Clarke, 1991:505).

As the comparison of personal data becomes progressively more external to the purpose of the initial transaction, the search tends to become less and less routine. In addition, the data against which the comparison is made are likely to be less and less relevant to the initial relationship between the data subject and the data user. Extrasystem or extraorganizational data matching thus confronts a central principle within information privacy or data protection law, that information collected for one purpose may not be used for another purpose without the data subject's consent.

Up-Front versus Ex Post Facto Dataveillance

Dataveillance can also be distinguished in terms of its timing. Some checking takes place *before* an individual receives a government benefit or service. This technique is normally referred to as *computer-assisted front-end verification*. Whereas computer matching is used to compare systems of records after an individual is receiving government benefits or services, front-end verification is anticipatory. It is used to certify the accuracy and propriety of an individual's claim at the time he or she applies. The information is verified on an individual basis rather than for an aggregation of people (as in matching and profiling), and "its purpose is to prevent and deter, rather than to detect and punish" (OTA, 1986:68).

Checks can be made through batch processing of several applicants (a form of mass dataveillance) or on an individual basis, typically through direct on-line inquiry. Clarke makes a more refined distinction between the routine screening or authentication of transactions and the front-end verification of transactions that appear to be exceptional against data collected and stored for other purposes (1991:503).

The front-end verification of transactions is normally considered to be less harmful to the individual, for two reasons. First, if the individual knows that his or her application may be checked against existing records, and that the receipt of a government benefit or service is contingent on that check, then there is at least implicit consent provided. The search for other information is proximate to, and related to, the transaction in question. Moreover, up-front checking is more likely to be guided by a set of a priori norms, often set out in law or regulation. The problem with dataveillance conducted after a benefit or service is already provided is that the individual normally cannot give consent, and the search is more likely to be guided by a less precise set of criteria. Post hoc matching encourages "fishing expeditions."

Single-Factor versus Multiple-Factor Dataveillance

In most of the surveillance techniques described above, the data analysis is conducted on one single factor about the individual—an application for a license, a traffic violation, a receipt of a benefit. The data user is interested in the individual only in terms of that person's specific role in society as a government claimant, an offender, a student, a driver, or whatever.

Some organizations, however, are interested in more complete pictures of individuals or classes of individuals. This procedure, known as *computer profiling*, follows a more inductive logic "to determine indicators of characteristics and/or behavior patterns that are related to the occurrence of certain behavior" (OTA, 1986:87). Thus databases are searched and multiple variables correlated to reveal a list of "red flag" characteristics. Profiles are then built of the typical drug dealer, tax avoider, violent offender, and so on. Profiles reduce the population of likely suspects and potentially increase an agency's effectiveness in targeting likely suspects.

Marx and Reichman (1984:430–31) make a further distinction between *singular* and *aggregative* profiling. The former focuses on discrete characteristics or events, which in combination suggest a greater probability that a violation will occur. For example, a segment on television's *60 Minutes* that aired on August 23, 1992, revealed that airline ticket agents in Miami, Florida, immediately inform police authorities whenever a single black male obtains a one-way airline ticket at the last minute and pays for it in cash. There is nothing illegal about any part of this scenario, but statistically such an airline passenger is more likely than others to be correlated with illegal drug trafficking. Aggregative profiling looks at the frequency of certain factors across different cases, and is often directed against systematic or repetitive violations, such as fraudulent personal injury claims or the repetition of fires involving the same person(s).

Negative versus Positive Dataveillance

Finally, we can distinguish dataveillance practices according to their likely impacts on data subjects. The word *surveillance* (and, by extension, *dataveillance*) has negative connotations, and the assumption so far has been that all techniques of dataveillance potentially have negative impacts on individuals. They have arisen in times of public expenditure constraint and out of a general concern with more efficient use of government resources (including personal information). And it is true that the unregulated use of these practices has led to many horror stories of unjustifiable denial of rights and services.

It is also worth noting, however, that the results of dataveillance need not be against the interests of the individual. For example, much data matching is used simply to detect and eradicate errors in data files. We know from bitter experience how the processing of incorrect, obsolete, or incomplete personal data can lead to wrongful arrests, the denial of benefits, unfair dismissals, and so on. To the extent that the comparison of personal data files can enhance data quality, these processes are in the interests of both the organization and the individual.

There are also isolated examples of what has been termed *positive matching,* in which data linkages are made to discover those who are eligible for government programs, but have never applied. An example would be the data matching program of the Australian Department of Social Security, which was used to identify families with children who may be eligible for additional assistance through the Family Allowance Supplement. The data match yielded the names of fifty thousand families to whom invitations were sent to test their eligibility for assistance (Department of Social Security, 1992:ix).[1] Positive matching exposes an interesting confrontation between privacy rights and other social values, such as the fair and equitable distribution of government benefits.

The Cross-National Recognition of Risk

The distinctions presented above are abstractions. They do not yield a neat typology of different practices that can be empirically observed and compared over time and space. They do, however, highlight the potential scope of dataveillance and the relative narrowness of national and international responses.

Dataveillance has not appeared on national policy agendas in the comprehensive way defined above. Indeed, with few exceptions, the concerns expressed so far have been confined to data linkages that are on a *mass* scale, that are *external* to the data-using organization, that are *ex post facto* rather than front-end, that are based on *single* variables, and that are deemed to have *negative* consequences for data subjects. The responses of most countries have been confined to the practice known as data or computer matching, the aggregate and ex post facto comparison of data systems according to single-factor analysis. The debate everywhere owes much to the initial definition of the problem in the United States, where the first big computer matching programs were conducted.

The concerns expressed about this practice have centered on two fundamental sets of problems. The first set might be termed practical; the second, civil libertarian. There is a typical convergence of concern as data protection advocates and officials have read and drawn lessons from the reports of their counterparts in other countries.[2]

On a simple, practical level, it is not clear that computer matching advances the effectiveness of government agencies in any significant way. This practice is by no means as simple or costless as was envisaged in the 1970s, when it first entered administrative practice. Costs include computing and programming time, which may be substantial if the two databases are not written in compatible computer languages or if variables have to be manipulated to facilitate comparison. There are also costs in terms of administrative time in planning the match and then following up to verify whether the "hits" are attributable to computer error, obsolete or inaccurate data, or real fraud.

Some matching guidelines, including those applied in the United

States and Canada, require a cost-benefit analysis before a matching program can be initiated. The American experience suggests that there has been no consistency in the manners in which costs and benefits are calculated (U.S. General Accounting Office, 1986). This leads to exaggerated claims by agencies about computer matching's effectiveness. Other analyses point to sometimes very small numbers of "hits" and paltry recovery of public funds (Regan, 1993). The U.S. Office of Technology Assessment found in 1986 that "no firm evidence is available to determine the costs and benefits of computer matching and to document claims made by OMB, the inspectors general, and others that computer matching is cost-effective" (p. 50).

Computer matching is also rendered suspect if the raw data are inaccurate, obsolete, or incomplete. The same OTA study also found that very few federal agencies conducted audits on record quality, and therefore had no idea about the integrity of their data (1986:111). The literature on privacy is full of horror stories about the denial of rights and services because of inaccurate, obsolete, or incomplete information held in files. Most data protection laws contain stipulations about the duty of organizations to keep accurate data. The U.S. Computer Matching and Privacy Protection Act requires an agency to submit a statement about the accuracy of its records when matching agreements are made, a rule that is not followed with any enthusiasm or diligence (Regan, 1993).

The practical problems of data matching are generally of interest to both data user and data subject. Organizations will not want to engage in a practice to which clear benefits cannot accrue. Nor is it in their interests to collect, store, and process inaccurate data. There are overlapping concerns on a practical level. On a more profound civil libertarian level, however, dataveillance can potentially compromise a number of individual rights and liberties that directly confront government interests. Four interrelated dangers can be noted; I address these in turn below.

First, most dataveillance contravenes a central principle of information privacy, namely, that information collected for one purpose should not be used or disclosed for another purpose without the data subject's consent. This right is not absolute, and privacy laws normally contain a list of exemptions, one of which is if the disclosure constitutes a "routine use" (in the American Privacy Act) or a "consistent use" (in the Canadian Privacy Act). The U.S. Privacy Act defines a "routine use" as a purpose "compatible with the purposes for which it was collected." U.S. federal agencies have found some creative and expansive definitions of the word *compatible,* with the result that this exemption has legitimated all kinds of intrusive record linkage and matching practices (Kirchner, 1981).

Second, critics have pointed to the "fishing expedition" character of the computer match in contravention of the limitations on "unreasonable search and seizure" in both the U.S. and Canadian Constitutions. Perhaps the Privacy Commissioner of Australia has expressed the concern the most vividly: "It is like investigators entering a home without any warrant or prior suspicion, taking away some or all of the contents, looking at them, keeping what is of interest and returning the rest, all without the knowledge of the occupier" (1990:vi). Whereas the courts in most countries have been careful to limit search and seizure to cases where there is "probable cause," there is no clear agreement that individuals can expect the same privacy for computer records held by government as they could if an investigator got those same records from their homes or offices.[3]

There is a third set of issues about the presumption of innocence. There is concern that anyone who appears as a "hit" in a computer match is presumed guilty and then has the burden to prove his or her innocence. This reverses the long-standing principle of Anglo-American criminal law that citizens should not be forced to bear a continuous burden of demonstrating to the government that they are innocent of wrongdoing (Shattuck, 1984:1002). Traditional investigations are triggered by some evidence of wrongdoing by specific individuals. Mass dataveillance (like matching and profiling) is directed at classes of persons, many of whom are (and have been proven to be) innocent. Principles of due process demand that the individual have the right to challenge and refute the government's information before a judgment is made. As a practical matter, that means notification of the match and an adequate opportunity for targeted individuals (the hits) to contest the findings and explain their situation.

A final problem concerns potential discrimination against certain classes of people. Matching and profiling are not neutral processes. They are conducted within a set of preconceived attitudes and institutional norms that may be subtly biased against certain social groups. Searches for categories of people most likely to be engaged in wrongdoing can never be wholly inductive. They are also informed by a collective sense of the kinds of people most likely to be suspect. In this sense, they are also deductive procedures and can discriminate (perhaps unintentionally) on the basis of race, ethnic origin, color, religion, gender, sexual orientation, and other socially constituted categories.

It is interesting as well as encouraging that each of these problems and risks has been recognized around the world. Very similar concerns have appeared in reports in Canada, the United States, the United Kingdom, and Australia. Partly, this is testament to the closeness of the "policy community" of privacy officials and advocates, which continually meet and read each other's work (Bennett, 1992:127–29). It is also testament to the convergence of information technology with the bureaucratic drive for efficiency that has a similar impact on organizations the world over.

Comparative Responses and Nonresponses

In some ways, the practices described above can be regulated within the framework of personal data protection law. Since the early 1970s, Western states have been enacting such legislation and, in most cases, establishing special regulatory instruments to oversee its implementation. The countries we are concerned with here enacted such legislation in 1974 (the United States), 1982 (Canada), 1984 (the UK), and 1988 (Australia).[4] These laws are based on a common set of "fair information principles," one of which is the principle of *relevance*— that information collected for one purpose should not be used or disclosed for another (Bennett, 1992:96–111).

The issue to be addressed here is the extent to which different states have recognized that new dataveillance practices require oversight and regulation beyond the basic provisions of data protection law. We have seen that concerns about dataveillance have generally been confined to the practice known as data matching. Those concerns have risen to the political agenda for the same set of practical and civil libertarian reasons. The convergence of problem definition, however, has not yet produced similar regulatory responses. Rather than provide a detailed commentary on the policies of individual countries, I will outline the options in more abstract terms, with references to specific jurisdictions where appropriate.

Administrative Denial and Outside Ignorance

The first option, so far observed in the British case, is to ignore the problem and rely on traditional institutional jealousies about administrative autonomy to control the sharing of data. There has been little official recognition that any of the practices discussed here occur (at least within central government). Furthermore, there has been no recognition that the rapid and extensive networking of British government through the Government Data Network (GDN) will facilitate interdepartmental transfer of data. Officials within the Treasury's Central Communications and Telecommunications Agency (CCTA) continue to claim that the network is to be used only for intradepartmental exchanges.[5] The former data protection registrar proclaimed that he was satisfied that the plans for security on the network are being "soundly and professionally developed" (U.K. Data Protection Registrar, 1988:13).

Officials also argue that data matching could not happen in Britain because that country has no extensively applied national identification number like the social insurance number (SIN) in Canada or the tax file number (TFN) in Australia. This is only partially true. The British national insurance number, like its equivalents overseas, is not subject to any specific statutory restriction, and thus has crept incrementally into a variety of uses for which it was not originally intended. The U.K. Data Protection Registrar first drew attention to data matching in the context of a discussion about the spread of personal identification numbers (1989:35). The subject has also been raised more recently in the context of the national debate about the introduction of a national identity card (U.K. Home Office, 1995).

Reformers have only vague suspicions rather than clear empirical evidence. Absent any firm evidence of the types of dataveillance practiced by British government agencies, the Registrar's knowledge is informed almost exclusively by developments overseas. In the U.K. Data Protection Registrar's *Eighth Report*, Eric Howe, the former data protection registrar, signals that "it may now be an appropriate time in the United Kingdom to seek a balance between the benefits which data matching might bring and the privacy of individuals." He defines data matching as "the computerised comparison of two or more sets of records. The objective is to seek out any records which relate to the same individual" (1992:52). He cautions also against the construction of profiles of individuals drawn from a number of different sources.

Ironically, there may be some value in the British obsession with secrecy that still permeates central administration. A combination of the constitutional principle of ministerial responsibility and a closed administrative culture creates a very segmented civil service (Bennett, 1985), which serves to protect information from outsiders. It may also create strong institutional rivalries that prevent the sharing of data across departments. This is a very fragile, and obviously unsatisfactory, control of the data matching process. We simply do not know the extent to which these techniques are used in Britain. A sine qua non of any data matching policy is transparency.

The Regulation of Automated Decision Making

Of central relevance to the British response is the emerging system of data protection at the European Community level. Since 1990, a general directive on the "protection of individuals in relation to the processing of personal data" has been making its way through the long and complex EC legislative process (Commission of the European Communities, 1990). This directive has aroused an enormous volume of lobbying, especially from British commercial interests (Raab and Bennett, 1994). Its effects on government surveillance practices have often been lost within more public debates about its effects on data-intensive industries, such as direct marketing and credit referencing.

In addition to its general provisions about the conditions for fair and lawful processing of personal data, the directive speaks explicitly to the issue of "automated individual decisions." Article 16 of the most recent version of the directive requires that "member States shall grant the right to every person not to be subject to a decision which produces legal effects concerning him or significantly affects him and which is based solely on automated procesing of data intended to evaluate certain personal aspects relating to him" (Council of the European Union, 1995:32).

Automatic processing is permitted only if there are suitable measures in place to allow the data subject to safeguard his or her legitimate interests, or if it is authorized by law. The intent of this section is to allow routine automated decisions, such as matching and front-end verification, if the decision is favorable, but to provide an explicit right of redress if it is detrimental. For the United Kingdom, and other European Union countries, this would certainly mean transparency for most dataveillance practices, as they inherently hold the potential for adverse automated decision making.

The Regulation of Personal Identifiers

A third method of control consists of attempts to regulate personal identifiers. The more extensive the applicability of universal identification numbers, the easier dataveillance becomes. Generally, personal identification numbers (PINs) have not proliferated through conscious political design, but rather through what Ronald Dworkin calls the "tyranny of convenience" (1990). The cross-national pattern is very similar, as numbers initially introduced for single and specified purposes gradually have become applied to functions other than those for which they were originally created.[6] The extent and timing of this spread may differ, but the pattern is generally the same for the social security number in the United States, the SIN in Canada, the TFN in Australia, and the national insurance number in Britain. This spread tends to support theories about the organic self-augmentation of technology through the process of "function creep" (Winner, 1977).

Both Australian and Canadian governments have formulated statutory guidelines to limit the use of the TFN and SIN, respectively (Privacy Commissioner, 1991; Treasury Board, 1989). By controlling the use of identifiers, one can potentially control the use of data matching; on a few occasions the Privacy Commissioner of Canada has been able to limit a data match because it relied on an illegitimate use of the SIN.[7] The problem is that many matches can still be conducted across other, less efficient, identifiers such as names and addresses. Moreover, there is of course considerable administrative resistance to the costs of developing new identifiers for old purposes.

Internal Review

A fourth form of control relies on internal review by the agencies in question. The American policy, enshrined in the 1988 Computer Matching and Privacy Protection Act (CMPPA), relies principally on this model. This legislation is the culmination of a typically lengthy and fragmented response to the proliferation of computer matching in federal and state agencies.[8] A number of executive and legislative bodies have involved themselves with the issue over the years. Initially, the response came in the form of guidelines pursuant to the 1974 Privacy Act produced by the U.S. Office of Management and Budget (the body with enforcement and oversight responsibility under that law) (1979). The weakness of the Privacy Act, and especially the broad and ill-defined "routine use" exemption to agency disclosures, created a widespread feeling that separate and stronger regulation of computer matching was needed (Flaherty, 1989:346-50). This point was made by the congressional Office of Technology Assessment, whose 1986 report *Electronic Record Systems and Individual Privacy* remains one of the most insightful analyses of dataveillance to this day, as well as by some key congressional committees (see especially U.S. House of Representatives, 1983; U.S. Senate, 1986).

The CMPPA has a limited scope, applying only to the "computerized comparison of records for the purpose of (i) establishing or verifying eligibility for a Federal benefit program, or (ii) recouping payments or delinquent debts under such programs" (U.S. House of Representatives, 1988:1). Thus it does not apply to matches performed for statistical, research, law enforcement, foreign counterintelligence, security screening, or tax purposes, or to those for state agencies or the private sector. Nor, of course, does it cover front-end verification or profiling techniques, identified as significant problems within OTA's 1986 study.

The CMPPA stipulates that computer matching can take place only pursuant to an explicit written agreement between the source and matching agencies. This should state the legal justification for the match, the records to be used, security measures, an assessment about the accuracy of the records to be used, and a cost-benefit analysis. The law also requires the matching agency to verify the information about hits before it acts on that information. The legislation requires each agency to establish a data integrity board to oversee the matching agreements, review the implementation of the matches, submit an annual report, and provide guidance on privacy-related issues.

Regan's (1993) preliminary evaluation of the CMPPA does not suggest that internal review places a significant check on the matching process. Regan found that the published matching agreements do not provide meaningful information, and that they are rarely read by either the public or the responsible oversight committees of the Congress.

Further, there are no clear criteria for establishing cost-benefit information and accuracy, and there is little evidence that the data integrity boards function as anything more than rubber-stamp bodies.

The American experience with this legislation is a reflection of the wider difficulty of implementing information privacy principles in a society where there is no policy instrument solely responsible for privacy issues. A Privacy Board was suggested in the Senate version of the 1974 Privacy Act, but this element was struck down by the House. The establishment of such a board has been constantly advocated ever since (Flaherty, 1984). The regulation of dataveillance in the United States has taken a very small step beyond the standards set within the 1974 Privacy Act.

External Review

In countries such as Canada, Australia, France, Germany, and Sweden, where privacy or data protection commissions do oversee the implementation of data protection legislation, an obvious body is available to provide some measure of external oversight.

At the federal level in Canada, dataveillance has come to the political agenda almost entirely through the efforts of the Privacy Commissioner of Canada, the oversight and advisory body established under the 1982 Federal Privacy Act. The government's policy was enshrined in a Treasury Board statement on data matching and the social insurance number issued in June 1989. It requires government institutions to provide prior cost-benefit analyses, to notify the office of the Privacy Commissioner sixty days prior to when the programs are due to begin, to account publicly for all matching programs, and to verify the information generated by matching programs before using it.

This policy has not been taken seriously by many federal agencies. The Privacy Commissioner complained in its 1990-91 annual report that "some departments seem to view the Commissioner's role as something of a rubber stamp to be applied after a last minute phone call" (Privacy Commissioner of Canada, 1991:47). In 1991-92, the Privacy Commissioner reported the receipt of only three notifications during the entire year, all from Agriculture Canada, and noted that "it would be credulous to accept that of more than 150 federal agencies subject to the government's data matching policy, only one began any new matches of discrete files during 1991-92" (1992:38). The Cana-

dian policy suffers from a lack of understanding about the requirements, as well as a certain reluctance to commit time and resources to
perform the necessary checks.

Australia is probably the country where the development of surveillance systems has been most politicized. Privacy issues have nowhere
been more publicly and vigorously debated than in Australia during
1986–87, when the government sought parliamentary approval for its
abortive "Australia Card" national identification scheme. The proposal was ultimately withdrawn in the face of enormous public opposition and intensive lobbying by a coalition of pressure groups and
government bodies such as the New South Wales Privacy Committee
(Clarke, 1987). The price of withdrawal was the enhancement of the
national tax file number, which, despite government promises to the
contrary, has slowly been extended to the point where some see it as a
de facto national identifier (Davies, 1992:45).

Data matching has also been more openly debated in Australia
than in other countries, and the oversight of data matching is express-
ly mentioned in the Australian Privacy Act of 1988. Many of the
largest and most controversial matches relating to social security are
also regulated through special legislation (e.g., the Data Matching
Program [Assistance and Tax] Act, 1990). This legislation established
the regulatory model that the Privacy Commissioner of Australia
(1992) subsequently adapted for its more general guidelines on data
matching. These provide for public notice of proposed data matching
programs; clear statements about justification, cost-benefit information, and safeguards; technical standards as to data quality, integrity,
and security; protection of the rights of individuals selected for
administrative action as a result of data matching; and oversight and
reporting by the Privacy Commissioner. This accountability is provided through published "program protocols" and nonpublic "technical
standards reports."

The Australian policy has been guided to some extent by a desire to
avoid the Canadian experience, where an overly broad definition of
data matching has left federal agencies confused as to their reporting
responsibilities. Thus the Privacy Commissioner's guidelines are both
narrower in focus and reflective of a variety of agency needs and interests. The overriding strategy has been to negotiate a practical set of
rules that will be taken seriously by Commonwealth agencies.[9]

Conclusion: Dataveillance, Bureaucratic Accountability, and the Structure of the State

The various techniques that are embraced by the term *dataveillance* are only now being understood and debated. Typically, legal and political responses have lagged behind the development and application of the technology. The control of a practice like this can be likened to trying to change a tire on a rapidly moving car. Any policy on dataveillance must be adaptable to the new surveillance practices that are continually being conceived and applied. The foregoing analysis suggests, however, that the extensiveness and complexity of dataveillance are straining the regulatory ability of existing data protection and information privacy regimes.

Dataveillance techniques are multiple. I have characterized them above according to five continuous variables. This classification alone yields at least twenty different types of data linkages. In reality, administrative practices are not so neatly distinguished, so the regulatory response in most countries has been directed toward those linkages that are most visible, and probably the least routine. Hence the emphasis has been on trying to regulate large-scale computer matching programs that are on a *mass* scale, that are *ex post facto* rather than up-front, that are based on *single* rather than multiple factors, that are *external* to the data-using organization, and that are deemed to have *negative* consequences for the individual.

The effect of trying to encompass the broader spectrum of dataveillance techniques under one regulatory regime is obvious in the Canadian experience—the policy is ignored by the majority of federal agencies. The result of the Treasury Board's (not the Privacy Commissioner's) definition of data matching is confusion as to what matching activities should be reported and how they might differ from routine use and disclosures. To control all dataveillance practices, societies need to develop different policies that are sensitive to the very different costs and benefits inherent in the different techniques. The regulation of data matching, sadly, reflects a problem with data protection legislation as a whole. As noted by Simitis, "Most legislators . . . restrict themselves to a few extremely abstract provisions that reflect both their hope of coping once and for all with the processing problems and their complete uneasiness in dealing with a technology the further developments of which are as difficult to see as their exact implications" (1987:741–42). We need a more exact understanding of these evolving practices and of their implications.

We also need to see these implications in societal, as well as individual, terms. In all countries, the analysis and regulation of dataveillance has flowed from a dominant liberal paradigm that has informed the theory of information privacy since the 1960s. One problem with this approach is that it tends to regard private sector personal data processing as inherently less harmful than that practiced by the agencies of the state (Peladeau, 1990). More generally, information privacy has as its fundamental premise the anticipation and reduction of costs on an *individual* basis. As Simitis reminds us, "Privacy considerations no longer arise out of particular individual problems; rather they express conflicts affecting everyone" (1987:709).

The debate about dataveillance has generally taken place between those who argue the social benefits and those who point out the individual costs. Recognitions of the social costs of dataveillance, or the social benefits of privacy, have been swamped by the pressing need to bring these new practices into existing privacy or data protection regimes (see Regan's essay in this volume). The civil libertarian implications are potentially enormous, but they express the dangers only in terms of the classic liberal relationship between the individual and the state. This, then, produces a response in terms of the procedural protections of the "fair information practices" inherent in data protection law.

One could argue that all dataveillance practices, even if they are cost-effective and pose no threat to civil liberties, are still not in the public interest. This risk is often expressed in terms of the potential for "surveillance societies" in which privacy is so compromised as to threaten our individuality and dignity as humans. The incremental growth in surveillance practices has the often unintended consequence of creating a social control system in which increasingly more refined information is collected in order to categorize individuals within the "panoptic sort" (see Gandy's essay in this volume).

There is plenty of evidence of these unintended consequences. The 1986 OTA study cited previously found that the "widespread use of computerized databases, electronic record searches and matches, and computer networking is leading rapidly to the creation of a *de facto* national database containing personal information on most Americans. And use of the social security number as a *de facto* electronic national identifier facilitates the development of this database" (p. 3). The "1984" nightmare, therefore, does not require intentional centralized planning by a Big Brother. The steady accumulation of justifications in cost-benefit terms is often enough to add another dataveillance practice on top of those that already exist.

Finally, and from the perspective of the political scientist (rather than the civil libertarian, the privacy advocate, or the sociologist), the spread of dataveillence, and thus the potential to regulate its worst effects, is also closely related to the structural and institutional features of different states. The early and widespread development of these techniques in the United States is partially attributable to a more fragmented political system than exists in parliamentary regimes. Weak and uncertain lines of hierarchical authority from both Congress and presidency allow a multitude of complex and interweaving horizontal linkages among lower-level bureaucrats. These "issue networks" facilitate the sharing of all kinds of data and information about public policy. Computer matching thrives between and within the diverse, nonintegrated, incoherent, and decentralized collection of agencies that constitute the U.S. federal bureaucracy.

Conversely, the slow and limited emergence of these techniques in Britain is attributable to the comparatively centralized, hierarchical, and formal structure of British central administration. Clear hierarchical lines of authority flow from top to bottom. Government departments are also characterized by relatively greater esprit de corps than is found in the United States, as well as a notable penchant for secrecy, both in relation to ordinary citizens and in relation to other administrative departments. Interagency sharing of data is thus less likely within this highly "sectorized" system.

The nature of dataveillance techniques is also dependent on the strength of the boundary between the state and civil society. The interconnectedness of the information economy and the information polity is itself breaking down these traditional barriers in all countries (Taylor and Williams, 1991). "Public" agencies regularly use information from banks and credit card companies for "public" purposes. "Private" bodies regularly use mailing lists derived from "public" agencies. "Public" functions, once performed by "public" agencies, are increasingly, in the era of privatization, performed by "private" agencies. The public/private distinction is breaking down for many reasons, as of course are the traditional functional definitions of agencies *within* the state (Bennett, 1991). The pace of these changes, however, is variable. It is probable that the boundaries are far more porous in the United States than they are elsewhere.

This comparative study of dataveillance has exposed the limitations of procedural regulation. New forms of dataveillance are straining the credibility of the theory of information privacy, of the data protection laws that it underpins, and of the agencies that have to enforce those laws. At best, these agencies can respond only on an individual level. They can ensure a certain transparency of the process; they can establish rules for data quality and integrity; they can insist on credible cost-benefit analyses before data matches are conducted; they can receive and resolve individual complaints—but they cannot *stop* dataveillance.

I would not conclude that a procedural response to dataveillance constitutes merely a legitimation of new surveillance. Significant, if limited, skirmishes have been fought and won by the most aggressive data protection authorities. I would conclude, however, that there are clearly normative limits on dataveillance techniques, however sound the procedural guarantees. Indeed, some laws already prohibit the collection of certain sensitive categories of information relating to race, national origin, sexual orientation, political views, and so on.[10] Substantive restrictions should clearly supplement the procedural ones.

There is an ill-defined line beyond which surveillance would be clearly excessive (Lyon, 1994:171). Until privacy protection is debated more actively and publicly in the political arena, however, that line will continually be pushed forward by the inexorable logic of bureaucratic efficiency and technological development. With very few exceptions, the problem of excessive surveillance has never been politicized. Politicians have almost never regarded surveillance as an issue over which they may lose votes; conversely, they have never seen privacy as a cause through which they can win votes. Dataveillance will continue to be managed to protect "privacy" rather than controlled to reduce "surveillance," until questions such as those addressed here become more central to political and public consciousness.

Notes

The research for this chapter was facilitated by grants from the Social Sciences and Humanities Research Council of Canada (SHRCC 410–90–1553) and from the Nuffield Foundation. I am grateful to my coresearcher, Charles

Raab, as well as to Cynthia Alexander, for their helpful comments on an earlier draft.

1. These invitations led to the lodging of 5,762 claims, of which 2,122 have been granted. Interviews, Australian Department of Social Security, November 18, 1992.

2. I discuss this phenomenon of cross-national "lesson drawing" about data protection in greater detail in Bennett (1992:123–27).

3. Relevant cases include *U.S. v. Miller*, 425 U.S. 435 (1976), and *Jaffess v. Secretary HEW*, 393 F. Supp. 626 (S.D. N.Y. 1975).

4. These laws are, respectively, the U.S. Privacy Act of 1974, 5 U.S.C. 552a. Sec. 3(a)(7); the Canadian Privacy Act, SC 1980–81–82–83, c.111, Schedule II; the United Kingdom Data Protection Act, c. 35; and the Australian Privacy Act of 1988.

5. Interviews, CCTA, December 17, 1990, and January 14, 1993.

6. See OTA (1986) on the American social security number as a de facto national identifier, and Flaherty (1989:283–84) for an analysis of the similar spread of the Canadian social insurance number.

7. Interviews, Privacy Commissioner of Canada, June 4, 1992.

8. The 1986 OTA study found that seven billion records were exchanged in just 20 percent of all matching programs between 1980 and 1985 (p. 49).

9. Interviews, Privacy Commissioner of Australia, November 12, 1992. As of the end of 1992, there were still several agencies, including the Tax Office and the Federal Police, that had declined to comply with the Privacy Commissioner's guidelines.

10. The latest draft of the EC directive mentioned previously prohibits the "processing of data revealing racial or ethnic origin, political opinions, religious beliefs, philosophical or ethical persuasion or trade-union membership, and of data concerning health or sexual life," except under certain defined circumstances (Article 8).

References

Bennett, Colin J. (1985). "From the Dark to the Light: The Open Government Debate in Britain." *Journal of Public Policy* 5, no. 2: 187–213.

———. (1991). "Computers, Personal Data and Theories of Technology: Comparative Approaches to Privacy Protection in the 1990s." *Science, Technology and Human Values* 16, no. 1: 51–69.

———. (1992). *Regulating Privacy: Data Protection and Public Policy in Europe and the United States.* Ithaca, N.Y.: Cornell University Press.

Clarke, Roger. (1987). "Just Another Piece of Plastic for Your Wallet: The Australia Card Scheme." *Prometheus* 5, no. 1: 29–45.

———. (1988). "Information Technology and Dataveillance." *Communications of the ACM* 31, no. 5: 498–512.

———. (1991). "Information Technology and Dataveillance." In Charles

Dunlop and Rob Kling (eds.), *Computerization and Controversy: Value Conflicts and Social Choices*. Boston: Academic Press.

Commission of the European Communities. (1990). *Proposal for a Council Directive Concerning the Protection of Individuals in Relation to the Processing of Personal Data* (SYN 287). Brussels: European Commission.

Council of the European Union. (1995). *Common Position on the Protection of Individuals with Regard to the Processing of Personal Data and on the Free Movement of Such Data*. Brussels: Council of the European Union.

Davies, Simon. (1992). *Big Brother: Australia's Growing Web of Surveillance*. Sydney: Simon & Schuster.

Department of Social Security, Australia. (1992). *Data Matching Program (Assistance and Tax)*. Canberra: Australian Government Publishing Service.

Dworkin, Ronald. (1990). *A Bill of Rights for Britain*. London: Chatto & Windus.

Flaherty, David H. (1984). "The Need for an American Privacy Protection Commission." *Government Information Quarterly* 1: 235–58.

———. 1989. *Protecting Privacy in Surveillance Societies*. Chapel Hill: University of North Carolina Press.

Kirchner, Jake. (1981). "Privacy: A History of Computer Matching in the Federal Government." *Computerworld*, December 14.

Lyon, David. (1994). *The Electronic Eye: The Rise of Surveillance Society*. Minneapolis: University of Minnesota Press.

Marx, Gary T., and Nancy Reichman. (1984). "Routinizing the Discovery of Secrets: Computers as Informants." *American Behavioral Scientist* 27, no. 4: 423–52.

Ontario Information and Privacy Commissioner. (1991). *Privacy and Computer Matching: Report for the Standing Committee on the Legislative Assembly*. Toronto: Ontario Information and Privacy Commissioner.

Peladeau, Pierrot. (1990). "The Informational Privacy Challenge: The Technological Rule of Law." In R. I. Cholewinski (ed.), *Human Rights in Canada: Into the 1990s and Beyond*. Ottawa: University of Ottawa, Human Rights Research and Education Centre.

Privacy Commissioner of Australia. (1990). *Data Matching*. Sydney: Privacy Commissioner of Australia.

———. (1991). *Tax File Number Guidelines*. Sydney: Privacy Commissioner of Australia.

———. (1992). *Data Matching in Commonwealth Administration*. Sydney: Privacy Commissioner of Australia.

Privacy Commissioner of Canada, (1991). *Annual Report 1990–91*. Ottawa: Minister of Supply and Services.

———. (1992). *Annual Report 1991–92*. Ottawa: Minister of Supply and Services.

Raab, Charles D., and Colin J. Bennett. (1994). "Protecting Privacy across Borders: European Policies and Prospects." *Public Administration* 72, no. 1: 95–112.

Regan, Priscilla M. (1993). "Data Integrity Boards: Institutional Innovation and Congressional Oversight." *Government Information Quarterly* 10, no. 4: 443–59.

Shattuck, John. (1984). "In the Shadow of 1984: National Identification Systems, Computer-Matching and Privacy in the United States." *Hastings Law Journal* 35, no. 6: 991–1005.

Simitis, Spiros. (1987). "Reviewing Privacy in an Information Society." *University of Pennsylvania Law Review* 135, no. 3: 707–46.

Taylor, John A., and Howard Williams. (1991). "Public Administration and the Information Polity." *Public Administration* 69: 171–90.

Treasury Board of Canada. (1989). *Guidelines on the Implementation of the Policy on Data Matching and Control of the Social Insurance Number.* Ottawa: Treasury Board of Canada.

U.K. Data Protection Registrar. (1988). *Fourth Report.* London: HMSO.

———. (1989). *Fifth Report.* London: HMSO.

———. (1992). *Eighth Report.* London: HMSO.

U.K. Home Office. (1995). *Identity Cards: A Consultation Document.* London: HMSO.

U.S. Congress, Office of Technology Assessment (OTA). (1986). *Electronic Record Systems and Individual Privacy* (OTA-CIT-296). Washington, D.C.: U.S. Government Printing Office.

U.S. General Accounting Office. (1986). *Computer Matching: Assessing Its Costs and Benefits* (GAO/PEMD-87-2). Washington, D.C.: U.S. Government Printing Office.

U.S. House of Representatives, Committee on Government Operations. (1983). *Who Cares about Privacy? Oversight of the U.S. Privacy Act by the Office of Management and Budget and by the Congress* (H. Rept. 455, 98th Cong., 1st sess). Washington, D.C.: U.S. Government Printing Office.

———. (1988). *Computer Matching and Privacy Protection Act of 1988* (100th Cong., 2d sess.). Washington, D.C.: U.S. Government Printing Office.

U.S. Office of Management and Budget. (1979). *Guidelines for the Conduct of Matching Programs.* Washington, D.C.: U.S. Government Printing Office.

U.S. Senate, Committee on Governmental Affairs. (1986). *Oversight of Computer Matching to Detect Fraud and Mismanagement in Government Programs* (hearing before the Subcommittee on Oversight of Government Management, 99th Cong., 2d sess.). Washington, D.C.: U.S. Government Printing Office.

Winner, Langdon. (1977). *Autonomous Technology: Technics Out of Control as a Theme in Human Thought.* Cambridge: MIT Press.

12

Surveying Surveillance: An Approach to Measuring the Extent of Surveillance

Simon G. Davies

The information technology developed over recent years is nurturing the development of surveillance societies throughout the world. Privacy advocates are finding that the development of new, more subtle, and more extensive methods of data collection and use is creating grave threats to privacy. And yet it is increasingly difficult to argue the case for privacy, and to set limits on surveillance. In this essay, I argue that the creation of a means of measuring surveillance is one approach that could be taken to raise awareness of surveillance. I propose a model that uses measures of the collection, use, and disclosure of personal data as the bases for scoring surveillance at a national level. The model is intended for use as a comparative device at an international level.

All societies tolerate a degree of surveillance for purposes of law enforcement and national security. Most endorse widespread surveillance in the course of government administration, revenue collection, and the management of welfare benefits. The mechanism of societal management has become technological in nature, and, as the technology becomes more cost-effective and interconnected, it has the potential to reach more comprehensively into the lives of all people.

Numerous authors have argued that technological societies are at risk of becoming surveillance societies (e.g., Flaherty, 1989; Simitis, 1987; Davies, 1992; Clarke, 1988; Madsen, 1992; Burnham, 1983). Figuring the point when a society has reached such a state is a complex task. Privacy and civil rights advocates have always faced difficulties in determining when "public interest" is outweighed by the right to privacy.

Such a dilemma is by no means unique in the world of civil rights. The rights of free speech and of free expression, for example, often conflict with other traditional human rights. Nevertheless, concern is frequently expressed about the impact of surveillance on the free, open,

260

and democratic nature of society. Not all privacy advocates agree on the nature of this threat or its consequences, but all view surveillance as a vehicle that threatens the loss of individual dignity and rights.

The concept of privacy is constantly eroded by "public interest" factors—real, alleged, or imagined. It is increasingly difficult to argue the case for privacy. Not only are threats to privacy often difficult to quantify, but arguments for privacy are often interpreted as selfish or hysterical. The rights of the individual appear to be subsumed by the alleged greater good.

The privacy advocacy community recognizes that this state of affairs must be reversed. The "golden age" of privacy, when the fear of Big Brother motivated many people to take action, has now passed. It has been transmogrified into a passive, pragmatic and legalistic interest. As a result, attempts to reform information systems in the interest of privacy are often thwarted or ignored.

In this essay, I propose that there exists a need to devise a method of measuring the extent of surveillance of individuals by governments, private sector organizations, and other individuals. I explore the challenges and options involved in such a scoring mechanism and propose a framework for measuring the extent of surveillance throughout a country.

This essay is intended as a proposal only. Its role is to explore the justification and feasibility of such an approach. The complexities involved in devising and refining a practical measurement system are beyond the scope of a single essay. Here I can do no more than argue the case for a measuring device and propose a simple formula.

Why Do We Need a Measuring Device?

Surveillance needs to be quantified because the justification for surveillance is so seductive and its acceptance so widespread. Article 19 and the Index on Censorship are able to quantify limits to freedom of expression by pointing out the extent of its repression. Amnesty International is able to point out the extent of infringement on the rights of the person by highlighting the extent of imprisonment and torture. Greenpeace can point out threats to the environment by publishing statistics. Privacy advocates share no such luxury. Surveillance, once perceived as a negative activity, is now often seen as a socially beneficial one. It allegedly improves equity and justice throughout society. It helps identify those who "owe" and those who "are owed." Whether it can really do these things is an issue that is often eclipsed by the image of surveillance as a beneficial and necessary activity.

In a sense, the advent of technological surveillance aims to return society to the days of the village, when the identity, activities, and even the thoughts of every inhabitant were known facts. In that small village society, as in our own, certain categories of knowledge about the individual were usually circulated within well-defined groups. The doctor, knowing certain things, would divulge this information to a coterie of colleagues and social acquaintances. In the modern context, personal information is passed by technology from one information user to another along set pathways.

This trend deeply worries privacy and human rights advocates. A return to the days of the village has limited appeal—certainly in the context of rampant technology without restraint. Sadly, efforts to restrict or limit the construction of surveillance societies have been mostly unsuccessful. Privacy advocates have failed to achieve the reforms and limits envisioned in the 1970s. Although it is true that many countries have established privacy and data protection laws, most of the particularly offensive invasions of privacy are exempted. The collection of personal information is largely unaffected by law. Legislation universally exempts collection of data for national security purposes, and usually excludes law enforcement and revenue collection uses as well. In countries such as the United States and Australia, the privacy debate in the private sector has been lost. Although Europe continues, in limited circumstances, to maintain relatively strong protections, the same cannot be said for most other countries.

Over the past decade or so, advocates have dealt with surveillance on a case-by-case basis, responding to each new project as it becomes known. Rarely is one category of privacy invasion discussed alongside another—unless there is a technological or policy link involved. Thus, the "big picture" that can be drawn in other fields, such as censorship, is not developed in the field of surveillance. No synergy exists. People cannot judge where the line should be drawn against further surveillance. What is occurring is a form of technological reductionism.

The surveillance scoring system discussed below has been developed from the perspective of privacy advocacy for use in measuring the extent of information collection and use. Currently, no such system exists. The situation in, say, the United States or Germany cannot be shown alongside that in another country. Neither, for that matter, can the protections be so compared.

The groups most likely to benefit from a surveillance scoring device are privacy advocacy organizations, consumer groups, and human rights defenders. Governments, and parliamentary oppositions, in certain circumstances might also find uses for such an instrument.

The watchdogs over surveillance fall into two categories: government-appointed privacy commissioners and ombudsmen and non-government privacy, consumer, and human rights groups. Both are facing increasing problems in dealing with the consequences of surveillance. In Australia, an extraordinary public revolt in 1987 over a proposed national identity card defeated the proposal and placed privacy at the top of the political agenda. Seven years later, the Australian Privacy Foundation, which organized the campaign, now fights inertia over the issue of surveillance and privacy. A similar situation exists in the Netherlands, where public concern in the 1970s over government collection of personal information has now all but vanished.

The establishment of a scoring system would also be useful for indicating the extent to which protections and safeguards need to be established in a particular country. The most recent draft *European Directive on Data Protection* stipulates that personal information should flow to countries with "adequate" protection (the former draft specified "equivalence" of protection) (Commission of the European Communities, 1992).[1] It is possible that a scoring system could assist authorities in determining how such a judgment should be applied.

The application of a quantifiable standard for judging surveillance has one other important basis. Privacy advocates have voiced concern in recent years over deficiencies in conventional legal safeguards and the extent to which legislation provides a legal basis for surveillance activities. In its fourth annual report, the Privacy Commissioner of Australia observes, "So, ironically, the Privacy Act is tending to supply a legal foundation for these [government surveillance] activities" (1992:3).

Dutch privacy expert Dr. Jan Holvast has recently explained that privacy legislation "corrects the mistakes and misuses but it does not attack the way in which technology is used. On the contrary, experiences with data protection law in several countries show that these laws are legalizing existing practices instead of protecting privacy" (1991).

If standard legislative mechanisms were adequate, and political responses uniform and sensitive, the need for a scoring system would be less pressing. Despite elements of convergence, however, nations respond in markedly different ways to issues of privacy and surveillance (Bennett, 1992).

Privacy legislation brings many obvious advantages. There is no question that some of the more objectionable activities of information users are reined in. Individual citizens are usually given some protection over the ways personal files are used. However, the privacy and data protection laws that exist in many countries have serious limitations. One of the most significant deficiencies is that many deal only with the ways certain conventional forms of personal data are collected, stored, used, and accessed. Many are not concerned, for example, with visual surveillance, drug testing, use of satellites, the extent and use of publicly available information, denouncement campaigns, or a range of other surveillance activities. Another important shortcoming of many data protection acts is that they do very little to prevent or limit the collection of personal information. Many laws stipulate only that information has to be collected by lawful means and for a purpose "directly related to a function or activity of the collector." Thus, a virtually unlimited number of information systems can be established without any breach of law.

Perhaps the most serious limitation of data protection laws is that they invariably provide extremely broad and well-used exemptions for the purposes of law enforcement, national security, and the collection of public revenue. It would be a mistake to assume that the law provides a blueprint for solving problems of privacy invasion and surveillance, or even that the net result of legislation is positive. The watchdog group Privacy International warns in its 1991 report:

> Protections in law, where they exist, are sometimes ineffective and even counter-productive. Extensive information holdings by government are invariably allowed under exemptions and protections in law. The existence of statutory privacy bodies, rather than impeding such trends, sometimes legitimates intrusive information practices. (p. 4)[2]

Professor David Flaherty has observed, "The public is being lulled into a false sense of security about the protection of their privacy by their official protectors, who often lack the will and energy to resist successfully the diverse initiatives of what Jan Freese [one of Europe's first data protection commissioners] has aptly termed the 'information athletes' in our respective societies" (1989:385).

It is for these very important reasons that the establishment of a method of quantifying surveillance would be one more step along the road to cultivating meaningful privacy protection. The calculation of a primary figure, representing the raw data in the hands of organizations, would provide an invaluable insight into the necessary responses at both policy and advocacy levels.

From the perspective of privacy advocacy, however, there is a risk that measurement of surveillance could be a two-edged sword. Although a measurement instrument may be a useful device for helping to raise awareness in countries that fall below the mean level of the international scale, it may also be used by government and information users to deflect criticism in countries that fall above the mean level.

Overview of the Scoring System

Comparative scoring has been useful for policy makers and advocates in a wide spectrum of areas, including the economy, the environment, health care, transportation, and social security. Such measurements depend largely on the existence of agreed-upon international standards and definitions. Such standards have not been established in the field of surveillance, and there is no doubt that more work needs to be done in the direction of achieving international agreement on terms and definitions.

The scoring system proposed here is a formula that estimates the extent to which information is known about the individual and the extent of collection, storage, use, and disclosure of those personal data. It takes into account the full range of surveillance methods and a wide spectrum of information uses. The surveillance model attempts to address four key questions:

1. How much personal information is known about individuals?
2. To what extent is this information kept "functionally separate" (maintained within the collecting organization and used for distinct purposes)?
3. Are adequate safeguards, checks, and balances in place?
4. How does the level of surveillance in one country compare with the levels in other countries?

The model consists of two scores:

1. a primary score, which is a measure of the extent of information collection, storage, use, and disclosure; and

2. a comprehensive score, which takes into account legislative and other protections, cultural factors, and aspects of public interest that may justify the extent of surveillance in a society.

I am concerned here principally with the development of the primary score.

To this point, no such scoring or measuring device has been developed. It is possible that this situation exists for four reasons:

1. Those working in the fields of human rights, privacy, and data protection have not perceived a need for such a device; they have instead relied on other approaches.

2. Surveillance is such a diverse and fragmented activity that such a process might have been viewed as too ambitious or arbitrary.

3. Surveillance may have been viewed as the end product of well-reasoned public policy (public interest issues such as law enforcement, national security, and the collection of revenue) and therefore was not seen as a tangible enough issue to quantify.

4. There has been no agreed-upon definition of surveillance. The lack of a widely accepted definition of privacy might also have implied that there would be a subsequent absence of a widely accepted definition of surveillance.

From a practical perspective, my conclusions in this essay are predicated on two assumptions: first, that a measurement of surveillance would be a useful device for advocates, independent privacy experts, and policy makers; and second, that it is ultimately possible to reach agreement on the definition and parameters of surveillance. This essay is intended to raise the issues for discussion and to propose a broad framework for measuring surveillance. I do not attempt to lay down precise parameters and procedures for such measurement.

Methodology and Approach

The proposed methodology uses a basic unit of personal data as the core of the scoring process. In this approach, each category (e.g., financial, employment) and each subcategory (e.g., spending patterns, employment monitoring outcomes) of personal data receives a certain value according to its sensitivity or significance. The weighting might be set internationally, or could be determined by experts or information users in individual countries. The value is then multiplied or diminished according to availability and use of the category of data. This produces the primary score.

The value of each category can then be altered through an assessment of the conditions for use (whether, for instance, there are cultural or legislative impediments limiting its use, or whether there are conditions such as a black or gray market that entice improper use). This produces the comprehensive score.

It is extremely important that the scoring process be divided thus. The idea of information as power demands a raw statistic. The concept that all data are potentially unsafe requires a primary statistic that provides a basis for assessment of surveillance within a society. A surveillance society, and a surveillance mentality, can still exist even if the "right" data are used by the "right" people for the "right" purposes (Bennett, 1992).

In order to find the most appropriate methodology, it is necessary to look to the work of people who have been involved in quantifying (a) personal information and (b) human and democratic rights.

Precedents for Quantifying Data

The model discussed here relies on the quantification of flows of personal data from the individual to information users, and the flow of data between information users. Several studies have attempted to quantify the flow of data across borders, and these will provide a valuable precedent for a scoring system.[3]

Precedents for Quantifying Rights

It is unusual to find examples of attempts to quantify basic rights. However, the Human Rights Centre of the University of Essex in England has undertaken a "Democratic Audit," which "is inquiring into the quality of democracy and political freedom in the UK." Reports are issued periodically (the first was released in 1993, the second will appear in 1999) to provide a comparative view of the state of democracy (see Beetham, 1993). Similar comparative studies of other countries are also being planned.

In the majority of transborder data flow studies, questionnaires have been used as a means of determining the value and the flow of information. The questionnaire system would be useful in a surveillance scoring test. It might be valuable to have two questionnaires: one administered to information users (private and government sector), requesting details of information collection and use, and a second administered to academics, advocates, and experts, seeking additional information and interpretation.

The approach taken by the Democratic Audit has been to establish sound parameters for viewing democracy and its value, and then, using a number of "auditors," to address a series of questions relating to elections, political systems, government institutions, government accountability, openness, judicial independence, definition within the law of civil and political rights, redress for damage caused by institutions, freedom of the media, and cultural imperatives. Although it could be argued that the results of such inquiries are at risk of being arbitrary, the Department of Government at the London School of Economics is developing statistical indices for certain processes of government, and these will assist the auditing process.

Defining Surveillance

There exists a very important relationship between privacy and surveillance. It has often been said that privacy and freedom of information are opposite sides of the same coin. It could equally well be argued that privacy and surveillance are opposing poles of the same magnet. Privacy protection is a defense against surveillance. Surveillance is an intrusion into privacy.

Surveillance might be marginally easier to define than privacy, possibly because it does not come with so much emotional baggage. It can also be argued that whereas the definition of privacy often begins with philosophic reasoning, the definition of surveillance can be built around actual events.

Collins English Dictionary defines surveillance as "a close observation or supervision maintained over a person, group etc, especially one in custody or under suspicion." *Chambers Dictionary* defines it as "spy-like watching." The idea of surveillance being an activity over people under suspicion is a recurring theme, and is particularly relevant in modern societies, where data matching has intensified surveillance over a large proportion of the population. However, the idea of surveillance being a covert activity seems to be obsolete. Surveillance (by way, say, of security cameras or employee monitoring) need not be invisible or covert.

David Flaherty describes surveillance (in the context of his study) as "supervision, observation or oversight of individual behavior through the use of personal data," rather than through such media as cameras or private detectives (1989: xiv). His definition of surveillance is as follows: "Any systematic attention to a person's life, aimed at exerting influence over it"(p. 409). Flaherty's interest in this work is the development of surveillance within the *information society*, which he defines as "a society dependent on information exchanges through the use of computers and telecommunications devices" (p. 409).

The definition of surveillance adopted by Flaherty and others relates to power and influence brought about by the use of information. The power definition of surveillance parallels a thread that runs through many definitions of privacy. The idea that privacy is a power relationship within society, the loss of which is brought about by surveillance, is not a new one. The idea of power and authority as the central component in the definitions of privacy and surveillance exorcises Alan Westin's often-quoted definitional curse, "Part philosophy, some semantics, and much pure passion" (1967:x).

Development of the Scoring System

Several key stages must be developed before the scoring system can be implemented. Much of this process is arbitrary.

1. The parameters of personal information must be developed. Which elements of personal information will be included (e.g., personal finances, property ownership, sexuality, mental health)?

2. These elements must be organized into categories and subcategories. *Example:* Category = personal finances; subcategories = spending patterns, personal debt, income, household expenditure, credit history. The categories form the key indices for the process.

3. The data categories must then be given raw weightings, according to a range of fixed characteristics (e.g., sensitivity of data, their vul-

nerability). *Example:* Property ownership, which might be publicly available information, could be given a weighting of 1, whereas criminal record information is weighted at 6. Criminal record data could be broken into subcategories. Thus, for instance, notification publicly of the fact of a conviction is weighted at 3, whereas disclosure as part of an employment record is weighted at 8.

4. Parameters and weightings must be developed relating to the processing of these categories of information (e.g., profiling, data matching). These processing outcomes may then, in turn, become separate categories of data; for instance, will the mass matching of social security files against health records constitute a new category of data? *Example:* A credit bureau record may be weighted at, say, 3.5. The automatic scoring function of the credit bureau may, in turn, be separately weighted at, say, 2.0. The inferential data arising from the credit information may be weighted at 0.5. These three weightings would be added together as part of the credit bureau (or credit file) category to achieve a score of 6.0.

5. Once the data category weightings have been established, the use weightings must be developed. The use weightings reflect the factors involved in information collection, use, storage, access, and distribution. The features that must be given use weightings include the agencies involved, the uses to which information is put, and the volume and extent of data held. *Example:* It could be decided that all categories of personal information held or obtained by police agencies are given an additional weighting of 3, whereas the same information in the hands of, say, the banks, is given an additional weighting of 2. Thus, if mental health information, rated at 8, is routinely given to police, its value increases to 11. If it also finds its way into bank records, the category weighting increases to 13, and so on through the agencies and information users.

The categories can be weighted by way of a survey form distributed to professionals in the privacy and information areas.

Once these five steps have been developed, we can establish an overall score for a country merely by adding together all categories. Again, the initial scores are likely to be unstable. The development of the second stage, the comprehensive score, requires a separate set of conditions, and these should be discussed elsewhere.

Implementation

The scoring process will not be a simple one. Even after the development of the needed weightings—a process that itself will consume considerable energy—the task of collecting data will be immense. The Canadian Department of Justice (1990) attempted to assess the extent of the flow of data across the Canadian border and encountered considerable problems collecting data from potential respondents. The project, commissioned by the Canadian government in 1989, sought information on data practices from more than 5,000 public and private sector organizations. Even after two written reminders were sent out over a three-month period, only 1,805 responses were received.

The privacy and consumer organizations that would potentially have most to gain from the development of the system described above would encounter difficulty administering the survey. Resources are scarce for these organizations, and most are already overburdened with a great many pressing issues. Cost would also be an important factor. Finding a source of financial support for the scoring process would be a herculean task.

There are several ways some of these problems might be overcome. Government privacy officials may be tempted to assist. Academic institutions that already have a demonstrated interest in the field might also become involved. These resources, together with the limited resources of nongovernment advocacy organizations, might provide enough structure for the project to commence.

Conclusion

The development of a scoring system for levels of surveillance may play a key role in sharpening public awareness and focusing interest on privacy issues. Although it is true that such a proposal involves substantial planning and complex design, the impact of the system may prove to be the shot in the arm that the advocacy community needs to overcome the current inertia. In the absence of any alternative approach to reviving interest in privacy at a public level, the approach deserves to be explored and developed.

Notes

1. The proposal for a Council directive concerning the protection of individuals in relation to the processing of personal data was originally put forward in 1990. The most recent version of the text was released in May 1995, and awaits approval by the European Parliament before February 1996.

2. Privacy International was formed in 1990 as an international response to privacy and surveillance issues. It is a nonprofit voluntary group based in Washington, D.C., and has members in forty countries.

3. These studies include those conducted by the Department of Justice, Canada (1990), the Intergovernmental Bureau for Informatics (1985), EDI Research Inc. (1988), the Computer Science and Law Research Group (1986, 1989), Kane (1986), the Organization for Economic Cooperation and Development (1989), and Sambharya (1985).

References

Beetham, David. (1993). *Auditing Democracy in Britain*. London: Charter 88 Trust.

Bennett, Colin J. (1992). *Regulating Privacy: Data Protection and Public Policy in Europe and the United States*. Ithaca, N.Y.: Cornell University Press.

Burnham, David. (1983). *The Rise of the Computer State*. New York: Random House.

Clarke, R.A. (1988). "Information Technology and Dataveillance." *Communications of the ACM* 31 (May).

Commission of the European Communities. (1992). *Amended Proposal for a Council Directive on Data Protection* (DG XIII). Luxembourg: European Commission.

Computer Science and Law Research Group. (1986). *L'identité piratée*. Montreal: Société Québecoise d'information juridique.

———. (1989). *Quelques donées empiriques sur les flux transfrontieres de donées personnelles en provenance et á destination du Canada*. Montreal: Société Québecoise d'information juridique.

Davies, Simon G. (1992). "Vulnerability Reaching Its Elastic Limit." In R. Clarke and J. Cameron (eds.), *Managing Information Technology's Organisational Impact*. Amsterdam: North Holland.

Department of Justice, Canada, Computer Science and Research Group. (1990). *Crossing the Borders of Privacy*. Ottawa: Department of Justice, Canada.

EDI Research Inc. (1988). *Respondent Report for the State of Canadian EDI 1988*. Oak Park, Ill.: EDI Research Inc.

Flaherty, David. (1989). *Protecting Privacy in Surveillance Societies*. Chapel Hill: University of North Carolina Press.

Holvast J. (1991). "Vulnerability of Information Society." In R. Clarke and

J. Cameron (eds.), *Managing Information Technology's Organisational Impact*. Amsterdam: North Holland.

Intergovernmental Bureau for Informatics. (1985). *Enquete de l'IBI sur les pratiques nationales et les pratiques des sociétes concernant les flux transfrontieres de donées*. Rome: Intergovernmental Bureau for Informatics.

Kane, Michael James. (1986). "A Study of the Impact of Transborder Data Flow Regulation on Large United States Corporations Using an Extended Information Systems Matrix Interface Model." Doctoral thesis, University of South Carolina.

Madsen, Wayne. (1992). *Handbook of Personal Data Protection*. London: Macmillan.

Organization for Economic Cooperation and Development. (1989). *The Internationalisation of Software and Computer Services*. Paris: OECD.

Privacy Commissioner of Australia. (1992). *Fourth Annual Report on the Operation of the Privacy Act*. Canberra: Australian Government Printing Service.

Privacy International. (1991). *1991 Interim Report to Members*. Sydney: Privacy International.

Sambharya, Rakeshkumar Bishanial. (1985). "The Impact of Transborder Data Flows on the Strategy and Operations of U.S. Based Multinational Corporations." Doctoral thesis, Temple University.

Simitis, Spiros. (1987). "Reviewing Privacy in an Information Society." *University of Pennsylvania Law Review* 135, no. 3: 707–46.

Westin, Alan F. (1967). *Privacy and Freedom*. New York: Atheneum.

Contributors

Jonathan P. Allen is a member of the faculty of the Management Studies Group in the Department of Engineering at Cambridge University. He has written about the social aspects of computerization and privacy and the dilemmas of using computerized models in manufacturing for production planning and control.

Colin J. Bennett is associate professor of political science at the University of Victoria in British Columbia. He has researched privacy and data protection issues in several advanced industrial countries, and is the author of *Regulating Privacy: Data Protection and Public Policy in Europe and the United States* (1992).

Simon G. Davies is a visiting fellow of the Department of Law of the University of Essex, and a visiting fellow in Information Law of London's Greenwich University. He is director general of Privacy International, a group that involves privacy experts from more than forty countries, and is a consultant adviser to the British Medical Association. He is the author of *Big Brother: Australia's Growing Web of Surveillance* (1992).

Oscar H. Gandy Jr. is professor of communications at the Annenberg School for Communication, University of Pennsylvania. He is the author of *The Panoptic Sort: A Political Economy of Personal Information* (1993).

Calvin C. Gotlieb is professor emeritus in the Department of Computer Science and the Faculty of Library and Information Science at the University of Toronto. He is the author of more than one hundred publications, including four books, the first of which, *Social Issues in Computing* (1973), was coauthored with A. Borodin. His editorial services include editor in chief of the *Journal of the Association for Computing Machinery* and *Communications of the ACM*, and he is a fellow of the Royal Society of Canada, the British Computer Society,

275

and the Association for Computing Machinery. In 1994 he was awarded the Isaac Averback Medal of the International Federation of Information Processing Societies.

Rob Kling is professor of information and computer science, and of management, at the University of California, Irvine. He has conducted extensive empirical and theoretical research about the social and political dimensions of computerized systems. He is the editor of *Computerization and Controversy: Value Conflicts and Social Choices* (2d ed., 1995) and editor in chief of *The Information Society,* a quarterly international journal.

David Lyon is professor of sociology at Queen's University, Canada. His books include *The Information Society: Issues and Illusions* (1988), *The Electronic Eye: The Rise of Surveillance Society* (1994), and *Postmodernity* (1994). He is a consulting editor for *Information Technology, Education and Society.*

Gary T. Marx is professor emeritus at the Massachusetts Institute of Technology and professor of sociology at the University of Colorado, Boulder. He is the author of *Undercover: Police Surveillance in America* (1988).

Abbe Mowshowitz is professor of computer science at the City College of New York, a member of the computer science doctoral faculty of the City University of New York, and professor of informatics at the University of Amsterdam. He is also a consultant to government agencies and businesses in North America and Europe on the policy implications of information technology. His current research interests include the economic, social, and political significance of computer-based information commodities and of virtual organization. He is the author of *The Conquest of Will: Information Processing in Human Affairs* (1976), *Inside Information: Computers in Fiction* (1977), and editor of *Human Choice and Computers,* volume 2 (1980).

Judith A. Perrolle is associate professor of sociology at Northeastern University in Boston, where she teaches in the College of Computer Science and in the Law, Policy, and Society Ph.D. program. Her research is on the social impacts of computers and communications technologies, environmental policy, and the sociology of risk. She is the author of *Computers and Social Change* (1987).

Mark Poster is professor of history at the University of California, Irvine. His books include *The Second Media Age* (1995), *The Mode of Information* (1990), and *Critical Theory and Poststructuralism* (1988).

Priscilla M. Regan is assistant professor in the Department of Public and International Affairs at George Mason University. She is the author of *Legislating Privacy: Technology, Social Values, and Public Policy* (1995). She was formerly a senior analyst at the congressional Office of Technology Assessment, where she was the principal author of *Electronic Record Systems and Individual Privacy* (1986) and *Electronic Surveillance Civil Liberties* (1985). She is a member of the National Advisory Board for the newsletter *Privacy and American Business* and is on the editorial board of *Media, Law and Society*.

James B. Rule is professor of sociology at the State University of New York, Stony Brook. He has written extensively on information technology and social change. His latest book is titled *Theories of Civil Violence* (1988); he is currently completing the sequel to this work, *Theory and Progress in Social Science*.

Elia Zureik is professor of sociology at Queen's University, Canada. He teaches courses on the sociology of science and the social aspects of information and communications technology. His published work deals with the ramifications of new technologies in the areas of work and telecommunications. With Dianne Hartling, he is coeditor of *The Social Context of the New Information and Communication Technologies: A Bibliography* (1987).

Name Index

Subject Index